OUTLINES OF CHRISTIAN DOCTRINE

BY THE REV.

H. C. G. MOULE, M.A.

Principal of Ridley Hall, and formerly Fellow of Trinity College, Cambridge

AUTHOR OF "VENI CREATOR: THOUGHTS ON THE HOLY SPIRIT OF PROMISE," ETC.

THIRTEENTH THOUSAND, REVISED

Wipf & Stock
PUBLISHERS
Eugene, Oregon

Wipf and Stock Publishers
199 W 8th Ave, Suite 3
Eugene, OR 97401

Outlines of Christian Doctrine
By Moule, Handley C.G.
ISBN 13: 978-1-55635-253-9
ISBN 10: 1-55635-253-0
Publication date 2/5/2007
Previously published by Hodder and Stoughton, 1894

TO MY BROTHER,

GEORGE EVANS MOULE, D.D.,

MISSIONARY BISHOP IN MID CHINA,

WITH LOVE AND REVERENCE

I INSCRIBE THIS BOOK.

PREFACE.

THE present short treatise was at first planned in the form of a Commentary upon the Thirty-Nine Articles. As the work proceeded the author was led to think that a sketch of the main doctrines of the Faith might be more generally useful, which, while always keeping in view the great historic Confession of the Church of which he thanks God he is a son and presbyter, should omit some topics contained in it and deal with others in a way somewhat different from that of a commentary.

The work makes not the least pretension either to originality or to fulness. It will have well served its purpose if in any degree it can stimulate its readers to personal study, and suggest lines for work and thought.

The author humbly trusts that what he has written has been written "at the foot of the Cross." Certainly, he has never willingly forgotten the presence of Him "whom truly to know is everlasting life." Before Him he desires ever to prostrate himself, and ever to recollect more fully that, as regards the depth and height of His Revelation, "we know in part, and prophesy in part."

Writing on the Day of the Annunciation, he reverently takes up as his own, in view of the holy truths he has here attempted to discuss, the words of its Collect, now thirteen centuries old:

We beseech Thee, O Lord, pour Thy grace into our hearts; that as we have known the Incarnation of Thy Son Jesus Christ by the message of an Angel, so by His Cross and Passion we may be brought to the glory of His Resurrection; through the same Jesus Christ our Lord. Amen.

CAMBRIDGE, *March 25th*, 1889.

CONTENTS.

CHAPTER I.

INTRODUCTORY: (1) NATURAL AND REVEALED RELIGION, (2) THE HOLY SCRIPTURES.

Certain data assumed, 1; Revelation, its possibility, 3; The Holy Scriptures, their characteristics, 4; Testimony of Christ to them, 5; their authority, spiritually ultimate, 7; Grades of authority, 7; Relation of Scripture to theology, 8.

CHAPTER II.

THE DOCTRINE OF GOD: (1) THEISM, (2) THE HOLY TRINITY.

Brief conspectus of the main lines of natural testimony to God, 10; Intuitions, 11; Order, 11; Consciousness, and its mode of witness, 12; Relation of these evidences to Revelation, 13; Polytheism, its error and its element of truth, 14; Pantheism, Brahmanism an instance of it, 14; Its error, and element of truth, 15; Atheism, rarely now held as a definite creed; why, 15; Agnosticism, its error and its element of truth, 16; Deism, 16; Christianity an element in theistic evidence, 17; Physical evidence for the being of God akin to that for the being of man, 18; Traces of divine handiwork not altogether like traces of ours, 18; Importance of Scripture doctrine of Creation, 19, Divine creative sovereignty, 19; The Holy

Trinity, a truth altogether of Revelation, 19; "Unitarianism" of Scripture, all-important to the enquiry, 20; Claim of God upon the creature, 20; Trinitarian evidence, 21; Statement of the doctrine, 23; Old Testament evidence, 24; Assumption of it in the New Testament, 24; Immanent and Economical Trinity, 24; Illustrations of the doctrine of the Trinity, 25; History of the doctrine, 26; Gnosticism, 26; Manicheism, 26; Monarchianism, 27; Arianism, 28; Point of contact between the above systems, an assumption of Unipersonality, 28; Modern alien theories—Unitarianism, Swedenborgianism, 29; The word Trinity, 30.

CHAPTER III.

THE DOCTRINE OF THE FATHER.

Best studied in the light of the doctrines of the Other Persons, 31; Creation by the Father, 31; Yet He is not Father of the Universe, 32; Redemption by the Father, 32; The Father loves the world, loves man, 33; Is He, therefore, in the proper sense, the Father of every man? 34; The Father "gives" the redeeming Son, 35; And lays our sins on Him, 35; Justifies, 36; Adopts, 36; Gives the regenerating Spirit, 36; Calls, 36; Keeps, sanctifies, glorifies, 36; Elects, 36; Mystery of election, 37; Necessary in such a subject of thought, 37; Scripture evidence, 37; Relation of the Father to the Son in the work of salvation, 38; All salvation is "in" the Son of the Father, 39; The Covenant between the Father and the Son, 40; Its matter, 41; Symmetry of the eternal purpose and method, 42; Election taught in Scripture in relation to other truth, 42; No force upon the will, 43; Moral purposes of the doctrine, 43; Other sides of truth equally true and important, 44; Sincerity of divine love and invitation, 44; Apparent contradictions of the highest truths, 44; "A Calvinist on his knees, an Arminian on his feet," 45; Scope of the Atonement, 45; Its double aspect, 45; Perseverance of the saints 46; Loss of grace, 47; Need of constant

CONTENTS. ix

personal communion with God, to study and to use truth aright, 47; Varying theories of Election, 48; National, 48; Ecclesiastical, 48; Conditional, 49; Election within election, 50; History of opinion on election, 51; Centuries ii.-iv., 51; Αὐτεξούσιον, 51; Centuries iv., v., 51; St Augustine and Pelagius, 51; Centuries v.-xvii., 52; Views on freedom of the will, 52; The Scholastics, 53; Trent, 53; The Jansenists, 53; The Reformers, 53; Calvin, 53; Luther, 54; Melanchthon, 54; Hooker, 54; Arminius, 54; Synod of Dort, 55; Baxter, 55; Century xviii., 55; Wesley and his English contemporaries, 55; Edwards, 55.

CHAPTER IV.

THE DOCTRINE OF THE SON.

(1) *The Person of Christ*:—Article II., 57; Scripture evidence for His Godhead, 57; and His Sonship, 58; The eternal Generation, 59; "The Word," 59; The Homöousion, 60; The Incarnation, 60; One Person, 61; Two Natures, 61; The Manhood perfect, 61; The Manhood never independently personal, 61; "Divine-human Personality," 62; Reality of Christ's human experience, 62; His sinlessness, 62; His Godhead and Manhood always, in Incarnation, present together, 63; Perfection of His knowledge, 63; The title "Son of God," 64; "Son of Man," 64; "Second Man," 64; History of the Doctrine of the Person of Christ, 65; Centuries i.-iii., 65; Centuries iv., v., Arianism, 66; Apollinarianism, 66; Nestorianism; Θεοτόκος, 67; Eutychianism, 67; Definition of Chalcedon, 67; Monothelite controversy, 69; Importance of ancient controversies, 69.

CHAPTER V.

THE DOCTRINE OF THE SON (*continued*).

(2) *The Work of Christ*:—In Creation, 70; Theory of pre-existence of Creation in the Son, 70; Is the Pre-existent Christ Primal Man? 72; Was the Incarnation irrespective of the Fall? 72; Difficulties, 73; The Atonement, 75; It

is central truth, 75; Scripture evidence, 75; Necessity of deep views of sin, 76; Reasons for present neglect of certain aspects of doctrine of Atonement, 76; Elements necessary to a true theory, 77; Scripture metaphors, 78; The word "at-one-ment," 78; What it does *not* imply, 79; Awful greatness of the problem of sin, 80; Godward aspect of the Atonement, 81; Its relation to other aspects, 81; Detached remarks, Purchase, 82; Equivalence, 83; *Lama sabachthani*, 83; Relation of Christ's life to His death, 83; $\dot{v}\pi\dot{\epsilon}\rho$, $\dot{a}\nu\tau\dot{\iota}$, etc., 84; "The blood of Christ," bearing of the phrase, 85; Penal suffering, 86; History of doctrine of Atonement, centuries i.-iv.; Clement of Rome, *Ep. to Diognetus*, Irenæus, Justin, Origen, 88; Athanasius, Augustine, 89; Was a price paid to the Evil One? 89; Centuries xi.-xvi.; Anselm, Bernard, Lombard, 90; Aquinas, the Mystics, 91; Age of Reformation, 91; Later currents of opinion, 91; The "Descent into Hell," 92; Hades, 93; 1 Pet. iii., 94 (and 95); Cautions, 94; History of belief about the "Descent," 95; Creeds, 95; Irenæus, Tertullian, Clement of Alexandria, 96; Apocryphal literature, 96; Supposed scope and nature of the Descent, 96; Reserve of Scripture, 96; Purgatory, 97; Prayer for the dead, 97; Scripture doctrine of the Intermediate State, 97.

CHAPTER VI.

THE WORK OF CHRIST (*continued*).

Resurrection, Session, Ascension, Return, 99; Purposes of the Resurrection, 99; Conditions, 99; The Second Adam, 100; Ascension; ubiquity, 101; Head of the Church, 101; Mediation, Suretyship, Covenant, 102; Intercession, 103; High Priesthood, 103; The Priest enthroned, 104; Is there an altar in heaven? 104; Does the Victim-state continue? 105; Kingship of Christ, 105; In what sense terminable, 106; The Lord's Return, why treated here with reserve, 106; Scripture evidence in various directions, 107; The future of Israel, 109; History of opinion about the Return; New Testament, 109; Justin, Iren-

CONTENTS. xi

æus, Origen, Dionysius, Augustine, 110; Middle Ages, 110; Later times, 111; Interpretation of the Revelation, 111; The Millennium, 111; The pre-millennial Return, 112; Considerations on both sides, 112; The Judgment committed to the Son, 115; Mystery of its conditions, 115; The Church judged, 116; And judging, 117; The Judgment an event, 117.

CHAPTER VII.

THE DOCTRINE OF THE HOLY SPIRIT.

The Spirit divine, 119; Personal, 120; John xiv.-xvi. and other Scripture evidence, 120; "Unitarianism" of Scripture, 121; Old Testament evidence, 122; Significance of the term "*The Spirit*," 123; The *Nexus* between the Other Persons, 123; Spiritual importance of the truth of the Personality, 124; The Procession, 124; The Dual Procession, 125; Its spiritual importance, 126; Work of the Spirit, in nature, 126; In mankind, 126; The universal Effusion, its meaning, 127; Does He work in the intermediate state? 128; His work in the Church, 129; Aspects of the Church, 129; Work in the individual, 130; Its order, 130; Conviction, 130; Its importance, 131; Union with Christ, 132; How it is "by the Spirit," 133; Work of the Spirit in the Incarnate Lord, 135; And in us in relation to it, 135; Christ our Life, the Spirit our Life-giver, 136; Illumination by the Spirit; His witness to Christ, 136; Freedom of the Spirit's work, 137; He maintains the life given, 138; How, 139; The Spirit is the true Author of Scripture, 139; Recognition of this by the earliest Fathers; Clement, 139; Justin, Theophilus, Irenæus, Tertullian, Cyprian, Clement of Alexandria, Origen, 140; Inferences from this doctrine, 141; The Spirit's work for the Community of the true Church, 141; Relation of member and body in view of this, 141; "Spiritual gifts," 142; "Grace," 143; Work of the Spirit in the Old Testament saints, 144; Difference of the New Testament period, 145; History of the doctrine of the Spirit, 146; Clement,

Ignatius, *The Shepherd, Second Ep. of Clement*, Justin Irenæus, Tertullian, Origen, 147; Athanasius, the Gregories, Basil, 148; The Dual Procession, 149; Augustine, Charlemagne, the Great Schism, 149; Council of Florence, 150; Modern views, Christian consciousness, 150; History of doctrine of the Spirit's work; Montanism, 150; Augustine, Bernard, the Mystics, the Reformation, 151; Present deepening of the sense of the supreme importance of the Spirit's work, 151.

CHAPTER VIII.

THE DOCTRINE OF MAN.

Nature of Scripture anthropology, 152; Creation of man, Gen. i., ii., 152; How far are the narratives to be understood "literally"? 153; The evolutionary philosophy, 154; Man a new departure, 154; Physical observation and philosophic theory, 155; The word "evolution," its ambiguity, 155; Antiquity of man, 156; Unity of mankind, 157; The Image of God, 157; Personality, 158; The individual, 158; Immortality, 159; The body, 160; Its relation to judgment, 160; To the Incarnation, 161; Soul and spirit, 161; Is man tripartite or bipartite? 162; Was his "spirit" lost in the Fall? 162; Body and soul, 163; Man essentially one, 163; The "heart," 163; The "inner man," 164; The "mind," conscience, freewill, 164; Its relation to the will of God, 164; Traducianism and Creationism, 165; Man's original state according to Scripture, 165; Other views, 165; The Roman Catholic doctrine of original man, 166; Greatness of human nature, 166; Sin unnatural, 167; Primal man a "son of God," how, 167; Adam the head of mankind, 168; Mystery of this, 168; The Fall, 169; At once fact and mystery, 169; The Temptation, and its sequel 169; Knowledge of good and evil, 170; Was it "a fall upward"? 170; Absolute origin of evil, unrevealed, 170; But evil is a fact, 171; Hateful to God, 171; Spiritual importance of full recognition of this, 171; Nature of man's bondage in the Fall, 172; "Depravity," 172; Testimony of doctrine

CONTENTS. xiii

of regeneration to it, 173; Original Sin, 173; Mozley on it 73; Coleridge, 174; The individual "totally" fallen, 174; Yet not under a binding fate, 175; Inherited sinfulness and guilt, 175; Mystery and mercy of the revelation, 176; Man restored, 177; Much of this subject anticipated, 177; "Antinomies" inherent in the subject, 177; Two Ways and Two Ends, 178; Is a universal hope possible? 178; Sin an unknown cause, 179; Attempt to indicate the eternal "plan," 179; Under what conditions this may be done, 180; The spirit proper to those who hold the view indicated, 180; Need of the Gospel in order to man's actual restoration, 181; Infants, 181; The normal process of individual restoration, 182; Regeneration and Conversion, 182; Repentance, 183; Union with Christ, 183; Justification, 183; Its revealed method, 184; Testimony of perversions to its real nature, 184; Meaning of "works," 184; Of "faith," 185; Bishop Bull, 185; St James' teaching, 186; First and second justification, 186; Hooker's dying words, 187; Essential importance and significance of the doctrine of Justification by Faith, 187; Imputed righteousness, 188; Is justification due to the divine foreview of glorified perfection? 189; Union with Christ and its relation to justification, 189; The justified still under discipline, 189; Sanctification; its relations to justification, 190; Absoluteness of sanctification in idea and purpose, 191; The work of faith in sanctification, 191; Eph. iii. 14-19, 192; The Indwelling, 192; Illustration from Old Testament, 192; Christ the Fountain of the holy life, 193; Faith the mode of derivation, 193; Yet the life so lived calls for full exercise of will, 193; Is the man thus living entitled to claim freedom in all respects from sin? 194; Promises, 194; Cautions, 194; Antitheses of Scripture on this subject, 195; The power and the presence of sin, 195; The flesh, 195; Crucifixion, 196; Rom. vii. 7-25 considered, 196; Does the life of sanctified deliverance begin with a crisis? 198; The Fulness of the Spirit, 199; Summary of the position and condition of man actually restored, in life, 200; In death, and eternity, 201.

CHAPTER IX.

THE DOCTRINE OF THE CHURCH.

Hooker on the two aspects of the idea of the Church, 202; The word *Ecclesia*, 204; Necessity of distinctions, 205; Illustrated by Rom. ii. 25-9, 206; Testimony of St Augustine, 207; Ridley, 207; Sacred claims of the visible Church, 208; Corporate re-union, 209; What is the most dangerous sort of schism? 210; The rule of order and its exceptions, 210; "Notes" of the Church 210; Earliest exposition of Art. XIX., 211; Hooker, Field, Pearson, 211; Is Episcopacy a "note"? 212; The word "Catholic," 212; Ignatius, Athanasius, 212; Claims of the Roman Catholic Church, 213; Need of caution in reasoning from patristic language about the Church, 213; One cause of separation, 214; Desirableness of temperate uniformity, 214; Authority of the Church; its nature, and limits, 214; Councils, 215; Art. XX., Church authority as regards order of worship, 216; Art. XX., XXXIV.; Prefaces to Prayer Book, 216.

CHAPTER X.

THE DOCTRINE OF THE MINISTRY.

Art. XXIII., 217; New Testament evidence, 217; Apostles, Deacons, Elders, "Bishops," 218; SS. James, Timothy, Titus, 218; Did the Community create its ministry? 218; Exceptions to primitive ministerial rule, 219; *Teaching of the Twelve Apostles*, Clement, Ignatius, 219; Peculiarity of the Apostolate, 219; How far it was, and was not, transmissible, 220; Succession, 220; Its rightness and benefits, 220; Yet not of the first order of truths, 221; Sacerdotalism, 221; Medium and Mediator, 222; The word $\iota\epsilon\rho\epsilon\upsilon\varsigma$ not used of the Christian minister in the New Testament, 223; Bishop Lightfoot on origin of Sacerdotalism, 223; Confession and Absolution, 223; New Testament evidence, 224; The Roman system 224; Contrition, Attrition, 224; In what sense the minister truly has an absolving authority, 225; History of the

CONTENTS. xv

Confessional, 226; Our Visitation Service, 227; Grace of
Orders, 227; Episcopacy, 228; New Testament use of
the word *Episcopus*, 228; Ignatius, Irenæus, 228; Asia
Minor and St John, 229; St Jerome's view of relations
between presbyterate and episcopate, 229; Non-episcopal
churches, 230; Anglican opinion, Jewel, 230; Whitgift,
Bancroft, Hall, Andrewes, 231; Ussher, Cosin, 232; Two
opposite tendencies to be avoided, 232; The Ministry
not meant to absorb the energies of the Church, 233.

CHAPTER XI.

THE DOCTRINE OF THE SACRAMENTS.

Art. XXV.; The word *Sacramentum*, 234; The Seven Sacraments of the Roman Church, 234; Roman theory of
grace and of sacramental conveyance, 235; New Testament evidence, 236; Special aspects of the "Body" and
the "Blood" in the Eucharist, 237; Bulk of New Testament teaching on Sacraments, its lesson, 238; Old Testament Sacraments, 239; The sacramental idea, 239; Place
of Sacraments under the Gospel, 239; Sacraments are
covenanting rites, 240; Bullinger's *Decades*, 241; Special
blessing of Sacraments, 241; St Bernard, 242; Aquinas,
243; The Sacrament described in terms of the Thing
243; Patristic idea of regeneration, 244; Baptism at
Easter and Whitsuntide, 244; Lombard, 244; Vogan,
244; Waterland on the work of Sacraments, 245; High
language of older Anglicans on Sacraments, yet "evangelical" language on grace, 245; Hall, Ussher, Beveridge,
Taylor, 246; Hooker, Augustine, 247; Two opposite
opinions to be avoided, 248; Definition of a Sacrament
in the Catechism, 248; "*A means and a pledge*," 248;
"Necessary to salvation," 249; Language of ceremony
and of related fact, 249; On the word "*in*," 250; Extension of the Incarnation, 251; It is by the Spirit alone,
251; Baptism; Art. XXVII., 252; Theories of the work
of Baptism; the Germ, 252; Bp Browne's view, 253;
Difficulties, 253; Change of *status*, 253; Ussher's view,
254; Characteristics of language of covenant, 254; Re-

mission of original sin in baptism, 254; Joh. iii. 1-8, 255; Ecclesiastical regeneration, 255; Church *and Church*, etc., 255; Confirmation, 255; Infant baptism, 256; Children and the seal of the covenant, 256; Circumcision, 256; Monnica, 257; Temperate language of our Article, 257; Wall's liberal statements, 257; Sponsors, 257; The infant viewed as a catechumen, 258; Baptism to be studied first in the adult, not the infant, 258; Sprinkling or immersion, 258; The Holy Communion, 259; Articles XXVIII., XXIX., XXXI., 259; What is the true meaning of "*The Body and Blood of Christ*"? 260; Words of the Lord at institution, 260; Importance of their full form, 260; And of the separateness of the Elements, 261; Transubstantiation, 261; Consubstantiation, 261; Teaching now current in the English Church 261; Bearing of the words of institution on these views, 262; Waterland, 263; What we "feed on" directly, in the Eucharist, 263; And on what indirectly but really, 263; The word "*is*," 263; Cannot be taken without explanation, 263; "*Do this in remembrance of Me*," 264; The hour of Communion, 265; Attitude at the Holy Communion, 266; *Realis Præsentia*, 266; Non-communicating Attendance, 266; Conclusion.

Addenda, 268, 269.

INDEXES, 270—288.

The writer has to thank his friend and colleague, the Rev. G. A. S. Schneider, M.A., formerly Professor of Divinity in Trinity College, Toronto, for very kind and valuable help in preparing the account of the History of the Doctrine of the Holy Spirit.

In preparing a Second Edition (July, 1889) the writer has received much help from his friend the Rev. Andrew Wood, M.A., Rector of Great Ponton, Grantham. Mr Wood has kindly revised with great care the whole text of the First Edition, including the references to Scripture and Fathers, and has made many important suggestions on points of detail.

In a Third Edition (Feb., 1890) Indexes have been added, and some corrections and alterations made. The writer is much indebted to his critics for indications of omission or error

CHAPTER I.

INTRODUCTORY.

I. NATURAL AND REVEALED RELIGION. II. THE HOLY SCRIPTURES.

WE are about to attempt a statement of the main doctrines of the Christian Faith, taken as the expressions of truths divinely revealed in the Scriptures, and divinely adjusted to the nature and needs of man. We desire to state and comment as always remembering not only the duty of accuracy and fairness, but also the presence of Him who is the eternal Life, Truth, and Love, the ever-blessed God, to whom be glory for ever.

As introductory to our study, we make a few remarks here on the Connexion between Natural and Revealed Religion, and on the Holy Scriptures and their authority.

I. Christian theology, as presented in Revelation, practically assumes, as otherwise given, certain great facts about man, the world, and God. It assumes the truth of inferences from general human consciousness, such as the reality of our personality, self-conscious, intelligent, and free to will; the reality of the material world, and of the immaterial; of their difference, and of our capacity really (not fully) to know both; the reality of the law of causation, that every change or becoming has an adequate cause really related to it; the reality of will as a true cause, an ultimate force. It assumes the fact of conscience, the unforced response of man's nature to evidence for the existence of an absolute law of moral obligation and accountability. It proclaims, but it even more largely assumes, the existence of God, the free Personal Creator, Himself eternally and necessarily *being*, and the sole ultimate cause and basis of all positive *becoming*; goal and repose of all that which in man seeks for original and perfect being, truth, and goodness; raised above condition and relation, as being self-existent and self-sufficient, but freely, sovereignly, and lovingly entering into relation with the creation of His will; Infinite, by the absence of all limit to His excellences, each in its kind, and meantime Personal, that is, knowing Himself, and intelligently willing—a view of Him which, far from limiting His nature, is of the essence of its greatness, for the absence of personality would be a vast imperfection. Revelation assumes that man, being what he is, and placed in the world, being what it is, has ground enough to be sure that that world exists because of the existence of One supreme Power of at least his own order; a Power which cannot *less than himself* know, will, and love (see further below, p. 12).

Christianity assumes and claims the facts of general developed human consciousness, as part of its evidence, and as necessary to a full estimate of its doctrines. And it deals with man, accordingly, not as with an abstraction, but as an actual being under actual conditions. It presents its doctrine of God, not *in vacuo*, but as to a being made in His image (below, p. 157). It presents its doctrine of salvation as to a being actually suffering from moral discord in his actual state of nature. Individual men may repel these claims. But Christianity invites them to reconsider their denial in the light of more general facts, and to listen again.

Meanwhile these assumptions prepare the way for articulate Revelation from God to man. Revelation assumes conscience, for, example, but it refuses to be thought of as its natural development. It is *for* man, and *to* him, but not *of* him. It speaks to man, conscious of the existence of supernatural power, as a direct message from the region of that power. It speaks to man, conscious of moral difference, and of internal moral discord, as a message, direct from the region of absolute right and love, about the nature and remedy of his own sin.

Christianity assumes of course the possibility of such direct messages. It assumes that the eternal personal Cause and Possessor of all creatures is supremely free amidst all ranges of His works, and in particular free to communicate, in His spiritual Personality, with the personal spirits whom He has made free to communicate with each other. And the independent study of physical phenomena only harmonizes with this assumption, by leading the observer, true to the deepest principles of thought in his own nature, along the chain of change and cause to the conviction of an ultimate Cause quite inscrutable to physical research. In other words, physical enquiry, often suspected of a tendency to materialistic atheism, really leads towards a region of being on which it can pronounce no positive verdict, and from which therefore may issue effects which it can neither predict nor preclude. That region, says Revelation, is God, supremely free to will and act. Physical enquiry, in its proper province, has no quarrel with that assertion. It has no proof to offer that He "who inhabiteth eternity" cannot speak from thence, amidst and through all that He has willed to exist; not treating His handiwork capriciously, or as unreal, but using it as entirely elastic under His wise and loving will.

The word Revelation may be used in a wider or a narrower sense. Man, rightly and fully studied, is to himself a revelation of the being of God. The external world is in some important respects a revelation, deeply connected with that conveyed through manhood. But common consent restricts the word Revelation to communications from and about God given otherwise than through the normal phenomena of man and the world. Such communications, Christianity holds, have been made from the very first to man. God has thus spoken sometimes by physical miracle, sovereign abnormal handling of material things and their successions; sometimes by spiritual miracle, as by disclosures of the future, or of present facts of the unseen world. Above all, Revelation has come through the Incarnation of the Son, the Christ, of God; through His manifested Person, Word, and Work. And if we ask for a sure *record* of Revelation in this its more definite and precious aspects, the Christian answer is, the Holy Scriptures.

II. The Holy Scriptures, whatever their origin and nature, are as a fact one of the great phenomena of the world. No other collection of writings exists which mysteriously combines, as they do, the widest diversities of date and authorship with the

INTRODUCTORY.

deepest pervading harmonies and unities. In one aspect they are a part of the national literature of a much isolated race; in another, they have been and are the spiritual oracle of many generations of precisely the most cultivated and vigorous races. Historical research affirms the accuracy of their pictures of men and manners of the remote past; but meanwhile they themselves refuse to separate from their firm texture of narrative and teaching the presence everywhere of the supernatural. From one side they are a long and solid chain of recorded and predicted events; from another, they are a continuous exposition of supreme spiritual principles, spiritual forces, and fears, and hopes.

They have been very often criticized in respect of their description, for example, of the origin and processes of the material universe. But among their defenders in these respects are found some of the chief exponents of the latest scientific knowledge.[1] They have been attacked in the region of history. But the past is full of verifications of their historical accuracy in matters once apparently hopeless of explanation; while it is also full of warnings against premature explanation of such difficulties.

But the Christian student sees the most impressive characteristic of the Holy Scriptures in the fact of the attitude towards them taken by Jesus Christ. Antecedent to all questions of its spiritual authority, the New Testament, as a whole, is a mass of valid historical evidence to the opinions of Jesus Christ. And in this character it attests beyond a doubt His profound veneration for the

---

[1] See Mivart, *Lessons from Nature*, Dawson, *Chain of Life*, and *Modern Science*, etc., Reusch, *Bible and Nature* (Eng. trans.), and Cave, *Inspiration of the Old Testament*.

Holy Scriptures then existing; that is to say, for the Old Testament, as in substance, and practically in detail, it exists to-day. For Him it possessed the peculiar and awful characteristic of Divine Authority. He stated no theory of its construction; but looking upon it as it existed, He recognized in it the decisive utterance of God, even in its minor features of expression. For the mind which recognizes in Jesus Christ all that He claimed to be, this verdict on the supernatural character and divine authority of the Old Testament is final.

And the transition of inference to the New Testament is not difficult. As a fact, Jesus Christ entrusted the exposition of His message to a selection of His contemporary followers. As another fact, within a very few generations, at furthest, from His death, the vast majority of His disciples recognized in certain writings, claiming to emanate from that circle, a divine character, identical with that of the older Scriptures.

The claims of some of these writings to authenticity were freely discussed, and in some cases long doubted. But this was never so with more than a small fraction of the whole mass finally recognized. And, what is most significant, doubt never extended, seriously or widely, to the point of refusing divine authority to an apostolic writing once ascertained. And it is certain that the "New Testament Canon," thus recognized from the first in idea, and in the concrete of its present contents within three centuries from the death of Jesus Christ, has shown itself ever since, by the evidence of spiritual and moral power, to be indeed of the same order with those older Scriptures before which the Incarnate Christ Himself bowed. And let it be remembered that the thoughtful and reverent study of the *internal* evidences of the Holy Scriptures will always contribute above all things to the solid belief in their divine character, and their claim to ultimate spiritual authority for the Christian.[1]

For in fact the attitude of Christ to the Old Testament Scriptures is decisive proof that they rightly claim *ultimate* spiritual authority. And it is well to remember, as a great subsidiary item of natural and historical evidence on this subject, that the early generations of the Christian Church held, with practical universality, this view of the Scriptures. On few subjects, if any, are the Christian writers of the first few centuries more entirely agreed than on the ultimate authority of the Holy Scriptures.[2] (See further, p. 139.)

It is important to observe that authority may be real, yet not ultimate. A Creed has authority; a Council has authority; a Father has authority, and still more, many consenting Fathers, witnessing to facts of belief. But none of these has ultimate authority. The Scriptures have it. (See below, p. 214.)

No thoughtful man will hastily urge his private judgment against the deliberate verdict of his religious community lawfully expressed; or against a great consensus of Christian witnesses or interpreters. That is, he will recognize authority in them. To him "private judgment" will be not so much a *right*, to be loudly asserted, as a sacred and searching *responsibility*, to be reverently remembered. But all this is not a concession of ultimate

[1] See Lord Hatherley, *Continuity of Scripture*, especially pp. xli-xliii.
[2] See this fully illustrated by Dean Goode, *Divine Rule of Faith and Practice*, vol. iii., ch. xi.

authority to anything but the Holy Scriptures. Reverently, but still lawfully and firmly, if the deplorable necessity should arise, the individual may appeal, from even Creed or Council, to the Holy Scriptures, asking to be tested by their sacred verdict alone, as the basis of the authority of all other lawful courts. On the other hand, he will cherish a high reverence *à priori* for the results of doctrine actually attained by those other courts, as against any isolated conclusions of his own.

The Holy Scriptures, then, are divine Revelation for the Christian who takes his place without reserve at the feet of the Jesus Christ of the Gospels. It remains to explain briefly what is the relation between them and systems or expositions of doctrine based upon them.

Scripture, it is obvious, is not in itself a formulated system of doctrines. But it does not therefore discountenance the construction of a system. The truth is that Scripture both contains in abundance the materials for a system, and in many of its parts, particularly in the Epistles, indicates a system. Up to a certain point Scripture is thus analogous to "Nature." The universe is not a system of science. But it contains the materials for the construction of theory and development of system, and by the orderliness of its phenomena it suggests an exposition in forms of mental order.

True, Scripture contains immensely more than the materials for a doctrinal system. It contains a mass of expressions and manifestations of Divine affections. It is a record of personal dealings of God with man, awful and tender, so presented as to caution us, at every step, never to study doctrinal method and order out of relation to the living and eternal Love. And Scripture contains, moreover, abundant warnings that its contents are in their nature so related to the inscrutable that in any systematization we soon reach the point of holy silence. With such provisos, however, we rightly approach the Scriptures with the aim first to ascertain their *data* of facts and truths, and then, knowing that their Author is the Lord of order, and has so constituted us that our minds must seek order through all phenomena, to endeavour to combine the *data* ; in other words, to trace a Theology.

CHAPTER II.

THE DOCTRINE OF GOD.

I. THEISM   II. THE HOLY TRINITY.

I. THEISM.

IN these pages, of course, no attempt is made to *elaborate* the argument for God from man and nature. We have seen already that the Christian doctrines, which are our real concern here, very largely assume that argument as, more or less consciously, carried out in the mind already. All that we do is to indicate some of the great converging lines of testimony outside the Scriptures, and to remark briefly on some systems of misbelief.

What then are the main lines of testimony, other than direct and miraculous, to the being and glory of the "One living and true God, everlasting, without body, parts, or passions; of infinite power, wisdom and goodness; the Maker and Preserver of all things, both visible and invisible" (Art. I.)?

Stated as simply and briefly as we can, they are —those testimonies which arise from man's observation of the world, and from man's observation of himself, and, as a special and profound fact under this last head, from man's possession of certain tendencies, or laws, of his nature, which, lying at the basis of all

THE DOCTRINE OF GOD. 11

his powers of observation and reasoning, conduct him also, with mysterious certainty of result, beyond them. We mean what are known as our "Intuitions;" man's constitutional recognition of certain primary facts as incapable alike of formal proof and of natural doubt.

Such facts are, the reality of our own personality, the reality of existence external to our own, the universal truth of the first principles of geometry, as that two straight lines cannot enclose a space, and the absolute difference between right and wrong. No logical process (in the popular sense of logical) can prove these truths. But when once the contemplation of them is occasioned to man by observation, and their bearing made clear, man is such that he cannot naturally doubt them, while in a state of mental and moral health.

The elements of evidence for God thus presented to man, apart from Revelation, work then somewhat as follows, so far as we can analyse a process which ordinarily takes place without the least conscious analysis. Man finds himself in the midst of a world, a universe, showing innumerable and ever-multiplying instances of *order*. We do not say design; for the word design takes for granted personal will behind order. Man sees order, the more closely he observes ; from the dust beneath to the starry skies above. His instinct is to infer personal purpose and action behind it. Why so? Because in that region of observation which to him is quite immediate, namely his own personal consciousness, he knows that the production of order inevitably implies purpose in action, somewhere, however far, behind the result. And he is certain that he is not his own cause, not his own maker ; that he himself is, in all the order of his being, an event, a production, demanding (for this is an intuition of the mind) a sufficient cause behind it. And he finds himself so related to things around him, so adjusted to and interlaced with the external world, that he naturally tends to recognize himself as, in some great respects, part of it; and so in its personal Cause to look for his own. And in himself he finds, immediately and inalienably, the facts of personal intelligence, will, and love, and the certainty that wrong and right in actions are absolutely different. And it is intuitive to him to be naturally sure that such consciousness is in a true sense *supernatural*, that it belongs to a higher order than other matters of observation, so that that which cannot know, and will, and love, and discern moral truth, is incalculably lower in the scale of being than that which can. The combined facts of the inner and outer worlds, watched by the one observer, man, thus naturally suggest to man Personality behind and above phenomena, recognized as exercising intelligent will, and as knowing good and evil. Meantime, the external things actually observed are always finite, and so cannot merely of themselves carry proof up to the infinite; but then the gulf is lawfully bridged by those intuitions which demand, by the constitution of the mind, the existence of the ultimate and uncaused; *being* behind all *becoming;* power than which nothing can be more strong, truth than which nothing can be more true, goodness than which nothing can be more good. Order, observed by the personal existence, man, who is himself profoundly related to that order, witnesses to personality behind it, personality of at least man's order, because man's cause. Conscience, known in himself by man, witnesses to that personal Cause as not only knowing good and evil, but as ranged on the

THE DOCTRINE OF GOD.

side of good. Intuitions of the infinite—as, for instance, in space and time—witness to that personal Cause as not only to a high degree knowing, willing, and good, but as being (because ultimate) *all*-knowing, *all*-powerful, *all*-good; a God of infinite attributes, that is to say, eternally exempt from imperfection in everything that can be predicated of Him; not a vague Something embracing all being, but the eternal One who is good so that He could not be better, wise so that He could not be wiser, strong so that He could not be stronger; perfect in Himself and to our true apprehension, infinite to our always finite comprehension.

It would indeed be idle to say that this idea of God so dwells in the human mind that it needs nothing to call it out, admits of no development, and demands no revelation. What we mean is that in its highest and noblest form it is still an inference as true as sublime from constant facts of the world and of man; that in the lowest manifestations of religion, even among savages, there are discernible the rudiments or the relics of it, and that Revelation finds in man's capacity for it and tendency to it the prepared receptacle for its glorious message, a message which meanwhile man's study of the world and himself could never by itself develope, and the essence of which, as Christians believe on good grounds, was accordingly given supernaturally to man even in the first days of his being.[1]

To this faint sketch of the lines of theistic testimony we append a brief notice of opponent or alien systems, with passing remarks.

---

[1] Among books developing the theistic argument we commend specially Flint's *Theism*, Harris' *Self-Revelation of God*, and Père Gratry's *Connaissance de Dieu*.

Polytheism is the belief of many invisible personal agents, more or less co-ordinate, behind or in phenomena. It is the belief of many races. In very many instances, if not practically in all, there lies however a theistic (i.e., as the word by usage means, *mono*theistic) background behind the polytheism, discoverable as the thought of the people is better observed and understood; one indication among others that polytheism is not the germ of theism, but a degradation. It is almost needless to say that polytheism as a belief is on the wane. Observation, now enormously developed, and ever developing, in its range and minuteness, tends to evince a unity in nature which effectually discredits polytheism. On the other hand, Revelation indicates an element of truth underlying it, telling us of innumerable existences other than human, personal, and therefore true causes, but all wholly subject (willingly or not) to the Supreme.

Pantheism is the view of things which may be roughly said to identify God and the universe, including man. More strictly, it views the universe, including the human consciousness, as a phase of the Absolute Being, held to be itself non-personal, non-conscious. God is the Ocean, the universe a wave, or waves. Ocean and waves alike are water, but the waves are not the ocean, only its surface in a certain state. In this view there is no separation between God and the world; all phenomena, good and evil, are equally and alike related to Him, or to It. The great existing instance of pantheism is Indian Brahmanism. To the Brahman all existences, material and personal, are transitory phases of the inscrutable Brahm, itself unpersonal, which for ever evolves and absorbs universes and persons,

THE DOCTRINE OF GOD.

yet without design, sovereignty, or distinction. It is remarkable that human instinct has so triumphed, however, as to make India the stronghold of developed polytheism, which is, in this case at least, the popular correlative of an inner pantheism.

Revelation wholly repudiates pantheism, above all by its witness to the eternal difference of right and wrong, and by always representing the Creator as the wholly free personal Cause of all other existence, and wholly sovereign over it. On the other hand, it fully responds to the element of truth in pantheism, by revealing the true God as not only distinct from His creation, and sovereign over it, but always and everywhere present and working in it; not so that "the universe thinks and knows," but so that His living, willing, and holy presence is the sustaining cause of all things moment by moment, in their nevertheless real existence, and while they work each in its sphere and order.

Atheism, although in theory the creed of the many millions of oriental Buddhists, is now rarely avowed, in a positive form, in thoughtful circles of unbelief. Practically, it involves the view that the world of phenomena explains itself. But observation shows more and more clearly that the universe, so far as its material resources and laws go, tends to quiescence and death. It is not self-sufficient for its existence. It must therefore have begun, originated *ab extra*, by a cause or causes not material. Non-theistic thought infers from this an impersonal eternal " force " as the cause; a cause not only mysterious, but unknowable; only, man can know that it is not the archetype of his own personality. To this view the abiding answer is our immediate certainty of personality, of self-conscious-

16 OUTLINES OF CHRISTIAN DOCTRINE.

ness, will, and conscience, and of the relative greatness of this amongst other kinds of being. In his personality man knows himself to be higher than even the most impressive of his surroundings, viewed as unconscious and without will. And he is assured, in the deepest sense of a reasonable certainty, that the true Cause of himself, a person, is not devoid of personality. His intuitions rest in an eternal Person as the ultimate truth, as they cannot rest in eternal non-personal being.

The non-theistic view just stated, as an alternative to material atheism, is what is known (with very many modifications of detail) as *Agnosticism*. It has affinities in some respects with pantheism, though widely differing from it in others. Like it, it leaves no real ground for the ideas of government of the world, of sin, of accountability and retribution. Meanwhile, it has in it elements of truth, recognized by Revelation. God, according to Scripture, is "unknowable" in the sense of being never "found out unto perfection;" in the sense that He only wholly knows His own infinite glorious being wholly as it is. He eternally invites, and eternally transcends, our thought. Only, we are sure that nothing unknown or unknowable in Him contradicts what He has revealed of Himself.

Deism is very much a word of the past. It denotes the belief of an almighty, or mighty, Contriver and Maker of the universe, who however is not actively sovereign over it, and is not immanent in it. In particular, it is a belief which declines to admit the fact (whether or no the possibility) of miraculous Revelation. Such a view of God and the world is discountenanced, not only by Scripture, but by independent observation and inference.

THE DOCTRINE OF GOD.

In closest connexion with the testimonies to God commonly adduced from man and nature, we lawfully claim, as a great concurrent evidence, Christianity, (or let us say, Jesus Christ Himself,) antecedent to any detailed study of the Christian doctrinal system. What, on the whole, is the testimony of mankind to Christ? There are many exceptions, real or apparent, to the testimony. But as a fact He has commanded not only the moral adoration of sixty generations of disciples, but also, to a degree quite without parallel, the moral reverence of those who have not submitted to His claims. In the languages of the foremost races the word "Christian" is practically synonymous with "righteous" and "good." And this Object of the homage of the human conscience not only confesses God, but claims unique connexion with and mission from God.

And Jesus Christ is no mere Ideal of the human conscience, evolved from its own materials. He is historical. His personality, character, utterances, and acts cannot, in the nature of things mental and moral, be the creation of the thought of Galilean peasants and a zealous Pharisee, of eighteen centuries ago, nor of their period. He appears before us as a fact of the past, with the practical alternatives that we see in Him either the supreme example of self-illusion or the supreme Truth. The natural verdict of human conscience is not on the side of the former.

This is not a book of Christian evidences. We can only point to the obvious fact that the evidences of Christianity are all evidences of course of theism, and direct us towards the highest answer to the further questions raised by natural theism. Only here, as everywhere else in the enquiry, the observer,

18 OUTLINES OF CHRISTIAN DOCTRINE.

man, as well as the phenomena observed, must be remembered.

In closing this section, we make a few detached remarks.

(1) Our physical evidence for the existence of God is akin to that for the existence of man. We infer, however unconsciously, the presence of human personalities around us, from observing matter around us acted on in a way which in ourselves we directly know to imply personality. So we infer the Supreme Personality, however dimly, from observing everywhere, around and within, the phenomenon of adjustment which we know implies, in the action of our own being, intention.

(2) A view of the Creator as working in His creation as well as ruling over it prepares us to find that the traces of His working differ in many respects from the traces of ours. "He leaves no chips." The hands and tools with which He works are, in the last analysis, His will, on which also the material rests for its existence and which gives it the power and law of its development from within.

(3) The dependence, absolutely and always, of creation on the Creator (Rev. iv. 11) is a truth more distinctive of Revelation than is commonly understood. The tendency of non-biblical systems of thought has been either to make the universe co-existent with God, who modifies and adjusts, but does not sovereignly originate and order, or to identify more or less the universe with God. The doctrine of Creation, with which Scripture begins and which is everywhere supposed in it, is all-important to the Scripture doctrine of Providence, which teaches us to regard the whole system of events as so related to the sovereign will that while every move-

THE DOCTRINE OF THE TRINITY. 19

ment of secondary causes is left truly free, the whole issue is such that " of Him, and through Him, and to Him, are all things " (Rom. xi. 36).

The One God stands in Scripture really and absolutely alone as the free personal Cause, the Creator, of all material and spiritual existence; as its true reason, not only of origin but of continuance in being; as its supreme and entirely just Lord, Lawgiver, and Judge; as its true Final Cause or *Raison d' être*; for He has made it "for Himself." He is not only greatest of Beings, first among many; He is the Being of Beings, such that nothing not being of His Essence can for a moment exist independent of it, or out of relation to Him. Being uncaused, He is in the fullest sense Eternal; His mode of being has nothing to do with either origin or close. Declining all analysis of the idea of eternity, Holy Scripture abundantly teaches that, whatever be the nature of matter or of spirit, the material universe, and the spiritual, are not conditions of, but consequent upon, the being and the eternally free will of God; never to be identified with Him, but never to be dissociated from Him as original and perpetual Cause, alike in their ultimate elements and in their whole combination.

II. THE HOLY TRINITY.

" In unity of this Godhead there be three Persons, of one substance, power, and eternity; the Father, the Son, and the Holy Ghost" (Art. I.).

For evidence on this supreme doctrine we go to the Holy Scriptures. A basis for it has often been sought, and thought to be found, in independent speculation on the nature of things, on the laws of being and of thought. But it is at least safer for those who accept the Scriptures to make them the whole basis. The *existence* of the supreme personal Cause and Lord may lawfully fall within the scope of natural evidence; but not so, surely, the *mode* of His existence. This He must Himself reveal. Nature and man may in certain ways harmonize with, or reflect, that mode of existence, but cannot be trusted to disclose it. A brief outline of Scripture evidence is accordingly presented.

(1) The basis of Trinitarian doctrine is Unitarian ––God is One. The divine Nature is not, like the human, distributed through or realized in a class of individuals; it is the Nature of One Being, who is at once the Individual and the Kind. He in the sphere of divine existence is One in such a sense that other claimants to Godhead can be called God only by direct usurpation or by figurative and well guarded designation, as when human judges are called *Elôhim* (Psal. lxxxii. 1, 6). As a few specimen passages of the "unitarian" doctrine of Holy Scripture, see Deut. iv. 35, vi. 4, xxxii. 39; 2 Sam. xxii. 32; 2 Kings xix. 15; Psal. lxxxvi. 10; Isai. xlii. 8, xliv. 8; Mark xii. 32. Further, this great truth appears in Scripture as a thing of warm and pressing practical importance. The Eternal One, being infinitely great, good, and holy, eternally and necessarily knows Himself to be such, and cannot, without ceasing to be Himself, "give His glory to another," nor approve the slightest transference of the allegiance, adoration, praise, and love, of the created being. Not in selfish jealousy but in eternal rightness, having justly caused all existence for Himself, He requires its right relation to Himself. And so far as that existence consists in personal wills, He eternally

THE DOCTRINE OF THE TRINITY. 21

and necessarily requires all wills, if they are to be in right relation to Him, to will His will, to find their highest utterance in His praise, to work always in the line of adoring and loving homage to Him, to recognize their creaturely relation in everything. Personal beings must personally live as those who live by, in, and for God. He meanwhile is always, and necessarily, and at once, alike the righteous claimant of such worship and love, and its infinitely good and satisfying Object; glorifying and beatifying the creature so related to Him. For evidence from the side of human consciousness to the supreme fitness and rightness of such a divine demand on human adoration, we may justly point to the spiritual experience of all true believers in the God of the Bible. To them, obedience to this sublime command is the most ennobling action of their will, understanding, and affections. With a joy that cannot be expressed they "give thanks to Him for His great glory," and recognize in that glory the true final cause of all His adorable ways.

Under this head see, for example, Exod. xv. 11; Psal. xlvii. 7, l. 23, xcix. 3, cxlvi.-cl.; Isai. xl. 12-28; Jer. v. 22, x. 7; Rom. xi. 33-36, xvi. 25-27; Eph. i. 6, iii. 20, 21; 1 Tim. vi. 15, 16; Jude 24, 25; Rev. xix. 5.

Such, faintly adumbrated—for even in Scripture we know Him but in part—is the One God; such is the consistent Unitarianism of Revelation.

(2) But here comes in the Trinitarian phenomenon of the Scriptures.

Throughout the Book, as we have seen, One God appears as the object and claimant of supreme love and worship; and His claim is guarded with holy jealousy. Yet meanwhile more Personal Existences than One are addressed, or treated of, in Scripture, in terms of supreme love and worship—in fact, as God. Let *both* these facts be given full and unreserved weight, and then compared and coordinated; and their convergence at least concurs with the catholic doctrine of the Holy Trinity. *Both* facts are necessary; for the evidence of the second will be weak out of relation to the first. It is the first which decisively forbids us to explain the second either in a polytheistic sense, or in the sense of a mere delegation of divine functions, or of a *quasi-*Godhead, to beings not properly divine. For the language used about the love and worship rendered in the cases instanced is such as to invade the prerogatives of Eternal Deity if it is not harmonized with them by being given to Those who are within It.

We do not here enter in detail on the statement of the evidence for the Godhead of the Son, and of the Spirit. See further below, in the proper places (pp. 57, 119, etc.). The inner relations of the Trinity will there find fuller consideration, so far as we may reverently attempt it.

Here, with a brief catena of passages, we rather assume the fact hereafter to be illustrated, and (*a*) make a short statement on the whole question, and (*b*) briefly outline the history of the doctrine.

The Deity of Scripture, then, is One Being, in a sense of oneness infinitely deeper than that in which, as in men, *man* is one—by a common nature in many individuals. The Oneness of Godhead is altogether unique, and implies a unity of the eternal Content ineffable, absolute, so that nothing can be more truly one; and necessary, that

THE DOCTRINE OF THE TRINITY.

is to say, such that Its eternal reason for so being is in Itself. Such is the Eternal Nature, which is also the Eternal One, that being eternally and necessarily not only Being but Love, It has more than oneness, It has relation, within Itself. In one respect One, it is in another respect Three; three eternally harmonious Wills, Agents, Persons; Persons, inasmuch as there is between Them knowledge, will, and love. Each has as His nature the entire Divine nature, which is quality, not quantity: Each is truly God. Each is necessarily and eternally one in Being with the Others: there are not Three Gods. Each is not the Others: there are Three Persons.

Meanwhile this Harmony presents with equal clearness the phenomenon of internal Subordination. The Father is not more divine than the Son, or than the Spirit; but He is the Father. Godhead is in Him as in the Eternal Fountain; in the Son and in the Spirit as in the Eternal Streams. They are not accidents of His will, any more than His holiness is an accident of His will (for without it He would not be God). Nevertheless, He is the Father of the Son, the Source of the Spirit. Such is His primacy that He is continually spoken of, by the side of mentions of the Son and of the Spirit, as simply God; while yet the other evidence forbids us, if we would submit, to explain this of a difference of Nature. It indicates a primacy of Relation, of Order.

See the following passages; Matt. xi. 25-27; Joh. v. 19-23, 26, 27, vi. 38, viii. 38, x. 29, xiv. 28, xvii.; and in general all passages where the phraseology of Sonship is used of our Lord in His divine Nature.

24 OUTLINES OF CHRISTIAN DOCTRINE.

Detached Remarks on Trinitarian Doctrine.

(1) In the Old Testament there is an adumbration. The plural noun *Elôhim* (singular, *Elôah*[1]) appears continually in the Old Testament with a singular verb. It would be too much to say that this reveals the Plurality in Unity, but it certainly is in deep and suggestive harmony with it.

Again, in a large range of passages a Being appears whose character is at once that of Messenger and Master, Angel of Jehovah and Jehovah. See e.g. Gen. xvi. 10, xxii. 12, xxxi. 11-13; Numb. xxii. 32; Josh. v. 13-vi. 2; Isai. lxiii. 9; Mal. iii. 1. Such passages at least adumbrate the truth that the divine Unity is not such as to exclude inner Relation.

Again, the divine Spirit is spoken of in terms which at least suggest that in God's mode of being His Spirit is not an impersonal Thing, but a Personal Being; not only Influence, but Agent. See Isai. xlviii. 16.

We may reverently add, as possible indications in the same direction, the threefold benediction, Numb. vi. 24-26; and the threefold ascription, Isai. vi. 3.

(2) The truth of the Trinity is accordingly in the New Testament less announced than assumed and developed, in the light of the Incarnation of the Son, and of the Mission of the Spirit to the world and to the Church.

(3) There is a recognized distinction in theology between the Trinity "Immanent," or Essential, and

---

[1] Whatever the ultimate derivation, there appears to be no doubt that the form of the words *El*, *Elôah*, *Elôhim* conveyed to the Hebrew the idea of power.

THE DOCTRINE OF THE TRINITY. 25

the Trinity Economical, or Dispensational. The Immanent Trinity is a phrase pointing to the eternal inner relation of the Persons. The Economical Trinity is a phrase pointing to what may be called with reverence the redeeming activities of the Persons. It views the Father as the Giver of the Son, the Supreme Author of the Incarnation and Resurrection, and the Adopter in Him of the saints. It views the Son as the Son, not only Eternal, but also Incarnate and Mediating. It views the Spirit as not only the eternal Bond of love between the Father and the Son, but the Glorifier of Christ in human hearts, and the Regenerator of fallen men into children of God in Christ, and the Bond of life and love between Christ and His Church. The distinction is helpful and important as a formulation of great revealed facts. Meanwhile it is obvious that there is a deep and necessary relation and connexion between the two aspects of the Holy Trinity.

(4) *Illustrations of the Doctrine of the Trinity.*— Up to a certain point illustration is lawful and helpful. Anything which illustrates the way in which apparent contradictions are often harmonized by remembering differences of point of view, may be thus in point. But the Trinity in Unity, being the mode of existence of the Eternal, is a thing essentially unique, and is therefore lifted far above the possibility of complete comparison or illustration. The student and teacher will do wisely therefore to deal very sparingly with such treatment of the doctrine, and will always guard what he does in this direction with a remembrance of the unique nature of the subject.

SUPPLEMENTARY.

HISTORY OF THE DOCTRINE OF THE HOLY TRINITY.

WE trace the history of the doctrine in the form of a very brief account of some chief misbeliefs, occasioning as they did closer examinations and definitions of the revealed Truth.

(1) In the *Gnostic* systems (say A.D. 60 to 200) the Trinitarian question is involved only by the fact that the terms Christ, Jesus, Holy Spirit, appear in them. A principle common to all these systems is the view of the Supreme as raised, not only above immediate contact with the world, but above all we conceive or define of personal existence and its attributes; so that in the scheme of Basilides, He, or It, appears as the *Non-Existent* (οὐκ ὤν). Such *quasi*-knowledge, however, as man can gain of Him is man's salvation; a *quasi*-knowledge purely speculative and contemplative, without love or service. This knowledge descends to man through a long chain of Emanations, in which the links are super-terrestrial existences. Among these existences appear a "Christ" (or, in one system, two Christs), and a Holy Spirit. The "Christ" appeared on earth either in mere semblance of, or as united to, a man, Jesus; but so that the higher being was in no way involved in the sufferings of the lower. What concerns the doctrine of the Trinity here is the tacit witness to the Christian belief that Christ is super-human, and the Holy Spirit personal.

(2) Akin in some respects to Gnosticism, but remote from it in others, is *Manicheism*. Its *floruit* begins about A.D. 280. Its feature was an explicit[1] doctrine of Dualism; the theory that the co-existence of good and evil in phenomena involves the eternal co-existence of two originals, God and Satan, Spirit and Matter, Light and

---

[1] Gnosticism, with its tenet of the essential evil of Matter, was implicitly dualist, and often explicitly so.

THE DOCTRINE OF THE TRINITY. 27

Darkness. What concerns us here is that the Manichean doctrine of Christ and the Spirit made a nearer verbal approach than the Gnostic to the catholic truth of the Trinity, and witnesses so far to its wide acceptance. From the Father, Lord of Light, emanated two Persons, subordinate to Him, the Son and the Holy Spirit. Jesus Christ was the Son, sent to enlighten souls, and to teach them how to escape from the prison of matter. His Body was not really material; His death, resurrection, and ascension were only mystical and visionary. There is no recognition of the mystery of eternal distinctions and relations *within* the Godhead. The Son and Spirit of the Manichean are little more than modes of the action of the good God.

(3) Somewhat earlier, and more within the Church, we find developed the *Monarchian* type of thought. Of its expounders the best known is Sabellius, a North African, an active teacher as early as A.D. 200. But the principle of the error was held about the same period by many and often mutually independent teachers; an often repeated phenomenon in the progress of both error and truth. Noetus, Beryllus, Paul of Samosata, and (later) Photinus, were all essentially Monarchian. The view indicated by this word is that God is essentially Unipersonal, and Three only in manifestation to us. The same Person, as the Father, decreed to save; as the Son, was incarnate and suffered; as the Holy Spirit, influences man. The Sabellian perplexed the orthodox with the question, often asked since in the same spirit, "*Have we one God, or three?*" And believers, in reply, sometimes used language about essential differences between the Father and the Son, such as to open the door to errors of the next type. The Monarchian theory is not a reverent induction from Scripture, but an attempt to harmonize its teaching with the *à priori* conception of a God necessarily unipersonal, devoid of inner relations of eternal love,

(4) The next great alien theory was the *Arian*. Arius (*floruit* A.D. 321-36) was the champion of the view which still assumed Unipersonality as essential in the Supreme. But, recognizing the personal difference given in Scripture between Father, Son, and Spirit, he taught, not three phases of the One, but that the One willed into existence Two Possessors of a subordinate *quasi*-Deity, to be His intermediaries with the world and man. Claiming to be scriptural, and insisting on the Personality of the Son and of the Spirit, he ascribed to the Son an existence pre-temporal, yet not eternal; a surpassing greatness and glory, yet not a *necessity* of existence. The Son's exalted being was yet originally contingent on the will of the Supreme. Conceivably, He *need not have been*; that is, He was a creature, though a creature who could in turn create, and could become incarnate in a *quasi*-man (below, p. 66). The doctrine of the Spirit was but slightly expounded by Arius. His followers arrived at the theory that the Spirit was willed into existence by the Son, and was thus God in a sense only *tertiary* (below, p. 148).

(5) Plainly, a common ground in the above systems is the assumption that the true God must be unipersonal. Each finds at least a hint of refutation when the Scripture is seen to assume and indicate interior and necessary relations of love in the unique Being of the Supreme. In that view, the supremacy of God over creation, and the sovereignty of His will, are as secure as ever; but a wholly new intensity is given to the truth that God is Love, and thus a new aspect to the reality and glory of the union of man with God in the Son Incarnate. To expound this truth was the great work of Athanasius and his immediate successors. It had been held before, but imperfectly set forth and vindicated. The truths whose harmony forms the true doctrine—the Unity of God, and the true Deity, yet Subordination, of the Begotten Son and the Proceeding Spirit—had been held, and held together; but very much as truths proposed to faith (as

THE DOCTRINE OF THE TRINITY. 29

some truths doubtless are), unrelieved by a harmony summing them up into one.

(6) *Leading Alien Theories of Modern Times.* — Of these perhaps the most distinct and important are those connected with the words *Unitarian* and *Swedenborgian*.

Of the "Unitarian" theology it is difficult to speak precisely, for it deprecates, on principle, dogmatic fixity. Its one really common tenet appears to be the necessary Unipersonality of the Godhead, involving the inferior nature of Christ. Within this lies a large gradation of views. The early Unitarians, at the era of the Reformation, held a doctrine akin to the Arian, and many modern Unitarians probably do the same. But the doctrine was early started that Christ was mere man (whether supernaturally born or not), and in no sense an object of worship; and this is perhaps the more prevalent modern view. Unitarians hold very various opinions on the authority of Scripture, from deep reverence to advanced rationalism; these, of course, are reflected in their theology.

Unitarians are often called Socinians, from the Italian teachers Lælius and Faustus Socinus (cent. xvi.). But the opinions of the Socini were Arian. The term Unitarian meanwhile is to be conceded only under reserve. The Trinitarian is an earnest Unitarian with regard to the Unity of the divine *Being*.

The theology of Swedenborg (1688—1772) is in some respects *sui generis*. A Trinity appears to be recognized within the Godhead. In Christ, supernaturally born, resides this triune Godhead, so modified, or manifested, as to be accessible to worship. The Holy Spirit is the influence communicated to churches and individuals by Christ. Worship is to be addressed to Christ alone, who is, for man, the One God.

The followers of Swedenborg are numerous; organized as the New Jerusalem Church, or the Church of the New Dispensation.

The Word "Trinity" (Τριάς, Triad)

The first formal adoption of the word to designate the Three in One, One in Three, dates A.D. 317, at a synod held at Alexandria. That the holy Mystery was long before this a common article of Christian confession appears from e.g. a passage in Lucian, the Voltaire of antiquity, (*floruit* probably about A.D. 160). In his *Philopatris* the Christian is made to confess "The exalted God, . . . Son of the Father, Spirit proceeding from the Father, One of Three, and Three of One."

"Trinity" properly means "Threefoldness." It is not, as it is sometimes said to be, a shortened form of *Triunity*

CHAPTER III.

THE DOCTRINE OF GOD (CONTINUED).

THE DOCTRINE OF THE FATHER.

ON this most sacred region of truth much is best said under the Doctrine of the Son, and that of the Spirit. The study of Their revealed glory, always related to that of the Father, who is Their fountain, best illustrates His. And thus, on the other hand, the Christian will always aim, not occasionally, but in deep purpose, in the study of Them, to study Him. All we know of Them is revealed, ultimately, "to the glory of God the Father" (Phil. ii. 11).

With this resolve we consider here, briefly, and only in some respects, what the Scriptures say of His will and work.

Creation.—In a sense special and supreme He is the Creator; "the Father Almighty, Maker of Heaven and Earth." Through the Son, by the Spirit, Creation was, and is. But in Their operation, the Father of the Son, the Giver of the Spirit, works His will, realizes His idea. Thus ultimately to Him, in a sense not of separation from Their work, but of operation through it, is due Creation, in its scriptural sense; that is, the willing of the finite into being, with the absolutely free volition of Infinite

Power and Goodness. We repeat it (above, pp. 18, 19), that nothing less or other than this is the Scripture view of the relation of Creation to God. It is not coeval with Him, nor necessary to Him, nor an emanation of Him. It is altogether contingent upon His will, so that He would not have been less Himself had it never been. It is observable in this connexion that Scripture never calls the Eternal Father *the Father of* the Cosmos, of the Universe; a term which might have favoured the thought of emanation, and perhaps suggested a co-eternity. He who is eternally the Father of the Son is freely and absolutely the Maker of the world. Finite being had a true beginning, at His *fiat*, however indiscoverable to us the distance of its date is. And Creation, as being thus the product of His mere will, is ever viewed in Scripture as wholly in His hands. It presents no difficulties to Him, as if matter, or finite being, were an alien something in His way. Nothing but sin is seen in Scripture as related so to God (below, p. 80).

Redemption.—It is out of the Father's Love, for the Father "is Love" (see 1 Joh. iv. 8, 9, 16, and the context), that the whole Redemption flows (Joh. iii. 16, vi. 38; Rom. iii. 21-26, viii. 32; Eph. iii. 3-12; 1 Pet. i. 3, 21; 1 Joh. iv. 9, etc.). Nothing is more unscriptural than any shadow of the thought that the Son is more merciful than the Father; that the Son interposed to make the Father willing to spare and save. Our Second Article (and so the Trent Catechism, *Pars* i., *c.* v., *Qu.* xiv.) says that the Son was sacrificed "that He might reconcile His Father to us"; and the purport of this phrase, though not the phrase, is fully scriptural. But the meaning is not that the Atonement induced the

THE DOCTRINE OF THE FATHER. 33

Father to have mercy, but that it liberated, so to speak, His mercy by satisfying His law. As Creator He loves His creatures. As Lawgiver and Judge He is the adversary of the law-breaker, pending vindication and satisfaction. But He Himself provided the sacred Satisfaction; "He spared not His own Son" (Rom. viii. 32). The satisfaction was eternally necessary, demanded by no mere exigencies of government, but by His own Nature, which alone is exigency to God. But His own uncaused Love found and gave it, in "sending" the Only Begotten, whose own free, divine, and blessed love, while indeed His own, is also of the Father; for the Son, in all He is, is "of the Father alone."

Thus the Father "loved the world;" a phrase to be read with unreserved adoration and thanks. It is a revealed truth that "His tender mercies are over all His works" (Psal. cxlv. 9); and that particularly He "loveth man as man" (Tit. iii. 4). Nothing must be allowed to negative this truth, or put it into the background. And accordingly "He willeth that all men should be saved" (1 Tim. ii. 4); "He willeth not that any should perish" (2 Pet. iii. 9); "as He liveth, He hath no pleasure in the death of him that dieth" (Ezek. xviii. 32, xxxiii. 11).

"We give Him thanks for His great glory," in which the central and intense light is Love. Infinitely unlike the Abyss of the Gnostic, or the unknowable Absolute of a modern philosophy, He is Love. To know Him, the Fount of Deity, by His Spirit, through His Son, is to touch nothing less than the perfectly tender and responsive Original of all personality, all love; paternal in a sense truly akin to, while infinitely transcending, the paternity of man's heart.

Is He accordingly the Father of every human being, so that each can say, as such, "I am a child of God"? If by Fatherhood is meant the divine side of that profound and tender relation which must exist between the all-loving Creator and His rational moral creature, made in His image (below, p. 157), and capable of true love to Him and an eternal likeness to Him, then the Father is Father of universal Man. Yet the use of the terms of proper Fatherhood to describe this relation is not fully in accord with Scripture. A few passages appear to look the other way; especially Luke iii. 38; Acts xvii. 28, 29. But it is plain that in Scripture the words Father, Son, Child, etc., in this connexion, tend habitually to refer, not to nature, but to grace; not to creation, but to redemption, and especially to adoption and regeneration; not to Adam, but to Christ; not to the world, but to the Church. See, out of a great mass of Scripture evidence, Matt. v. 9, xiii. 43; Joh. i. 12, viii. 42; Rom. viii. 14, 15, 17, 21, ix. 7; Gal. iv. 5, 6; Eph. i. 5, v. 1; 1 Joh. iii. 1, 2, 9, 10, v. 1; and cp. Deut. xiv. 1; Psal. ciii. 13; Isai. lxiii. 16. The "Lord's Prayer" (Matt. vi. 9) was expressly taught to "His disciples" (Matt. v. 1, and cp. 45). Along with this reference of the words Father and Son, goes the truth of the absolute and universal need of Regeneration (Joh. i. 13, iii. 3, 5, 7; 1 Pet. i. 23; 1 Joh. iii. 9, iv. 7, v. 4, 18; cp. 2 Cor. v. 17; Gal. vi. 15), in order to right relations with God. This *new birth*, along with the kindred revelation of the *adoption* of grace, is in Scripture the foreground aspect of the whole subject of Divine Fatherhood.

THE DOCTRINE OF THE FATHER. 35

Compared with this Fatherhood, under which we become "partakers of the divine nature" (2 Pet. i. 4), the Fatherhood of Creation appears rather as a profound relation analogous to the paternal idea than as Fatherhood in its proper meaning, which demands a true and proper impartation of nature.

Thank God, the circle of the true Fatherhood, immovable in its holy limits, is graciously open to faith. "Whosoever will" is welcome to step into it, met by a divine embrace, in the name of the Only Begotten and infinitely beloved Son of God, "Firstborn among many brethren" (Rom. viii. 29).

These reflections lead us to the revealed action of the Eternal Father in the provision made for the redemption, salvation, and glorification of the Church (on the Doctrine of the Church see further below, p. 202, etc.). The gift of the redeeming Son is the act of the Father's supreme love. And thus, through the Son, One with Himself, the Father also redeems (so often in the Old Testament; e.g. Isai. lxiii. 16); whether Redemption is taken in its larger and *potential* sense, of full provision for deliverance, or in its (much more frequent) *actual* sense, of accomplished deliverance, the experienced rescue of its objects from condemnation and from the power of sin.[1] But more particularly it is the Father who "lays on" the Son "the iniquities

[1] "God the Son hath redeemed me and *all mankind*" (Church Catechism). These words are referable to the *kind*, the *genus*. So has the Son of God dealt for and with that kind that it is restored, and more than restored, in Him, to acceptance and holiness, and that restoration is ready to be realized in any individual of it believing on Him. But actual, biographical "redemption" of the individual, if the Scripture use of the word "redeem" is observed, is not an accomplished fact till his incorporation into Christ by the Spirit, nor fully realized till resurrection (Rom. viii. 23).

of us all" (Isai. liii. 6), and who, on the other hand, "justifies," or pronounces accepted, all who are found united to the Son in faith by the Spirit (see Rom. iii. 24, 26, 30, iv. 5, viii. 30, 33, and see further below, p. 183). It is He who "adopts" (Rom. viii. 15; Gal. iv. 5; Eph. i. 5) these same persons to be His children, as members of His Son (see just above, p. 34), thus meeting with an act of sublimely legal acceptance His concurrent gift of new birth and new creation. He sends and gives not only the redeeming Son, but the regenerating Spirit, by whom our will, understanding, and affections are so dealt with that the man, coming in willing faith to the Son, receives the mystery of regenerate life in Him (see Luke xi. 13; Joh. i. 13 with iii. 8, xiv. 16, 26; Rom. v. 5; 1 Pet. i. 2; cp. Joh. vi. 44, 45). Thus, ultimately, it is the Father who gives the regenerate life, "calling" the soul into it, with a "call" which not only proclaims, but actually, without the least violation of the will, prevails.[1] Those thus "called" and "justified" by the Father are by Him "kept" (Joh. xvii. 11, 15; 1 Pet. i. 5), and "sanctified" (Joh. xvii. 17); and finally "glorified" (Joh. xvii. 24; Rom. viii. 30); "to the praise of the glory of His grace" (Eph. i. 6).

These revelations lead up to the revelation of an Election, or Choice, on the Father's part, with a view to this call, justification, and glorification. On this great mystery we speak with humble reserve and reverence. It has been and is an occasion of even agonizing perplexity to many hearts dear to God.

---

[1] See, for this meaning of "call," e.g., 1 Cor. i. 23, 24. It is regular in the Epistles. In the Gospels the meaning is rather invitation successful *or not* (Matt. xxii. 14).

THE DOCTRINE OF THE FATHER. 37

A very few steps of thought into it bring us to a stand, on the brink of the unknown. And every inference upon it needs always to be governed and qualified by the unalterable facts that the Lord's tender mercies are over all His works, that He willeth not the death of a sinner, that God is Love. Never for a moment is God either unmerciful or unjust. Never does He magnify one of His attributes *at the expense of* another. Yet in the revelation of His ways we must be prepared for phenomena which, at least at present, are to us absolutely mysterious; for instance, for actions of His will as He is Sovereign, and as He is His own eternal End, and as He is Infinite, which we cannot formally harmonize with His explicit assurances and proofs of pure and universal Love.

Such insoluble elements are inherent in all thought on the action of the Infinite on the finite. Our thought must very often come to its end when we have to study, e.g., the use of means by infinite Will, the action in time of the Eternal, the relations between us who become and Him who is "I AM."

Here we have such necessary mystery specially around us. In Scripture, we find an element of unexplained divine will and choice regarding the actual participants in salvation. We carefully say, "*an element.*" The sacred thing in question is not the *ruling truth* of the Gospel. It does not hold there the place of Incarnation, Atonement, or Regeneration. But it is there. See in particular Rom. viii. 28, 29, 30, 33; Eph. i. 4; 2 Thess. ii. 13; 1 Pet. i. 2. See Rom. ix. 6-25 for a strong assertion of the principle of an inscrutable action of the will of God in choice; action based not on caprice, or mere force (God forbid!), but on relations between Creator and creature which lie beyond us. See 2 Tim. i. 9 for a similar aspect of this truth; that this action of His will is "not according to our works;" not to be accounted for by anything of merit in the objects of it. With this compare such Old Testament passages as Deut. vii. 7, 8, ix. 4, 6, where the choice of Israel to peculiar blessings is described as similarly sovereign. With this again compare Rom. xi. 2, where this sovereign resolve and choice is called "foreknowledge;" an indication of the meaning of that word in still deeper connexions (Rom. viii. 29; 1 Pet. i. 2; and cp. Acts ii. 23). See further Rom. xi. 5-7. Another aspect of the same truth appears in 1 Cor. i. 27, 28. In that passage the Apostle speaks of a special and distinguishing divine action on human hearts, not to be accounted for by anything in them, but just such as to illustrate the triumph of grace over sin. See, on this side of the subject, the passages where the Christian is taught to refer every link of his salvation to the will and gift of God (1 Cor. iv. 7; Eph. ii. 8); and where the Father is seen as "giving" to the Son those who actually "hear the voice" of Christ and receive "life eternal" from Him (Joh. vi. 37, x. 29, xvii. 2, 3, 6, 9, 11, 12, 24).

This work of electing grace is consistently assigned to the Eternal Father. In a very few passages (see Joh. vi. 70, xiii. 18, xv. 16, 19; Acts i. 2, 24, ix. 15, and cp. Joh. v. 21), the Son is seen to "choose." But in most of these passages the reference is rather to work and privilege than to acceptance and holiness. And in Joh. v. 21 the context explicitly connects the choice of the Son with that of the Father as with its eternal basis.

The language of Joh. xvii. (and vi. and x.), just

THE DOCTRINE OF THE FATHER.

referred to, leads to the doctrine of the relation of the Father to the Son in the work of the salvation of the Church. With this we close the treatment of this aspect of the doctrine of grace, and then append some remarks on questions of detail, and on history.

Nothing shines more radiantly in the New Testament than the eternal love of the Father for the Son (Joh. i. 18, v. 20, xvii. 24, etc.). The Son is "His well-beloved" (Mark xii. 6), "in whom He is well pleased" (Matt. iii. 17), whom it is His eternal will to "glorify" (Joh. xvii. 5; Eph. i. 10, 11; Phil. ii. 9-11; Col. i. 16-18). So here, not only is the Son the one infinitely meritorious Sacrifice, and Risen King and Head of the Church, but in the antecedent work of covenant and choice, it is with Him that we see, as through a cloud of light, the Father dealing. "In Him" the saints were "chosen, before the foundation of the world" (Eph. i. 4); "through Him predestinated to the adoption of sons" (*ibid.*, 5); "in Him," in the same premundane purpose, "made an inheritance" (*ibid.*, 11). "In Him," in the same purpose, they "received grace" (2 Tim. i. 9), "according to" which, and not to their "works," they are "called" and "saved" in time. To the Son the Father "gave" them; a phrase plainly of like reference. Their "predestination" is, "to be conformed to the likeness of the Son" (Rom. viii. 29); "to be holy and without blame before the Father in love" (Eph. i. 6), as accepted in the Son. Accordingly, when the process descends from eternity to time, they are actually united by the Spirit (1 Cor. vi. 17; Eph. iv. 4) to Christ, as limbs to Head (1 Cor. xi. 3; Eph. i. 22, iv. 15, v. 23; Col. i. 18, ii. 19); so joined to Him that He and they are one "Christ" (1 Cor. xii. 12; cp. Gal.

ii. 20). They are "in His hand," and "in His Father's hand," so that "no one can pluck them out" (Joh. x. 28, 29). The issue is that they are "glorified together with" the Son (Rom. viii. 17); "in Him" (2 Thess. i. 12); "obtaining His glory" (*ibid.*, ii. 14); "being with Him, beholding His glory" (Joh. xvii. 24).

Through the whole plan and process, from "before the world was," we see the Eternal Father loving the Son with immeasurable love, conducting Him to a peculiar and supreme glory as Lamb, Priest, King, Head, Bridegroom, of the Church, ordaining Him to be not only Head and Bond of Creation (Col. i. 17), but, far more prominently, the one Fountain—for the New Creation, for man regenerate, for the Church—of "all spiritual blessing" (Eph. i. 3); of "eternal life" (1 Joh. v. 11). Union with the Son, true and vital, after the order of grace, not nature, is the one indispensable way of acceptance, peace, holiness, power, and final glory. Towards this union with Him of those whom the Father has "given" Him, all the processes of providence and grace converge, under the Father's will (Rom. viii. 28). The construction of the Church in Christ, the glorification of Christ in the Church, and of Himself in that fact (John xvii. 1), is the central thing in the Father's will and ways (Eph. ii. 7, iii. 11, etc.).

It is in this connexion that we find the provision of salvation presented as a *Covenant* made between the Father and the Son. (See Gal. iii. 17; Eph. ii. 12; Heb. vii. 22, viii. 6, ix. 15, xii. 24, xiii. 20; cp. Mal. iii. 1.) This side of Scripture truth (below, p. 102) calls for careful study if we would see the indicated symmetry of the plan of grace. What

THE DOCTRINE OF THE FATHER. 41

the *matter* of the Covenant is appears from, e.g., Heb. x. 16, 17 (cp. Jer. xxxi. 33, 34). It is a magnificently full acceptance, and then (second in idea, though not necessarily in time) an "inscription" of the will of God "on the heart and on the mind."[1] It is Justification and Sanctification, to use familiar terms. It is divine release from the guilt of sin, and from its power (see also 2 Cor. iii. 6-8). Now this, in explicit statements, and in wider indications also, is presented in Scripture as secured under eternal promise by the Father *to the Son*, for His members, out of the free will of divine love, and under the holy condition of the finished work of the Son, whose Blood of Atonement is "the Blood of the Covenant" (Matt. xxvi. 28; Mark xiv. 24; Luke xxi. 20; 1 Cor. xi. 25; Heb. ix. 15-22, xiii. 20). The Son, our blessed Representative in this supreme matter, triumphing as Man over sin and death, is, in the Father's plan and will, the Trustee and Depositary, for His members, of "pardon, holiness, and heaven;" He "is made unto us, of God (the Father), wisdom, even righteousness, and sanctification, and redemption" into glory (1 Cor. i. 30). Potentially, in the sense of undistributed grace, He is all this for *man*. Actually, in the sense of distributed grace, He is this for *His "members,"* His limbs, His body. And they are those designated Rom. viii. 28, 29. They are men "chosen out," "called out," "not according to their works" (2 Tim. i. 9; cp. Eph. ii. 8-10), but "according to the purpose of Him (the Father) who

---

[1] From Jer. xxxi. it is plain that the grace of remission comes, in idea, first; then, the grace of the new "heart" on which "the law is written." The objects of the Covenant are morally transfigured, being freely welcomed (see further, p. 190).

worketh all things after the counsel of His own will" (Eph. i. 11).

Thus, with the symmetry of an eternal plan, "all things" concur for the fulfilment of the Father's will, in the glorification of the Son, and of His members in Him, and of Himself in all. From this sublime point of view rays of relation traverse the whole region of salvation. Nothing is vague, contingent, variable. The will is divine, and so is the foreknowledge (that is, foredecision: see above, p. 38) and the provision for the actual full "spiritual blessing" of its objects. The same "determinate counsel" (Acts ii. 23) of the Father "chooses" the true Church, "calls" member after member in, and has also provided, in the sacrifice and triumph of the Head, for the actual acceptance and new life of every member.

SUPPLEMENTARY

REMARKS ON CERTAIN DETAILS.

CAUTIONS FOR THE STUDY OF THE DOCTRINE OF ELECTION.

(1) The divine Choice is presented in Scripture, like other spiritual truths, never *in vacuo*. It is not an abstract problem, a mere instance of Infinite Will as such, still less the result of a necessity inherent in things. It is connected, on the one hand, with the will of a God who gives *otherwise* magnificent proof that He is All-Good, All-Kind; on the other hand, with the fact, not of mere creaturehood, but of sin. The mankind contemplated is not mankind simply as God's work, but as God's work

THE DOCTRINE OF THE FATHER. 43

perverted from God's will. Even in Rom. ix. it is plain that the fact of *sin* in the creature is in view ; while the creature is enjoined to be silent before the Creator, not because He is merely strong, but because He, as Creator, is, by a deep necessity, beyond the creature's full comprehension as to the whole relations of His ways

(2) In Scripture the divine choice does not work through force upon the will. "He enforceth not the will" (*Westminster Confession*, ch. iii., § 1). It is as certain from Scripture as from our intuitions that man's will is a reality, and is truly free. In its every act it really expresses personal choice, and is not the mere result of material circumstance. A strong drift of modern thought favours "necessitarianism," under which, in effect, man's will is but a phantom, and our consciousness that "we might have chosen otherwise" an illusion. Scripture says nothing of the kind. It appeals everywhere to the will as a true centre of free though finite causation. What it does put before us is the mystery and fact of the Supreme Will, in its absolute and all-embracing freedom, dealing with all things from the eternal centre, so that finite personalities shall all have free play in genuine volition, and so that evil and its results are wholly of the creature, and not of God, and yet that in the summing up of things God shall be seen to have carried out His most holy will in the sum of all events.

(3) The divine choice is so presented in Scripture as to produce certain definite moral impressions. It is not a problem thrown before the disputant, but a fact presented to the convinced conscience, and then to the believing heart. To the awakened conscience it says, " Sinful man has no right to divine mercy ; do you own this *for yourself?*" And where that is owned, the truth has done one side of its work—the work of Rom. ix. To the believing heart it says, first, " Who maketh thee to differ ?" (1 Cor. iv. 7), and then, " All things work together for good to them that love God, to them that are called according

to His purpose" (Rom. viii. 28). And so the truth does the other side of its work—the work of Rom. viii.

(4) The doctrine of the divine choice is not the scriptural foreground, and certainly not the scriptural total, of the doctrine of salvation. There are other sides of truth, so presented as to be in their turn taken as they stand. Scripture isolates for treatment truths which converge in experience. The divine choice, isolated for study, stands out real, sovereign, unalterable, persevering; realizing with divine efficacy the symmetry and detail of a divine plan. On the other hand, the Christian's need to watch and pray, and the perfect reality of the risk of ruin otherwise, and the necessity of missionary and other *labour* in order that the divine plan may be carried out (2 Tim. ii. 10), are just as little to be explained away. As a fact of spiritual experience, no man can use the doctrine of a divine choice in order to give himself comfort during one moment's willing sin, without obscuring his every evidence of grace.

(5) Scripture asserts with loving iteration that the Eternal Father who chose, no less than the Eternal Son who suffered, "willeth not the death of a sinner," "willeth that all men should be saved" (1 Tim. ii. 4). His solemn warnings and most tender invitations are divinely sincere. The feeblest stirring of the human soul towards Him, we may be very sure, is met with a willingness and warmth of attention past our thought. Never, in His holy Word, is the Gospel presented as a message whose scope the messenger is to limit to the "foreknown." The Christian preacher is not only to uphold Christ before men, but to "pray men, in Christ's stead, *be ye reconciled to God*" (2 Cor. v. 20).

To refuse to do so is to forget that Scripture deals, for us, with the sublime truths of the will of God under the limits always imposed on thought and its expression, whenever thought touches upon dealings between the Finite and the Infinite. At that mysterious line of contact, as we have seen already, there tend to occur to the human mind

THE DOCTRINE OF THE FATHER. 45

apparent contradictions, in which the contrasted statements are each a known truth, a fact, not an illusion, while yet the relation between them is unknown, and perhaps knowable only to the Eternal Mind, to Him to whom Time, for example, is related as it is not to us. Under such contradictions falls the truth that the same Eternal Person who "willeth not the death of a sinner," "worketh all things according to the counsel of His own will," and, among all things, the retributory death of the sinner.

(6) It is only to illustrate this to say that the scriptural Christian should be, and will be, "a Calvinist on his knees, an Arminian on his feet." For himself and for others he will pray to, and trust in, a God who has all wills in the hand of His will. To himself and to others he will appeal as to those whose wills and responsibilities are realities indeed. Not that truth lies equally in the systems associated with the names of Calvin and Arminius. But there is that in Scripture which responds from its depths to emphatic points in both. And the full secret of the harmony lies with God.

(7) Here best a few words may be said on the question of the *purposed scope* of the Lord's Atonement. Was its benefit intended for every human being equally, or for man actually and ultimately regenerate only, the chosen Church? For the former view appear, e.g., Isai. liii. 6 (?); Joh. i. 9; 1 Tim. ii. 6; 1 Joh. ii. 2; and cp. 2 Cor. v. 19; also, Rom. xiv. 15; 1 Cor. viii. 11. For the latter appear, e.g., Joh. x. 15, with 26, 29; Eph. v. 25-27; and all passages which limit the actual benefits of the Atonement to the sphere of union with Christ by faith, taken with the truth of God's never-disappointed purposes (Eph. i. 11, etc.). It is plain that on the whole the atoning work appears as not only competent to procure and secure salvation, but as efficaciously doing so. And indeed nothing, from the divine view-point, is loose and contingent; all is within a covenant.

But are we not entitled here also to read the lesson of

parallelism, of apparent contradiction? We are on the border-line where the Eternal touches the temporal, the Infinite the finite. The actual issues of salvation and redemption most surely and exactly realize the eternal purpose, and as it were define it. From this point of view the purpose of the Atonement is limited within the vast (Rev. vii. 9) circle of the true Church. Yet, on the other hand, Scripture not only expressly testifies (as above) to a universal "gracious aspect" of the Atonement, but, by its appeals and invitations, takes such an aspect for granted, in the sense not only of an ample provision, but of a divine willingness and love in offer. The mystery, and at the same time the indication of where the unknown solution lies, resides in the relations of Infinite and finite. The Eternal, as the Eternal, purposes and carries out; as the Eternal condescending to gracious relations with the temporal, He invites all to a full and actual provision.

(8) *The Perseverance of the Saints.*—As we are here concerned with divine plan rather than human action, let us rather say, *the Perseverance of God.* Now here, too, the principle of apparent contradiction enters. Scripture abounds with assurances of perseverance (see Joh. x. 28 for most explicit words) and an exulting anticipation of it, as an element of experience (Rom. viii. 31-9; 1 Pet. i. 8, 9), *and* with warnings and cautions of the deepest earnestness (e.g., 1 Cor. viii. 11, ix. 27 [1]). In a sense, both sides of its language have to be adopted heartily, by the teacher dealing with concrete experiences. But the Scripture evidence as a whole goes for the permanence, in the plan of God, of the once-given "eternal life." As

---

[1] Heb. vi. 4-6, x. 26, 27, have struck deep into human hearts. Rightly, in the case of the man satisfied with himself and his light, and relaxing his watch. But in very different cases they have given an alarm surely not meant by their divine Author. In both the thought is of the possession of intense *light*, rather than divine *life and love.* Balaam's story illustrates every detail of Heb. vi. 4-6.

THE DOCTRINE OF THE FATHER. 47

we patiently compare the Scriptures on the two sides, we shall be struck with the mass, and emphasis, of the positive statements. It is as if the positive side conveyed a ruling spiritual principle,—the negative, a warning not to distort or divorce it; the positive, an assurance for the *Christian* as such,—the negative, a caution to the *man* as such not to delude himself about his Christianity, above all, not to allow anything to palliate a moment's sin. It is remarkable that in the divinely-chosen *biographies* of Scripture no person appears who, at one time certainly a saint of God, at a later time was certainly a lost man.

(9) Is grace, in any sense of the word, ever finally withdrawn ? Yes, if by grace is meant any free gift of God tending to salvation, or more specially any action of the Holy Spirit tending in its nature thither. Spiritual knowledge and light, alarming intuition into judgment, pleasing intuition into the beauty of holiness, are given where, through the sinner's fault, no salvation results (Acts xxiv. 25, with Joh. xvi. 8). A certain special connexion with Christ may be given, and lost (Joh. xv. 6). But if by grace is meant the dwelling and working of God in the truly regenerate, there is no indication in Scripture of the withdrawal of it. The opposite is powerfully indicated (Joh. x. 28 ; cp. xvii. 2, 3, 24). Nowhere occurs the thought of the mortification or amputation of a true *limb* of the mystical Head.

(10) To close ; the practical solution of many spiritual problems lies in the fact that revealed truths, dark and bright alike, are never rightly studied apart from a view of the Real Personality of God. *Solvitur ambulando cum Deo.* This is eminently true in the matter of *Assurance*, whether of present acceptance and divine life, or of final glory. This the Christian will enjoy both the more warmly and the more lawfully the more he actually deals, not only with the promises, but with the Promiser. In adoring intercourse with HIM, through His Son, in His Spirit, it shall be delightfully possible to enjoy without

misgiving the certainty of present spiritual life and its development in glory, and, as a deep element in the joy, to be on the one hand calmly sure that His tender mercies are over all His works, and that in every step of His ways He is both just and merciful, and on the other hand to recognize, with "sweet, pleasant, and unspeakable comfort" (Art. XVII.), that the individual believing soul is the object of a totally unmerited, divinely free, and tenderly special love and call, and of an almighty "keeping, unto salvation ready to be revealed in the last time" (1 Pet. i. 5). In this adoring communion with God, the man thus believing will find in his humble assurance the very opposite of a contraction of sympathies and efforts. If it is indeed GOD IN CHRIST whom he thus knows, trusts, and worships, the joy of possession will by its very nature ask to be communicated. The man will "yield himself" in deep peace to be an implement in the hands of his immeasurably gracious Father, who "so loved the world that He gave His only-begotten Son, that whosoever believeth in Him should not perish, but have everlasting life." He will be, if true to his belief, at once humble and strong, deeply yet wakefully at rest, "at leisure from himself" to be God's means of good for others, as He, sovereign in wisdom, love, and power, shall choose.

THE DOCTRINE OF ELECTION: VARIOUS THEORIES: SKETCH OF THE HISTORY OF OPINION.

Very various theories of this great mystery have been held in the Church. We give a very brief enumeration.

(1) *National Election.*—The Scripture doctrine has been explained as meaning a sovereign choice of nations, or races, to light and privilege. Such election—in the case of the Jews at least—there is. But the theory cannot *satisfy* such passages as Joh. xvii., Rom. viii.

(2) *Ecclesiastical Election.*—It is held, much more widely, that the chosen are, in effect, the members of the Church,

THE DOCTRINE OF THE FATHER. 49

explained as the community of the baptized. On the surface, Scripture gives much support to this ; e.g., St Peter (i. 1, 2) addresses the Christian body in Asia Minor as "elect according to the foreknowledge of God the Father." But here arise great questions connected with the word "Church" (see further below, p. 202, etc.) ; particularly, whether an address to a community in such cases does not inevitably assume its ideal, and not necessarily its concrete and individual, condition. As to the fact of baptism, no reserves would need to be made. But not so as to the reality of faith, hope, and love in a given individual. Yet the whole community is addressed as believing, hoping, and loving. So with the choice of God. If it was a choice "unto salvation through sanctification of the Spirit and faith in the truth" (2 Thess. ii. 13), there would be need, in order to know that any given member of the given community was the object of it, to ascertain the reality of his faith and sanctification. Rom. viii. 33 plainly identifies the chosen with the justified. But the justified are the truly believing (Rom. v. 1). Certainly such passages as Joh. xvii., Rom. viii., indicate by their very tone and manner a mystery and glory in the choice of God ranging above observable organization, however sacred. They point direct, not only to opportunity or privilege, but to glory.

(3) *Conditional Election.*—Under this are grouped all views which regard election as to life eternal, but as going upon a personal difference, in some sense antecedent, between the chosen and others. The chosen man is thus the man who is foreseen as about to believe, to submit to Christ, and whose difference from others is simply that he has not resisted the common grace. As one form of statement puts it, God graciously chose believers, as a class, to life eternal : whoever, making use of grace, entered that class, became *ipso facto* one of the chosen. Such statements have a manifest side of truth. God "enforceth not the will ;" the believer "wills" to come to Christ as genuinely

4

as the unbeliever "wills not" to come. But we think that the view fails to harmonize with Scripture in one crucial point. It fails to do what the Scripture doctrine of election manifestly aims to do, to emphasize the guilty impotence of man and the mystery of the ways of grace. Practically, it makes man, not God, the chooser. It may be fairly put somewhat thus : God has in His sovereign wisdom appointed faith in Christ to be the way of life ; He has provided means whereby faith in Christ is in the power of all fallen human beings ; those men who choose to exercise it place themselves on the register of life. But is such a statement true to *that side of Scripture truth* which exalts the wonder of any given salvation ? We think not. But it is with *that side only* that the doctrine of election is concerned. The other limb of the "contradiction" (p. 44) stands untouched ; "God willeth all men to be saved." But *this* limb must be untouched too, if we would be true to Scripture. It must be owned a mystery whose explanation and harmony lie within the secret things of God.

The conditional theory has been held by Christians who hold the necessary perseverance of the saints, and by Christians who deny it. In the first case, the truly believing and the elect would always be identical terms and persons ; in the second case they would not.

(4) *Election within Election.*—It has been held that in Scripture the word "election" is, like many others, elastic ; that all the baptized are chosen, but that the living and loving among them are chosen in an inner sense, whether the "choice" in their case be conditional or not. Or again, that all true believers are a chosen people, but that only some of them have a grace *securing* their final glory. These are the elect in the highest sense.

Here again are clear elements of truth. The merest external Christian membership is a grant of divine kindness ; the most imperfect exercise of Christian conduct is an occasion for thanks to God. But the mystery

THE DOCTRINE OF THE FATHER. 51

and greatness which the leading New Testament passages attach to the divine Choice, lead us deeper and higher for *an adequate account of this side of truth. Abit in mysterium.* It is only one side of the apparent "contradiction;" but one side it is. "The Son quickeneth whom He will " (Joh. v. 21) ; " All that the Father giveth Me shall come to Me . . . and I will raise him up again at the last day " (vi. 37, 39).

History of Opinion.

(1) *Second to Fourth Centuries.*—No controversy about election appears in this period. And the then Church teachers, from Clement of Rome (cent. i.) downwards, emphasize earnestly and largely the freedom of the will, the αὐτεξούσιον of man. On the other hand, there are many references—e.g., in Ignatius (cent. i.)—to the glory of a divine election. Ignatius identifies the elect body with the baptized Church ; but see above (p. 49) for remarks on inferences from this. And as to the assertion of the freedom of the will, it is to be noticed that such assertions were made mainly in the face of Rabbinic or pagan fatalism. In our time, the thoughtful Calvinist would be as earnest as his Arminian friend in vindicating the αὐτεξούσιον of the will against materialistic necessitarianism.[1] Yet he would reverently hold that wherever a will, as the free and true expression of a human personality, genuinely chooses Christ, it acts, in a very special sense, " according to the purpose of Him who worketh all things after the counsel of His own will."

(2) *Fourth to Fifth Centuries* (the age of Augustine). —This great saint (A.D. 354—430) was once a Manichean necessitarian. Convinced of sin, with deep intensity, he came to the feet of Christ. One great controversy of his life was with Pelagius, who practically asserted the sufficiency, for holiness, of the natural human will. This controversy occasioned Augustine's full treatment of grace

[1] See Dr A. A. Hodge, *Lectures on Theological Themes*, p. 158.

and nature, and, in connexion, of divine sovereignty. True to the principle explained above (p. 43), he held firmly that the will is always the genuine unforced expression of the personality, but that God's choice is sovereign, and His call effectual where He wills. Augustine's position, as the first great patristic teacher in this direction, is largely explained by his spiritual history. It would seem that no previous great teacher, since the Apostles, had had his own soul so pierced by conviction of sin, and so filled with a sense of the wonder of mercy. And it is in the region of such convictions that the doctrine before us finds its moral response.

Augustine's teaching was, in outline, this. Adam freely fell; God, for reasons good and wise, but hidden in Himself, willed to save some, not all, of Adam's race. That salvation is within the visible Church alone. And of the baptized, regenerate, and godly, not all have the grace of perseverance, without which glory is not attained.

In the sternness of his views on Infant Salvation he clearly outruns Revelation. But the essential mental attitude of this great, tender-hearted, and heavenly-minded man was that of one who, in the awful light of personal conviction, had seen the fallen heart, and thus, with spiritually quickened insight, found (as it were) an element in Scripture less fully found before—the *wonder and sovereignty* of mercy.

(3) *Fifth to Seventeenth Centuries.*—The divine choice and its working was a subject of discussion all through the medieval times, in Western Christendom far more than in Eastern. The Easterns always tended to a view less stringent than Augustine's, attributing on the whole to the human will, since the Fall, not only the freedom which lies in its being always the expression of unforced personal choice, but freedom in the sense of full moral ability to choose good, to choose God; that is, to love holiness, not only to approve it. In other words, liberty for the Latins

THE DOCTRINE OF THE FATHER. 53

meant, in effect, self-determination, unforced from without ; for the Greeks, balance between opposite choices.[1]

Of the Schoolmen, or Scholastics, of the West (cent. xii.-xiv.), who laboured to apply logical method to theology, many great representatives were Augustinian ; e.g., Anselm, Lombard, Thomas Aquinas, Bradwardine. Others took a line almost, in some cases, Pelagian ; e.g., John Duns Scotus, a Northumbrian monk. The Benedictine and Franciscan Orders followed the *Thomist* and *Scotist* systems respectively. Divergence of opinion on these points has been continuous in the Roman Church. At the Council of Trent (1546—1563) Augustinianism was practically reaffirmed, though a large party were for freer definitions. All rejected the doctrine of necessary final perseverance. The Jesuits, who are at present dominant in the Roman Catholic Church, favoured a semi-Pelagian doctrine. In 1640 Jansenius, Bishop of Ypres, published his *Augustinus*, a powerful restatement of strict Augustinianism. He attracted eminent followers, e.g., the Abbè de St Cyran, the theologian Antoine Arnauld, the great lay thinker Blaise Pascal, who powerfully attacked Jesuit theology and ethics in his brilliant *Lettres Provinciales* (1656-7), and, later, the expositor P. Quesnel. The *Augustinus* was censured by the Pope, 1642, and the Jansenists were ultimately repressed. They survive as a seceding community.

The leaders of the Reformation were not agreed on the details of the doctrine of divine sovereignty. But they were, as a body, decided Augustinians in all main respects.[2] Perhaps their chief difference lay in their greater or less tendency to put the facts of sovereignty into the foreground, and to follow them logically into remoter conclusions. The *Institutes* (1536) of the great Frenchman John Calvin (1509—1564) do this certainly beyond Scriptural warrant ; while in his admirable Commentaries,

[1] See Shedd, *Hist. of Doctrine*, ii., 60, etc.
[2] See Goode, *Effects of Baptism*, ch. iii., for a mass of evidence to this effect.

written later, he shows a full sense of the solemn mysteries of the subject, and the desire to take practically the plain lines of revealed love and promise. With Luther (1483—1546) the subject lay more in the background, though he was an ardent disciple of Augustine. Melanchthon (*ob.* 1560) assures Calvin that his views, on the whole, are Calvin's; still, Melanchthon certainly allowed more *balance* to the will of sinful man than Calvin did. Our great theologian Richard Hooker (1554—1600), who had before his luminous mind the Reformation literature, as well as the Patristic and Medieval, was an Augustinian,—indeed, a moderate Calvinist.[1] He puts the doctrines of personal election and perseverance always in proportionate connexion with other truths, as one convinced that they are present and important in Scripture, but not that they are the central and ruling revelation. He was the type of a large English school in the first half of the seventeenth century.

By the middle of cent. xvii. came a reaction from extreme Calvinism, bringing in a new dominant form of theology in the English Church. It may be called popularly Arminian, from James Arminius, of Leyden (1560—1609). It held, in effect, only a conditional and contingent election to life eternal. (See above, p. 49.) The divine fore-knowledge was not effectual fore-will. The ultimate account of salvation in any given case lay in the human will, choosing to come, determining to persevere. Most reverently and strongly Arminius emphasized the necessity of grace for salvation, and as the source of all good in man. But still, as no grace was in its nature certainly prevalent, the *difference* lay outside grace, and in the self-action of the will.

In such a statement lie large elements of Scripture truth. The will, and so the responsibility, are real indeed, in Scripture. But, on the other hand, the Arminian doctrine fails to give due place to the mysterious tone

[1] See Mozley. *Baptismal Controversy*, note 38.

THE DOCTRINE OF THE FATHER. 55

of Scripture on divine sovereignty *as one side of truth*, and to the instinct of the convinced and pardoned man to recognize mere mercy in the *whole* saving process.

The Arminian controversy came to a sort of climax in the Synod of Dort (Dordrecht), in Holland, 1618. Representatives of Protestant churches, including the Anglican, met there, and the distinctive articles of Arminianism were finally censured. But the English delegates were more favourable than the continentals to a moderate positive statement.

Still in the seventeenth century, that acute thinker and saintly pastor, Richard Baxter (1615—1691), advocated a theory akin to that described above (p. 50) as election within election. Final perseverance was possible for all the regenerate, but was left contingent for all but an inner circle.

(4) *Eighteenth Century.*—In the great spiritual Revival in England, and New England, the controversy revived. The Wesleys (John, 1703—1791 ; Charles, 1708—1788) were decided Arminians ; Whitefield (1714—1770) a moderate Calvinist ; and so Doddridge, Venn, Newton, and Scott. Romaine and Toplady were strong Calvinists.[1] In New England, the great thinker and saint, Jonathan Edwards (1704—1758) wrote profoundly on the theology of the subject. With him, God's Holiness and Supremacy were the possessing thoughts, for rapturous adoration at least as much as mental enquiry. He made, however, an undue application of metaphysical method, particularly in discussions on the will, and used arguments soon appropriated by non-Christian fatalism. The very nature of this range of truth, as *presented in Scripture* as a " part of the ways " of God, is a warning in this direction. All truths are connected in God, and so everything is, ultimately, an ordered system.

[1] For a deeply interesting comparison of views between a " moderate Calvinist " and a great Arminian leader (C. Simeon and J. Wesley) see Carus, *Memoir of Simeon*, ch. viii.

56 OUTLINES OF CHRISTIAN DOCTRINE.

But Scripture continually warns us that in the matter of spiritual truths we inevitably "know in part." Thus the Christian student will always guard his use of revealed premises by revealed, rather than merely inferred, conclusions.

CHAPTER IV.

THE DOCTRINE OF GOD (CONTINUED).

THE DOCTRINE OF THE SON.

I. THE PERSON OF CHRIST.

WE approach the subject of the Person and Work of our most sacred Lord and Saviour Jesus Christ. He is " the Son of God, the Word of the Father, begotten from everlasting of the Father, very and eternal God, of one substance with the Father." Being such, He "took Man's nature in the womb of the blessed Virgin, of her substance; so that two whole and perfect Natures, that is to say, the Godhead and the Manhood, were joined together in one Person, never to be divided, whereof is one Christ, very God and very Man; who truly suffered, was crucified, dead, and buried, to reconcile His Father to us, and to be a sacrifice, not only for original guilt, but for all actual sins of men " (Article II.).

At His name let our spirits bow and adore, and " confess that He is Lord, to the glory of God the Father" (Phil. ii. 11). He is "the First and the Last, and the Living One; He became dead, and behold He is alive for evermore. Amen" (Rev. i. 17, 18).

For direct Scripture assertion of His Divine Nature, His proper Deity, see, e.g., Joh. i. 1-4,

viii. 58, xx. 28 ; Acts xx. 28 (probably) ; Rom. ix. 5 (probably) ; Tit. ii. 13 ; Heb. i. 8. For the implied assignment to Him, in the New Testament, of the name Jehovah, see Joh. xii. 41, compared with Isa. vi. 5; and cp. 1 Cor. xii. 3 ; Phil. ii. 11. But it is all-important to remember that such passages are all the while only the crown, or nucleus, of a far wider phenomenon, the assumption, expressed in many various ways all through the New Testament, that He is divine. Thus He appears as fully knowable only by the Father (Matt. xi. 27); as the object of boundless trust and love to the human heart (Phil. iii. 7-10 ; Eph. iii. 19, and cp. ver. 8) ; the offerer of rest to all mankind (Matt. xi. 28); the Lord, Head, and Bridegroom of the universal Church (Eph. i. 22, 23, v. 25) ; the sovereign Disposer of the life and death of His servants (Joh. xxi. 22 ; Rom. xiv. 7-9); and again as wholly devoid of that sense of imperfection in Himself which He unvaryingly inculcates on man.

All this evidence, to give it full weight, must be studied with real research in the Holy Scriptures, and in constant view of their jealous "Unitarianism" (above, p. 20).

Meanwhile, being divine, being properly God, He is Filial, He is the Son. For Scripture evidence on the eternal (as distinguished from the human) Sonship of Christ, see e.g. Joh. i. 18, xvii. 5, 24 ; Col. i. 13-17; Heb. i. 2, 8, ii. 14-17 ; 1 Joh. iv. 9. Not only as He is Man, but as He is God, He is so related to the Father that in divine reality, eternally and necessarily, He is the Son; as such, truly possessing the whole nature of "His own Father" (Joh. v. 18), and truly subordinate to Him, not in nature, but in order.

THE DOCTRINE OF THE SON. 59

The inscrutable mode of this blessed Filiation is named in the theology of the Christian Church "the Eternal Generation." The phrase is due to Origen (cent. iii.), and was, like the word Trinity, an instance of the happy *denomination* which at once collects and clears up truths already held. Scripture reveals that the Christ is the Son antecedent to Incarnation. It also reveals that He is eternal. "Eternal Generation" (γέννησις ἄχρονος, προαιώνιος) combines these truths in the thought that the Begetting is not an event of time, however remote, but a fact irrespective of time. The Christ did not *become*, but necessarily and eternally *is*, the Son. He, a Person, possesses every attribute of pure Godhead. This necessitates eternity, absolute being; in this respect He is "not after" the Father. But Fatherhood is peculiar to the blessed First Person, and in this respect the Father is the Origin (ἀρχή) of the Son, "greater than the Son" (Joh. xiv. 28). See further above, p. 23.

The Divine Son is called "the Word," *Logos* (Joh. i. 14; Rev. xix. 13. The reference of Heb. iv. 12; 1 Joh. i. 1; to the Son, is not certain).

The *Logos* of St John has been connected with the Logos of the Alexandrian Jewish thinker Philo (cent. i.). But Philo's Logos is rather the divine inner *Reason* (the alternative meaning of the word λόγος) than the forthcoming *Word*, God's utterance of Himself. A truer antecedent to St John's inspired use is the Aramaic word *Memra* (*Word*, root *âmar, dixit*), employed by the Palestinian Rabbis to convey the thought of *God in intercourse*. It was this "Word" which the Apostle seems to have been led to adopt, or explain, as the title of Him (not It) who is the Supreme Revealer of the Father, and the Living Way of union and communion between God and the creature.[1]

The phrase "*of one substance with (the Father)*," ὁμοούσιος (*homöousios*), *consubstantialis*, was the battle-word of the Arian controversy (see above, p. 28); a controversy of permanent significance, affecting as it did problems inseparable from the Scripture doctrine of Christ. The Arians rejected the word ὁμοούσιος in favour, some of them, of ὁμοιούσιος (*homœousios*), *simili-substantial*; while others, more extreme and explicit, preferred ἀνόμοιος (*anomœos*) *dissimilar*. To a modern the word "substance" is misleading, as it suggests in common parlance the idea of material mass. But *substantia*, in the early centuries, represented the Greek οὐσία, Being; a thing wholly immaterial. It means properly that which *stands under* phenomena, that which they manifest; in fact, the essence of a thing. Thus the "substance" of God is Godhead.[2] The Arian debate thus really turned on the Attributes of Christ; were they fully divine, or only *quasi*-divine, or positively *non*-divine? Had He fully, or only proximately, or not at all, the Divine Nature? And the only real alternative was between the first and last. The Son could not be almost almighty, almost eternal, almost necessary; for such conceptions are self-destructive. He is either true God or not truly God.

The Incarnation.

For Scriptures bearing on this holy subject, the palladium of the revealed Gospel, see Joh. i. 14, the

[1] Cp. Westcott, *Introduction* (p. xv) to St John's Gospel (*Speaker's Commentary*).

[2] In the definition of Chalcedon (below, p. 67) the Incarnate Son is said to be consubstantial (coessential) *with us*, ὁμοούσιος ἡμῖν; that is, partaker of true manhood.

THE DOCTRINE OF THE SON. 61

central passage, and around it, e.g., Matt. i. 1, 18;
Luke i. 31-5; Joh. vi. 51, viii. 40, 58, xvii. 5;
Rom. i. 3, 4, viii. 3, ix. 5; Gal. iv. 4; Phil. ii. 5-8;
1 Tim. ii. 5; Heb. ii. 9-18, iv. 15; 1 Joh. i. 1, 2,
iv. 2, 3; and, in the light of New Testament fulfilment and illustration, e.g., Gen. iii. 15, xxii. 18;
Isai. vii. 14; Micah v. 2; Zech. xiii. 7.

From these and other Scriptures emerge the
following elements for a true theory of the blessed
Incarnation.

(1) *One Person* is in view throughout. He who
undergoes birth, growth, suffering, death, says,
"Before Abraham was, I am;" "I had glory by
the Father's side before the world was." He who
"was in the form" ($\mu o \rho \phi \acute{\eta}$), i.e. who possessed the
manifested essence, "of God," "took the form of a
bondservant, and obeyed, even unto death."

(2) *Two Natures* are in view, the divine and the
human, in equally real relation to this Person. He
is God; JEHOVAH (cp. Isai. vi. 5, with Joh. xii. 41):
He becomes man. And He becomes *complete* man;
possessing body, soul (Matt. xxvi. 38), spirit (Luke
xxiii. 46); developing in physique and in wisdom
(Luke ii. 52); capable of surprise (Matt. viii. 10),
and of tears (Joh. xi. 35); feeling man's instinctive
and necessary aversion from suffering as such (Matt.
xxvi. 39). His manhood, by its mode of becoming,
namely, birth of a mother, is not an alien and
strange manhood, but *solidaire* with ours. It
descends from Adam, though in its actual production
a supernatural power takes place. Its materials are
created materials, and derived (see below, p. 68).

(3) *The Human Nature of the Son never*, for a
moment, *stood or stands apart from His Divine nature
and person.* "God sent forth His Son, born of a

woman" (Gal. iv. 4). He did not send His Son to join a man born of a woman; which would have been an alliance of two persons, not a harmony of two natures in relation to one person. The Manhood was, and is, never independently personal. It is better to say Christ is *man*, than Christ is *a man*.

(4) The divine Person of the Son thus, in Incarnation, took human nature, besides divine nature, into the field of personal consciousness. This is sometimes expressed by the phrase, "divine-human Personality." It is better to say that the Incarnate Son is Divine-Human; His ultimate Personality, Divine.

(5) Meanwhile this absolute and necessary dependency of the Manhood does not mean the least unreality in the human experience of our Incarnate Lord. Here the phenomena of the Gospels are clear. Christ, as man, is seen to learn, to trust, to bear, to do, to contemplate past, present, and future, with perfect naturalness. Peter is in these respects no more human than Christ. *In some sense*, the solicitations of evil appear as a trial as real for Him as for His followers.

(6) On the other hand, He not only did no sin; He "*knew* no sin" (2 Cor. v. 21). Not for one moment did sin *enter* the human field of His being. In the highest sense He was incapable of sin; not physically, (for every physical faculty and limit which in us, as men, is an avenue for temptation, and ministers to the sinning spirit, was in Him,) but morally and spiritually. *In this respect*, His position is expressed by "ability not to sin," *posse non peccare*, rather than by "inability to sin," *non posse peccare*.

(7) Yet, from another point, the ultimate truth is *non posse peccare*. The Manhood of Christ is to

THE DOCTRINE OF THE SON. 63

be studied not in the abstract, but in its actual, absolute, necessary harmony with His Deity, under His divine Personality. Had the Manhood sinned, the Christ would have sinned in His Manhood; the highest moral impossibility.

In this subject, we are reduced to the acceptance of revealed phenomena as yet, at least, imperfectly harmonized to our thought. Our blessed Lord was really tempted. Our blessed Lord could not sin.[1]

(8) We read in the phenomena of the Gospels the truth that our Incarnate Lord, whatever the conditions of His humiliation, still was always God as truly as Man, and Man as truly as God. Real temptations, real hunger, thirst, and surprise, leave Him still able to offer rest to all the weary of mankind; to assert His own eternity, and His eternal Being in heaven (Joh. iii. 13); to exercise omniscience so far as He wills.[2] In Him full Godhead and full Manhood were always present, in harmony.

---

[1] As St Anselm points out (*Cur Deus Homo*, ii. 17), to say "God," or "Christ, cannot sin" is a phrase not of impotency but of potency. It expresses the utter *inability of temptation* to deflect the nature and will.

[2] Mark xiii. 32 is quoted as invalidating His perfect knowledge. It no doubt limits His knowledge on that one point. But the very phrase, from His lips, looks like an implicit claim to knowledge otherwise complete. And the doctrine of the Eternal Sonship, in the Gospels, makes it surely inconceivable that even that limitation of conscious knowledge should be imposed on the Son because of limitation of capacity. It was for unknown purposes of dispensation; and it was the one thing of the kind. The Christian who deals eclectically with *any* positive statement of His, about fact as well as about principle, is on very dangerous ground indeed.

As regards Luke ii. 52, the "increase in wisdom" no more implies stages of defective wisdom than the "increase in favour with God" implies stages of defective favour. What is implied is developed application to developed subject-matter. Cp. by all means Liddon, *Bampton Lectures*, Lect. viii.

64 OUTLINES OF CHRISTIAN DOCTRINE.

(9) On certain titles of the Incarnate Lord.

(*a*) *Son of God* (Luke i. 35). The words, in the light of the context, indicate the divine action, analogous to human paternity, in the generation of the Manhood. Compare the same words used of Adam (Luke iii. 38), with reference also to special divine action in his production.

(*b*) *Son of Man*. This designation is used only by our Lord, never by His disciples. It is remarkable that in the Old Testament the phrase "Son of Man" habitually refers to the weakness and dependency of *mere man*.[1] In the Gospels the Saviour uses it in a sense apparently new, designating Himself as the True Man, the Man of men.

(*c*) *The Second Man* (1 Cor. xv. 47). In the light of the last remarks, this title explains itself. As Adam sums up and represents humanity as created, and as fallen, so Christ, incarnate and "perfected" (p. 74), sums up and represents humanity as regenerated and holy. Individually, every man, as man, is "in Adam," as to derivation of nature and bond of covenant; every regenerated man is "in Christ," as to reception of renewed nature and grant of new covenant. Adam is the head of humanity, Christ of new humanity. On the question whether the Manhood of Christ was pre-existent, see p. 72.

---

[1] In Dan. vii. 13, a Messianic passage, we find the True King represented as, "like unto (a) *Son of man*"; perhaps in contrast to the "beasts" symbolizing the usurping world-powers. See Westcott on Joh. i. 51.

THE DOCTRINE OF THE SON. 65

SUPPLEMENTARY

HISTORY OF THE DOCTRINE OF CHRIST'S PERSON.

Our outline of this has been in part anticipated under the History of the Doctrine of the Trinity.

(1) *First to Third Centuries.*—That *divine worship* was from the first paid to Christ can be amply proved. In the second century the records of martyrdoms, as of Polycarp and of the martyrs of Lyons and Vienne, and the Letters of Ignatius, fully show the intensity of faith in the Lord's Godhead. So does the frequency with which heathen observers fix upon the *adoration of Christ as God* as a phenomenon of Christianity. Side by side with this more popular phase of the facts, the early teachers of the Church do, on the whole, steadfastly and with deepest earnestness, both in replies to assailants and in instruction to disciples, avow and glory in their adoration. From the first, as even the New Testament bears witness, there were alien drifts of opinion; but the broad fact remains that a main stream of conviction not only allowed, but jealously guarded, the confession of the Godhead of Christ. The more and more careful definitions of it were made in face of attacks upon a truth felt to be inestimably precious, and which had been not carelessly held, but inadequately analysed and stated.

This last remark accounts for exceptional language found in orthodox writers earlier than the Nicene Council (325), language which favours later theories openly heterodox; e.g., that the Son is "*another God* under the Creator" (Justin); or of a nature "*very near* to the Supreme" (Clement of Alexandria). But the whole evidence gives the inference that such language is accidental, not essential; an aberration from a central truth which had not yet received full analysis under the process of attack. From the same writers a far larger mass of testimony to a full doctrine of our Lord's Godhead can be adduced.

(2) *Fourth to Fifth Centuries.*—In the Arian controversy the question lay, as we have seen (above, p. 28), between a Christ only *quasi*-God (we do not yet speak of His Manhood) and a Christ fully God. It is remarkable that on the whole the Arians posed as the original thinkers, as against a stationary traditionism ; a fact suggestive of the past state of belief. The *Homöousion* (above, p. 60), and not simply the *Godhead* of the Son, was the crucial word of the discussion, because the Arians patronized a secondary, illusory, use of the word "God," which thus ceased to be a test-word.

Meanwhile, the Arians taught only a *quasi*-manhood as well as a *quasi*-Godhead. To them, the manhood altogether lacked the spiritual element ($\pi\nu\epsilon\hat{v}\mu a$) ; its place was taken by the *quasi*-Godhead of "the Son."

" Far from spanning the infinite abyss which philosophy, not revelation, had placed between God and sinless man, the Arian Christ is nothing but an isolated pillar in its midst " (Gwatkin, *Studies of Arianism*, p. 28).

The Arian controversy left the general Christian confession of our Lord's proper Godhead historically unmistakable. But the following century saw three great after-waves raised over related questions.

(*a*) *Apollinarius* (cir. 380) represents the opinion that in the manhood of the Christ the highest natural element, the rational soul ($\nu o\hat{v}s$, *mens*) was lacking, and that the Godhead took its place. This he taught, apparently, as if necessary to the impeccability of the Incarnate; ignoring the surer inference from it that it leaves Him not truly "one with us." He also held, in some sense, the eternal pre-existence of this *quasi*-manhood, and that the Crucified suffered not only *being* God, but *as* God. Apollinarianism was repudiated at the Council of Constantinople, 381.

(*b*) *Nestorius* (Bishop of Constantinople, 428) held, in effect, a dual Personality in the Incarnate. With him,

THE DOCTRINE OF THE SON. 67

the Manhood was not only entire, but *independent*. A human being, supernaturally produced, the Virgin's Son, was then taken into an ineffable connexion by the eternal Son of God. The term "Mother of God" (θεοτόκος), then recently adopted as a title of the Holy Virgin, in testimony to the Godhead of her Son, was earnestly censured by Nestorius. His theory seriously obscures the relation of our Lord, as "the Second Man," to manhood in general. The Nestorian Christ, from the human side, is not Man, but a man. Nestorianism was rejected at the Council of Ephesus, 432. The followers of Nestorius became a dissentient body, still existing in the East. Their bishoprics extended at one period across the whole length of Upper Asia, to China.

(c) *Eutyches* (abbot at Constantinople, 448) represents the opposite tendency of opinion, the *Monophysite*, or *Uni-natural*. With him, Incarnation resulted in a Single Nature, that of "God made flesh and come to dwell in man" (θεοῦ σαρκωθέντος καὶ ἐνανθρωπήσαντος). This opinion was condemned at Chalcedon, 451. The Council issued a Confession, known as the "Definition" (ὅρος), a memorable document, alike for its fulness, clearness, and balance. We translate here that part of it immediately in point.

After reciting certain circumstances, and after solemn recognition of the Creeds of Nicæa and Constantinople, the Fathers proceed:—

" This wise and saving Watchword of the grace of God would have sufficed for the true knowledge and establishment of our religion. But since those who seek to spoil the proclamation of the Truth through their own wilful errors (αἱρέσεις) have produced their idle utterances, some daring to undermine the Lord's Incarnation (οἰκονομία) for our sakes, and to reject the term 'Mother of God,' and others to introduce [the theory of] a compound and mixture, foolishly feigning that the nature of the Flesh and the Godhead is one, and unnaturally asserting that the divine Nature of the Only Begotten is, by the compound, passible . . . . [the Synod] opposes those who seek to rend the mystery of the Incarnation into a Pair of Sons, and thrusts from the assembly of holy worship those who dare to say that the Godhead of the Only Begotten is passible, and resists those who invent a mixture or compound concerning the two Natures of the Christ, and casts forth those who teach that that 'Form of the Bond-servant.' which He took from us is of celestial or any non-human essence (οὐσία), and bans those who fable two Natures of the Lord before the Union, but invent one Nature after it. Following then the holy Fathers [of Nicæa and Constantinople], we confess One and the Same Son, our Lord, Jesus Christ, and all with one voice teach that He is perfect in Godhead and perfect also in Manhood, God truly, and also Man truly, of reasonable soul and body consisting, consubstantial (coessential, ὁμοούσιον) with the Father as to the Godhead, and also consubstantial (coessential) with us as to the Manhood, in all things like to us without sin, begotten of the Father before the ages as to the Godhead, but also in the end of days, for us and for our salvation, [born] of Mary, the Virgin, the Mother of God, as to the Manhood ; confessed One and the same Christ, Son, Lord, Only Begotten, in two Natures without compound, without change, without division, without [possible] separation, the difference of the Natures being nowise removed because of the Union, but rather the property of each Nature being preserved, and concurring in one Person (πρόσωπον) and one substance (ὑπόστασις), not as if He were to be partitioned . . . into two Persons; but One and the same Son, and Only Begotten, God, Word, Lord, Jesus Christ ; as of old the Prophets concerning Him, and also He, the Lord Himself, instructed us, and as the Watchword of the Fathers hath handed it down to us." [1]

[1] For the original, in a generally accessible form, see Heurtley *De Fide et Symbolo*, p. 19 ; or *Canons of the First Four General*

THE DOCTRINE OF THE SON. 69

(3) *Seventh Century.*—A subordinate ancient controversy was the *Monothelite*, or *One-Will* controversy. The Monothelite held that as there was one Person only, there could be but one Will, though acting through two Natures. Against this Scripture is practically clear; and, indeed, the conclusion seems to be direct that, granting the full *spiritual* element to manhood in the Incarnate, we grant the presence of human *will*. The doctrine of Two Wills, separable in conception, but perfectly and always harmonious in divine plan and historic fact, was laid down at Constantinople, 635.

Our sketch of controversies is inevitably meagre and eclectic. But it may in part be supplemented from the previous section. Its aim is to present great specimens, suggestive of closer study. The ancient controversies are significant for all time; not specimens of fossil species, but fossil specimens, singularly instructive by their surroundings, of existing and permanent species of thought.

Councils (Clarendon Press, Oxford), p. 81. See also Hagenbach, *Hist. of Doctrines*, Eng. Trans., ed. 1850, vol. i., p. 300; and by all means Hooker, *Eccl. Polity*, bk v., 51-4.

CHAPTER V.

THE DOCTRINE OF GOD (CONTINUED).

THE DOCTRINE OF THE SON (CONTINUED).

II. THE WORK OF CHRIST.

(1) AS regards *Creation* generally, Scripture reveals the Eternal Son, the Logos, the living *Fiat* of the Father's will, as concerned specially and vitally with the act of creation. "*Through* Him all things" (which begin to be) "came into being" (Joh. i. 3); cp. Col. i. 16[1]; Heb. i. 2, iii. 3, 4. "*In* Him all things were created" (Col. i. 16); words which receive illustration from others just below (ver. 17), "all things consist, hold together, in Him." He is so related to Creation that all its orders and their life have their reason and basis in His being. On their creation, they came forth as *ab initio* rooted in the life and will of the Son. And only as so remaining do they remain in being.

The language of Col. i. 16 may suggest, taken by itself, the thought of a pre-existence of the Creation in the Son, or, if it may be so put, the Son as the pre-existent and archetypal World; so that every thing, and inclusively every person, has

[1] In Eph. iii. 9 the words "*by Jesus Christ*" are not genuine.

THE DOCTRINE OF THE SON. 71

a mysterious existence in Him, as the Eternal Idea, and not so much begins as is developed and realized in time and history. And it has been definitely held that some such existence in the Logos is true of all human souls. But as we look round on the whole evidence of Scripture there is, to say the least of it, the very scantiest support for such a view. Nothing in Scripture is more emphatic than its teaching of the vast *disparateness* of the universe and God, in this respect, that all things which become are the result, not of an inner necessity in God to evolve and realize, but of a divine volition as sovereign as it is benignant (Rev. iv. 11).

All that Scripture entitles us to affirm is that, Creation *being* divinely willed, there was an eternal fitness in the function of the *Son* as its immediate Head and Root. Through Him the Father, never passive and quiescent, works. In Him, as Cornerstone, the work held, and holds, together. The secret force and substance of things has, for its true account, His will. And Creation is related to Him as, under the Father, its Final Cause, its *Raison d'être:* "all things have been created *for* Him" (Col. i. 17).

He is thus "the Beginning" ($\dot{a}\rho\chi\dot{\eta}$, Origin) "of the creation of God" (Rev. iii. 14); "Firstborn of all creation" (Col. i. 15); that is, "Elder with reference to all created being" (see ver. 16); not the first thing brought into being, but antecedent causally to every such thing, whether material or immaterial.

In the Old Testament see Prov. viii. 22-31 for a passage which harmonizes with this New Testament revelation.

(2) As regards *Man*, the doctrine of the work of

the Son is of course included, in a measure, under the last heading. Man is a part of the created world. But he also stands apart in some great respects.

The doctrine of the Incarnation is sometimes so stated as to place the Eternal Word in a union aboriginal and necessary with every man. The view indicated is that manhood stands in so near a revealed relation to God that it must be eternal, *a parte ante*, in the Person of the Son. He is thus, eternally, Primal and Archetypal Man, summing up in Himself all mankind, all man, all men. In Incarnation accordingly He did not *become* man, but became "flesh" (Joh. i. 14); entering in His own Person on the conditions of human "life *in the flesh*" as a special phase of that life, for special ends.

And thus, it is maintained, Incarnation was divinely inevitable, quite irrespective of the Fall. It was a thing of original and supreme purpose, in order to the realization of the eternal Idea of Humanity, the glorification of man in the Son, and the Son in man. The Fall occasioned an application, as it were, of this sublime process to a special end by the way. In passing towards the original goal of a final and universal glorification the Incarnate deals with the intruding, isolated, and finite problem of sin, by suffering and dying with relation to it. That relation, however, is not of a substitutionary kind, or at least not nearly so much of that kind as of the kind of a mysterious effusion of Christ's life and power into humanity through the liberating process of His self-sacrifice in death.

From such a doctrine one result appears to be that the Eternal Christ is in a necessary and eternal union, as Primal Man, with every man;

THE DOCTRINE OF THE SON.

holding a connexion, vital and federal, with him, antecedent to and independent of the work of atonement and of regeneration. In the original constitution of the Christ, on this view, every man is in Him, and He in the man. The spiritual awakening of the man, on this view, may be explained as a discovery of the Archetypal Christ latent in him, and his place in that Christ in the eternal order. Gal. i. 16 has been so explained.

But this refined and abstruse theory has very slight semblance of support in Scripture. There the creation of man is "in the image of" not distinctively *Christ*, but *God* (Gen. i. 26, 27; Jas iii. 9). And a New Creation (2 Cor. v. 17), New Birth (Joh. iii. 3), of the individual is revealed as wholly necessary, and as expressly related both to a previous spiritual death, and disunion from God (Eph. ii. 1, 12), and to a pre-temporal choice and adoption in Christ, redemption by His Death, incorporation into Him, and likeness to Him (Eph. i. 4, 7, 13). And the view stated fails to harmonize with Scripture as regards the position of man, as man, before God. Scripture does indeed represent man as made in the image of God, and capable of a most wonderful and blissful union with Him. But this is represented as due not to an eternal and necessary order, but to divine free goodness and condescension. Humanity is certainly not, in Scripture, either a phase of Deity, or one of Its contents.

The above view of the relation of Christ to man plainly has no necessary connexion with a doctrine of Propitiation. And, in fact (above, p. 72), it is often found combined with theories of our Lord's Death which deny, or minimize, its expiatory purpose.

Certain Scriptures seem at first to favour the view of a necessary relation between Christ and men, such as would harmonize with an archetypal and eternal Manhood in Him. Such are Joh. i. 9; 1 Cor. xv. 22, 47. But Joh. i. 9 does not reveal an archetypal connexion between the Word and man. And 1 Cor. xv. 22, like its whole context, is concerned with the resurrection not of man as such, but of those who "are Christ's" (ver. 23); a distinct limit to the reference of the "all." 1 Cor. xv. 47, in view of its context, speaks of the Lord's coming "from heaven" as the Second Man, not at the Incarnation, but at the Second Advent. It in nowise makes Him the Second Man in His pre-existent state.

Meanwhile it is amply revealed that the Son of God, in eternal regard to Incarnation and Atonement, *has* deep and gracious connexion not only with certain individuals, or sections, of the race, but with man. To Him, as the Eternal Word Incarnate "for us men and for our salvation," every man is so related as to have the right to say, "I am of that nature which in Christ is united to God; I am of that human world (1 Joh. ii. 2) for which Christ is the Propitiation; I am of that mankind which He redeemed."

As a fact, the unity of the human race, taken along with the historical Incarnation, places every man of all time in natural, while most wonderful, contact with the Incarnate Lord. And this fact is preliminary to all truths of regeneration and incorporation.

But now comes up for study what we hold to be, from man's actual point of view, the central truth in the work of Christ for man:

THE DOCTRINE OF THE SON. 75

(3) THE ATONING SACRIFICE OF CHRIST IN HIS DEATH.

We have already noted the fact (p. 72) that many thinkers find the central point elsewhere, as in the Incarnation. But we affirm that the Scriptures teach otherwise, largely and distinctly. From the point of view of fallen and sinful man, the Cross is central. True, there is little definite teaching about it in the *Gospels* (but see Matt. xx. 28; Joh. vi. 51, and all the accounts of the Institution of the holy Supper). But the business of the Gospels is narrative; and the narrative gives an overwhelming prominence to the close of the Lord's life, and to the indissoluble other side of His death—the Resurrection. The death and its work is the main truth of almost all the discourses in the *Acts*. In the *Epistles* and *Revelation* it appears in still larger development, culminating in the vision of "the Lamb as it had been slain," the object as such of universal adoration.[1]

Nor must we forget the Old Testament; the New forbids us to do so. If the Old Testament is to us what it was to our Lord, definitely prophetic of Him, we shall see in it His sacrifice foreshadowed on a scale, and in a detail, to which predictions even of His Incarnation afford no parallel. See, e.g., the Levitical ritual, especially of the atonement day (Lev. xvi.), as interpreted in the Epistle to the Hebrews (ch. ix.); the Passover and its

[1] See, among the wealth of references, Acts ii. 23, iv. 10, viii. 35, xiii. 28-39, xx. 28; Rom. iii. 23-5, v. 6-9; 1 Cor. xv. 3-11; 2 Cor. v. 14, 21; Gal. i. 4, iii. 13, vi. 14; Eph. i. 7, ii. 13, v. 2; Phil ii. 8; Col. i. 14, 20; 1 Thess. v. 10; 2 Tim. ii. 11, 12; Tit. ii. 14; Heb. ii. 9, 14, vii. 27, ix. 11-28, x. 10-12, 19, xii. 24, xiii. 10-12, 20; 1 Pet. i. 2, 11, 19, ii. 24, v. 1; 1 Joh. i. 7, ii. 2, iii. 16, iv. 10; Rev. i. 5, 7, v. 9, 12, vii. 14, xiii. 8.

application; and above all Isai. liii., of which almost every verse is quoted in the New Testament. According to the Risen Lord Himself (Luke xxiv. 26, 46) the main burthen of prophecy was that He should *suffer* and rise again. The Pauline Gospel had for its main article ("*first of all*") that "the Christ died for our sins *according to the Scriptures*" (1 Cor. xv. 3).

The reason of this prominence is plain, from one point of view. We shall say more hereafter (p. 169) of the Fall, Sin, and Guilt of Man. But it must be affirmed at once here that an indispensable requisite to a just view of the Scripture doctrine of the Atonement is a profound personal view of the guilt of human sin. In Holy Scripture sin is not only calamity, disease, disturbance of the constitution of humanity. It is *guilt;* it is the violation of the categorical authoritative Law of God, bringing with it a liability to holy punitive retribution. No consideration is more important than this *in limine*, if the Atonement is to be studied in its revealed proportion.

The first requisite of man in this view is a righteous Acceptance, despite his guilt. The first requisite of the holy Law is a righteous Satisfaction, good for man. Antecedent to all man's needs of elevation, or development, or realization of his ideal, is his need of a Propitiation for his sins.

Meanwhile, no view of the matter is more liable to be forgotten and ignored in our own time. . The claims connected with the great words Law, Guilt, Retribution, have been greatly obscured and lost sight of in cultivated thought in general. The cause is to be sought sometimes in an exclusive attention to the blessed truth of divine Benevolence,

THE DOCTRINE OF THE SON. 77

but much more in less worthy directions; in slackening of conviction about the eternal difference of right and wrong, in lowered views of the authority of Scripture, in a growth of indifference or doubt about the supernatural altogether.

However, we venture to assert that a study of the doctrine of the Cross cannot be successful where the recognition of sin, as guilt, is not present in strength. And we venture to assert also that to this recognition the deepest instincts of unsophisticated man, really awakened, respond.

Now what, on the whole, according to Scripture, is the purport and significance of the Death of the Son of God?

To a true theory, the following elements, presented in Scripture, are necessary.

The Person in question is the Blessed Son, Incarnate His Sufferings are ordained in eternal purpose (Matt. xxvi. 24; Acts iv. 28). They are essential, not accidental, in His work (Luke xxiv. 26, 44-6; Acts iii. 18, xxvi. 23; 1 Cor. xv. 3, etc.). They stand in a vital connexion with the pardon and acceptance of sinful man.[1] They are the supreme evidence of divine Love. We may add that Scripture represents the Eternal Father as

[1] Take, e.g., 1 Cor. xv. 14-18. The immediate subject is the Resurrection, but evidently as the crown of the work of the Death. Now the Apostle teaches that, without the objective fact and work of the Resurrection, the faith of the Corinthians would be "vain"; they would be yet in their sins. But as a matter of fact they were penitents and believers; the subjective conciliation of their wills had taken place; they were no longer rebels, or victims of sin. He therefore means that if, *per impossibile*, these spiritual results could have taken place without the objective fact of the Atonement and its triumph, they would be unpardoned still. The reasoning implies a work done by the Lord's Death not only man-ward but primarily God-ward.

78 OUTLINES OF CHRISTIAN DOCTRINE.

"giving" the Sufferer (Rom. viii. 32), and, in some sense, inflicting the suffering (Psal. xxii. 1; Isai. liii. 6; Acts ii. 23). And the suffering is felt by the Sufferer to be ineffable and unique; and, observe, ineffably *His own*, so that He would, if the end were otherwise attainable, put aside the awful "cup." On the other hand, it lies with Him, to the last, to put it away, *if He pleases;* so that the suffering was no mere inevitable result of His collision with the sinful will of man (Matt. xxvi. 53; Joh. x. 18).[1]

Another element for a true theory is the fact that this suffering procures not only the pardon of the guilty, but their pardon, full and gracious, *at once, upon acceptance of the Crucified*. It is a pardon *for His sake;* not for the sake of their own moral revolution caused somehow by His sufferings. The procuring reason, the merit, lies always in Him.

Again, the effects of the suffering are expressed in such terms as these: *redemption*, or deliverance by ransom (Matt. xx. 28, etc.); *purchase*, as by a price (1 Cor. vi. 20); *covering*, as by an interposition (Rom. iv. 7); *undertaking of responsibility*, as by a surety (Heb. vii. 22); *bearing*, in the sense of endurance of penalty (Heb. ix. 28; cp. Lev. xxiv. 15; Numb. xviii. 22, etc.); *acceptance*, as of a propitiatory sacrifice by an offended God (see 1 Joh. ii. 2, 3); *deliverance from the death-sentence of a Law*, by virtue of one who has borne it (Gal. iii. 13). As to the word *Atonement* itself, it has been said that its etymology, "at-one-ment," reconciliation, indicates that the true work of the sufferings of Christ is such a bringing of God and man together as would be needed if the need of conciliation lay wholly on man's side. In this view, the difficulty

[1] See Crawford, *The Atonement*, Part I., sect. i.

THE DOCTRINE OF THE SON. 79

lay wholly in man's unsubdued will; in God there has never been anything but pure benevolence, yearning for the alienated to see it and come, and asking no condition but such coming. But, on this theory, the Atonement resides in *whatever* Christ was, or did, with a view to break down man's misconceptions of God. And thus Christ's Death stands in no *unique* position in His work; for what did He ever do, or be, or bear, that did not tend, if studied aright, to illuminate the eternal beauty of the Character of God? On such a view "at-one-ment" would be effected, for many minds, not by His Death, but by the self-sacrificing beneficence of His Life, including the mingled majesty and love of the miracles, or by the divine charm of His words.

But an inductive study of Scripture negatives such a view. For the Lord's *Death* stands there in a place mysteriously unique. And besides, the words "atonement," "reconciliation," in Scripture, do not lend themselves to such applications. Usage is often a safer guide than etymology to the meaning of words. So it is with "atone." The word is used in the Old Testament to represent the Hebrew "cover,"[1] in connexions sacrificial and propitiatory. In the New Testament (Rom. v. 10) it is used, in the Authorized Version, for the Greek καταλλαγή. That word, and its cognates, habitually point to the winning rather the pardon of an offended King than the consent of the rebel to yield to His kindness.[2] Thus "be ye reconciled to God" (2 Cor. v. 20) will mean not so much, "bend your

[1] כפר in the *Piel*.
[2] See, for illustrations from *non-theological* passages, 1 Sam. xxix. 4, where the LXX. has διαλλαγήσεται; Matt. v. 24; 1 Cor. vii. 11. See Pearson, *On the Creed*, p. 365.

pride to His unalterable benevolence," as "secure, while you can, His acceptance;" an acceptance connected (ver. 21) with the sufferings of His Son.

We believe that an impartial review of these elements, and of the whole manner of the Scriptural presentation of the Saviour's death, will tend to the conviction (antecedent to many further possible enquiries in detail) that the immediate necessary purpose of the blessed Death was propitiatory, expiatory; not the moral suasion of man, nor even the procurement for man of new spiritual power, but expiation as towards God. It was the *sine quâ non*, under a divine plan, in order to lodge in the Sufferer, being Man, being the Second Man, a *Merit*, such as divine Holiness, without which God would not be God, should recognize as capable of more than balancing the demerit, the guilt, of sin. In the recognition of that guilt in its mysterious greatness lies some approach to a solution of the mystery of such an Atonement. There, certainly, lies the true secret of sympathy and submission as regards the fact of it.

It has been well said that Creation, relatively to God, is little, "a very little thing," but that Sin is not. Sin—shall we dare to say it?—is the one formidable fact, the one difficulty, before God. Its pardon, with Him, is anything but "a very little thing." That He may deal with the awful fact of its guilt, in view of His Law, in view of HIMSELF as Holy Legislator and Judge, there must be brought in something which shall also be, in His sight, great and wonderful. This something, according to a Scriptural induction, is the propitiatory death of His Son, One Divine Person, united in His manhood to man; a Victim most willing, and whose unique union of

THE DOCTRINE OF THE SON. 81

Natures in one Person secures for that death perfect human reality along with absolute wonder and merit.

The death of Christ, thus viewed, looks rather towards God than towards man. The death, or rather the glorious Person whose holy willingness put, so to speak, HIMSELF into the death, possesses for ever a *merit* on the ground of which goes the pardon and acceptance of guilty man, once brought into connexion with Him.[1] The holy and blessed Sufferer takes a position of awfully real relation to the Law, viewed as carrying with it the death-sentence of the guilty. He does not only suffer, or only sacrifice self, or only go all lengths in sympathy with the demands of the Law; He presents Himself to be "made sin," to be "made a curse," to be the Antitype of the sin-offerings of the altar.

Seen thus, the Cross is meanwhile the supreme manifestation of divine Love. Let the Godward, expiatory aspect be fully recognized, and it will be seen to carry fully with it this tender manward aspect. Divine Love, as seen in Scripture, is in its nature absolute, but in its action limited, by the limits not of external constraint, but of God's own Nature, in His absolute jealousy against evil; in brief, by all that is involved in His being holy. By His Nature, His Love cannot act along any line but one which shall glorify at once both love and holiness. Nothing can do this, to the unsophisticated conscience and instincts of man, like the willing giving, by the Father, of the infinitely good and beloved Son, as a willing Altar-Victim, through His holy Humanity, with reference to the doom of the Law, for man and in his place.

[1] See, at large, *The Doctrine of the Atonement*, by L. Edwards, D.D.

Thus the strictly expiatory view of the Atonement carries along with it, as its sacred accessory, one of the views often preferred to it—the view of the Atonement as a moral attraction of man's will, and enlightening of man's eyes, towards God. The same may be said of other alternatives to the expiatory view. Thus, the expiatory view fully allows for the fact that the Saviour's holiness, colliding with man's sin, was the occasion of action to those who actually slew Him. It fully allows for the martyr-aspect of His death. It fully allows for all sides of its work of example. It fully allows for His agonizing sense of the evil of man's sin and the misery of the sinner's position. Only, it includes all these precious things under the sacred centre of a real, proper, valid ransom of and propitiation for the guilty, and bids us, in the awful light of Divine Holiness and Law, recognize its main purport there.

Detached Remarks on Atonement Doctrine.

(1) From some remarks above, it appears how deep is the significance of the phrase (1 Joh. ii. 2), "*He*" (emphatic in the Greek) "is the propitiation for our sins." It is He, not it; the Sufferer, rather than the death. The Doer gives its absolute and eternal merit to the Work.

(2) The imagery of "purchase" is entirely scriptural (see e.g. Rev. v. 9).

But Scripture regards the price rather as paid *for us*, to buy us to be the Lord's possession, than for our pardon. The importance of this will appear later.

(3) To whom is the price paid? (below, p. 89). To eternal and necessary Holiness; to divine Law;

THE DOCTRINE OF THE SON. 83

to the claims of God, who is, by His Nature, the holy Lawgiver. He who was "made a curse for us" "bought us from the curse (death-sentence) of the law" (Gal. iii. 13).

(4) Did our Lord suffer a precise *equivalent* for the sufferings due to man? The question is not really raised by the Scripture doctrine. There we see absolute merit, in view of the broken law, lodged in guilty man's Representative, by virtue of sacrificial death. This is a thought concerned with quality, not quantity.

(5) Were our Lord's sufferings the same *in kind* as those due to guilty man? In some respects, indeed not. They could not include that personal remorse which must be one awful element of the future woe. But the *Lama sabachthani*, as well as the horror of Gethsemane, inexplicable on common human grounds,[1] at least favours the belief that the all-blessed Sufferer willed to bear, and the Father to ordain, the personal experience of a desertion such as enters into the final doom. But the reverent disciple will avoid all *detailed* speculation in such a matter.

(6) Is our Lord's Life a constituent, with His Death, in the Atonement? In some very important respects, it is not. In Scripture everywhere the death stands in a position *distinctive and apart*, as the Sacrifice. But, on the other hand, the connexion of the life with the death is deep and necessary. The life was a necessary qualification for the death, not only as *manifesting* Christ's absolute worthiness, but as *making* it, in the sphere of His holy manhood.

---

[1] Voltaire said to Rousseau, "When you say that the death of Jesus, compared with that of Socrates, was the death of a God, you forget the sweat of blood."

If, *per impossibile*, He could have gone to Calvary having lived an imperfect life, He would not have been the all-worthy Sacrifice. His life had to do with His being all-worthy. But it did not, in whole or part, constitute the Sacrifice.

(7) *On certain New Testament phrases.*—The Lord "suffers," or "gives Himself," or the like, (*a*) "*for* us," "*for* sinners," etc.; (*b*) "*for* our sins," "*for* sins," etc. The two classes of expressions mean, in effect, the same. The second may be described as an ellipsis for the first. He died for us, in respect of the guilt of our sins.

The *Greek prepositions* vary under both classes. Oftenest, we find ὑπέρ, "*on behalf of*" (etymologically, "*over*," as of protection); see e.g. Rom. viii. 32; Gal. ii. 20; Tit. ii. 14. Sometimes ἀντί, "*instead of*" (Matt. xx. 28; Mark x. 45; cp. 1 Tim. ii. 5, 6). Sometimes περί, literally "*about;*" but by usage the word is strongly sacrificial and propitiatory, in contexts at all open to such ideas; see e.g. Rom. viii. 3; Gal. i. 4; 1 Pet. iii. 18; cp. Heb. x. 6. Sometimes διά (with the accusative), "*on account of;*" Rom. iv. 25. These phrases all harmonize in substantial meaning. The Lord died "*on account of*" the fact of our sin and need; "*about*" us and our sins, as sin-offering; "*instead of*" us, as our substituted Representative, substituted in the obvious sense that He so gave Himself, and was given, to suffer, as lawfully to procure our exemption; "*on behalf of*" us, in a sense including all these, and further implying the personal will and love with which He suffered. Observe further that, in Greek literature generally, where the preposition ὑπέρ, apart or in compound, occurs in connexion with ideas of *death*, the thought suggested tends to be that of substitution; death

THE DOCTRINE OF THE SON.

" on behalf of " another in the sense that the other therefore does not die.

(8) *"The Blood of Christ."*—Some expositors draw a distinction between this phrase and " the *Death* of Christ," maintaining that the ideas of blood and *Life* are deeply connected in Scripture, and inferring that the blood-shedding of the Redeemer has to do less with propitiation, by the immolation of life forfeited, than with vivification, by surrender to God and impartation to man of life strengthening. Thus to be "cleansed by the blood of Christ" (1 Joh. i. 7) would mean to be morally purified by the inflow of the surrendered, and now infused, life of the risen Christ. To " drink the blood of the Son of Man " (Joh. vi. 53) would mean, not to appropriate His propitiatory sacrifice, but to imbibe the powers of His risen life. Against such a view, we think, the Scripture speaks on the whole decisively. The text appealed to as the first warrant for the view is Lev. xvii. 11 ; as if it so connected " blood " and " life "[1] that where the blood goes the life goes, as life. But observe the wording ; "*the life of the flesh* is in the blood." The thought is directed to the deadness of the " flesh " when the blood is shed ; not to the persistence of " life " in the shed blood. And as the word " blood " in anything like kindred connexions is traced through Scripture, the preponderating idea is that of death, not life. Where " blood " denotes not the current in the veins but the stream poured from them, the suggested idea is by no means life surrendered for service, or transfused for another's invigoration. Blood *shed* is not a vehicle of power, but an evidence of death,

[1] Observe that ψυχή not ζωή is the word used by the LXX., Lev. xvii. 11.

especially by sacrifice or execution. (See among the numerous examples, Gen. ix. 4, 5; Deut. xxi. 8; 2 Sam. i. 16; Psal. lxxii. 14 (cp. cxvi. 15); Micah vii. 2; Matt. xxvii. 4; Acts v. 28). A remarkable detail of its usage is in connexion with *making covenants* (Exod. xxiv. 8; Zech. ix. 11), an association quite alien to ideas of infusion.

The following are the passages in which the word "blood" occurs in connexion with the work of Christ:

Matt. xxvi. 28; Mark xiv. 24; Luke xxii. 20; 1 Cor. xi. 25 (in all which the word *covenant* occurs); Joh. vi. 53-6; Acts xx. 28; Rom. iii. 25, v. 9; 1 Cor. x. 16, xi. 27; Eph. i. 7, ii. 13; Col. i. 20; Heb. ix. 12, 14, x. 19, 29, xii. 24, xiii. 20; 1 Pet. i. 2, 19; 1 Joh. v. 6, 8; Rev. i. 5, v. 9, vii. 14, xii. 11. (In Col. i. 14 the words "in His Blood" are to be omitted from the text.)

It is not too much to say that the bearing of these passages *as a whole* is decisively towards ideas of not life but death, not of infusion but of effusion, of the blood of death, the striking of covenant, the propitiation wrought at an altar, the sprinkling of a mercy-seat, the signified acceptance of pardoned suppliants, the lawful purchase of condemned men from death by death.

On the meaning in particular of 1 Joh. i. 7 compare by all means Lev. xvi. 30, especially in the Greek.

(9) Were our Lord's sufferings properly *penal*? It has been earnestly maintained that they were not. But the denial appears to arise from a too limited definition of the word "punishment." If punishment can only mean judicial retribution for the sufferer's own transgressions, personally done, of course HE could not suffer personally. But nothing forbids

THE DOCTRINE OF THE SON. 87

the use of the word "penal" when suffering is *judicially* inflicted on a person who, by whatever process, is legally liable. If the Redeemer, in His own gracious freewill, laid Himself actually under liability for our transgressions, then the "curse of the law" dealt penally with that liability, laid on Him. His sufferings had regard to broken Law and its satisfaction; they were thus penal.

The language of Isai. liii. certainly points in this direction: "the chastisement of our peace was upon Him"; "the Lord hath laid on Him the iniquity of us all"; "it pleased the Lord to bruise Him"; "my righteous Servant shall justify many, for He shall bear their iniquities" (5, 6, 10, 11). And see ver. 8, with the alternative rendering of the Revised Version: "He was cut off out of the land of the living, for the transgression of My people, to whom the stroke was due."

SUPPLEMENTARY.

HISTORY OF THE DOCTRINE OF THE ATONEMENT.

(1) *First Four Centuries.*—The *controversies* of these centuries turned more upon the Person than the Work of Christ. But, nevertheless, there was a practically continuous sub-reference to the Work, as that which gave the problem of the Person its supreme importance. That Work, under many variations of language and thought, as different aspects of its central idea come up, was viewed on the whole as no mere means of influence on men, as by witness or example, but as a transaction related to God. We append a few out of the wealth of possible refcrences.

Clement of Rome (cent. i.)—*Epistle to the Corinthians*, c. 7: "Let us fix our eyes on the blood of Christ, and see how precious it is to His God and Father, because, being shed for our salvation, it won for the whole world the grace of repentance." Cp. *ibidem*, cc. 12, 16, 21, 49. In this last place the words are; "Our Lord Jesus Christ gave His blood for us in the will of God, and His flesh for our flesh, and His life (ψυχή) for our lives."

The Epistle to Diognetus[1] (early cent. ii.)—c. 9: "When our unrighteousness had reached the full, God Himself gave His Son a ransom for us (λύτρον ὑπὲρ ἡμῶν) ... the just for the unjust. ... For what else was able to hide our sins, but His righteousness? ... Oh blessed exchange! ... That so the iniquity of many should be hidden in One Righteous, and the righteousness of One should justify many iniquitous."

Irenæus (cent. ii.)—*Against Heresies*, bk v., i. 1: "The Lord ransomed us by His own blood, and gave His life for our life and His flesh for our flesh" (cp. Clem. Rom. *supra*). In the immediate context Irenæus dwells on the fact that the Atonement had for a main end the satisfaction of the claims of justice. The "persuasive" power of the Atonement appears in the same context as grounded on an effected redemption. See further, bk v., xiv. 3, 4.

Justin Martyr (cent. ii.)—*Dialogue*, c. 95: "The universal Father willed that His own Messiah, on behalf of men of every race, should receive on Him the curses of all, knowing that He would raise Him up after crucifixion and death."

Origen (cent. iii.)—*On the Romans*, iii., c. 8: "'*God set Him forth to be a propitiation, through faith in His blood*'; that is, through the sacrifice of His body (*per hostiam sui corporis*) to make God propitious to men. ... For God is just, and the just cannot justify the

[1] Anonymous; printed with the works of St Justin Martyr.

unjust; therefore He willed the intervention of the Propitiator, that through faith in Him they might be justified who could not be through their own works." See further, towards the close of the same chapter.

Athanasius (cent. iv.)—*Oration i. against the Arians*, c. 60: "The Son of God came into the world, not to judge the world, but that He might redeem all men, and that the world might be saved through Him. For of old the world as an accused person was judged, under the Law; but now the Word (Λόγος) hath received on Himself the judgment, and, suffering in His body on behalf of all men, hath granted salvation unto all." *On the Incarnation*, c. 20: "He offered His sacrifice (τὴν θυσίαν) for all (περὶ πάντων), giving up to death His own Temple (ναόν) in the stead (ἀντί) of all; that He might set all free from the guilt (ἀνυπευθύνους) of the original transgression," etc.

Augustine (cent. iv.-v.)—*On Psalm* xc., § 2: "The transgressions belong to us; the suffering for us belongs to our Head. But because of His suffering for us, all that belongs to us of transgressions is discharged."

These are only specimens of a great store of doctrine. All along there appears in the Fathers the recognition of a profound propitiatory value in the Lord's death; certainly no tendency the other way, no reluctance akin to modern objections.

One curious phase of patristic teaching was the view that the Lord's Death was in some sense a ransom paid to the Evil One for his captives, and that the purpose and full value of the Death was hidden from the Evil One till all was over. This latter thought appears as early as Ignatius, early cent. ii. (*To the Eph.*, c. xix.; often quoted by later Fathers). But this relation of the Atonement to the supposed claims of the Enemy is, as a fact, no main or vital element in patristic teaching, either in quantity or logical weight. It is more than balanced by constant unreserved assertions of the iniquity of the enemy's action, and Christ's mighty triumph over him for us. It is an excrescence of doctrine, not a genuine limb. Meantime it witnesses to a belief in the truth that underlay it, the need of far more than moral suasion, or even spiritual change, for our redemption.[1]

(2) *Eleventh to Sixteenth Centuries.*—In the eleventh century appeared the short treatise of Anselm (Abp. of Canterbury 1093—1114), *Cur Deus Homo? Why was God made Man?* This is a discussion, as reverent as it is logically clear and subtle, of the nature and purpose of the Atonement. The thought which it emphasized is the satisfaction of the claims of (not the Enemy, but) the Lawgiver. This was only a clearer statement of what the Church belief had always implied, though previous thought had dwelt rather on *fulfilment of divine threatening* (of death for man's sin) than on satisfaction of the inherent claims of God's holy Nature. In Anselm's view the Lord, as Man, satisfies those claims by a co-ordinate obedience, which results in His infinite merit, applied to win our remission. Anselm speaks less strongly than Scripture on the "bearing of the curse" as the central mystery of the obedience. But it is plain that he felt no aversion to this aspect of the truth.

Bernard of Clairvaux, commonly known as St Bernard (cent. xii.), writes (*Epistle* cxc.) : "Man it was who owed, Man it is who hath paid. . . . The Head satisfied for the members, Christ for His own vitals."

Peter the Lombard (cent. xii.-xiii.), the "Magister" of the Schoolmen, dwells at some length on the Merit of the Lord (*Sententiæ*, Bk iii., *Dist.* xviii.-xx.). The relation of the Atonement to the devil's power appears in his discussion. But he regards the Enemy not as

---

[1] A passage is sometimes quoted from Gregory of Nazianzus (cent. iv.) to the alleged effect that error regarding the purpose of our Lord's sufferings is not spiritually dangerous. But it refers to the question of the nature, not the purpose, of the sufferings (*Oratio* xxxiii.).

a power entitled to contract for ransom, but as one whose actual grasp on man came only of man's unpaid debt to God. This debt the death of the Sinless One discharges. Throughout the discussion, with all its logical clearness, runs a certain confusion, due to an imperfect apprehension of the Scriptural meaning of justification (below, p. 250). But this leaves untouched the view of our Lord's Death as a proper "sacrifice, oblation, and satisfaction for the sins of the whole world."

Thomas Aquinas (cent. xiii.), following Lombard, brought out more fully the relation between the Atonement and *the Union of Christ and His members*.

The *Mystics* are among the most interesting phenomena of the Middle Ages. But clear statements of Atonement Doctrine are not to be looked for in them. Their absorbing theme was the union of the soul with God, and they tended to lose sight of the guilt as compared with the disease and power of sin. See Dorner, *Person of Christ* (Div. ii., vol. ii., Introduction), for an account of the German Mystics, and of their failure to see "in the Cross on the one hand the condemnation, on the other the atonement, of guilt."

(3) *Age of the Reformation.*—The Reformers, continental and English, were more concerned to vindicate the Scriptural doctrine of the application of the Atonement (Justification), than of the Atonement itself. (See below, p. 187.)

(4) To trace the history of opinion on the Atonement, in detail, *onwards to our own time*, would far overstep our limits. But through the mass of theories and explanations there are apparent two *main* directions of thought; the one, towards an insistence upon the need of propitiation Godward, in view of divine Holiness and Law; the other, towards explanations in which this view is denied, or minimized, in favour of either a moral work of reconciliation, an exhibition of divine love

92 OUTLINES OF CHRISTIAN DOCTRINE.

persuading and alluring men, or of a deeper mystic belief in the "liberation," by death, of the life-power of Christ, for the animation of His members. The appeal between real divergences must be to the Holy Scriptures. And in the theory rejected on such an appeal, elements of important truth may yet very probably be present for which place must be found in a true theory, though the *characteristic* of that theory will remain not the less distinctive.

In close connexion with the Atoning Death occur other points of doctrine concerning the Work of Christ. And first

THE DESCENT INTO HELL.

The precise wording of this belief is not Scriptural; we nowhere find in Scripture the words "*descent*" and "*hell*" used together, with reference to our Lord. But the substance is Scriptural. See Psal. xvi. 10, interpreted Acts ii. 26, 27.

Of no other passage can it be affirmed with certainty that it refers to, much less that it teaches, this belief. Those commonly adduced are Luke xxiii. 43; Eph. iv. 9; 1 Pet. iii. 18-20, iv. 6 (on which further below). But only Acts ii. 26, 27 is unmistakable in its reference. What is its interpretation?

The word *Hell*, etymologically akin to *heal*, *i.e.*, to *cover* (a wound with skin), and meaning *the covered, hidden region*, represents the Hebrew *Sheôl*, and the Greek *Hades*. Around these two words a mass of interpretation has gathered. But their prevalent reference is to the state of the immaterial part of

THE DOCTRINE OF THE SON. 93

the dead, viewed as a state of awful, abnormal separation of man from his proper state of being. That state receives the good and the bad, and may contain abodes of comparative bliss, or of woe. But in all cases it is *in that respect evil* that it is for man a state of separation and dislocation; of abnormal mystery; of connexion with the sentence of death.

Hell, as rendering *Hades*, must thus be distinguished clearly from Hell as rendering *Gehenna* (γεέννα, Matt. v. 22, 29, 30, x. 28, xviii. 9, xxiii. 15, 33; Mark. ix. 47; Luke xii. 5; Jas iii. 6). Gehenna is the place, or state, of final woe; a word of unrelieved awfulness.[1]

No doubt the words *Hell* and *Inferi* (Art. III.) represent Hades, not Gehenna. The truth taught is that our Lord entered the State of Spirits, accepting all its essential conditions. To teach as revealed truth anything beyond this fact is an intrusion into the Unseen. And to lay stress upon the local cast of the phrase, and on the word *descend*, is unsafe; for all local conceptions are unsettled in the absence of bodily conditions. Nothing is demanded by Scripture phraseology but that the descent of the body into the earth transmits its idea to the motion of the soul into the Unseen. In the light of New Testament language about the presence of the believer with Christ now at death (2 Cor. v. 8; Phil. i. 23), and of the apocalyptic visions of redeemed and praising multitudes " before the throne," in what seems to be a pre-resurrection

[1] But *Sheôl* and *Hades* are often also used *in connexions* which point the same way. E.g. Psal. ix. 17, where the meaning must be deeper than that "the wicked shall enter, or return to, the state of departed spirits." But this lies in the context. not in the word.

state (Rev. vii. 9, xix. 1),[1] the belief of a literal "underworld" of departed spirits may be dismissed from thought.

The substance of the doctrine thus relates to our Lord's submission to all the essentials of the Separate State, for our sake. As His human body entered a grave, His human spirit entered Hades. Whatever awfulness that entrance had for any of His saints, it had for Him.

1 Pet. iii. 18-20 is often quoted as plainly referring to this Descent. But St Augustine recognized it as difficult of interpretation, and inclined, at one time at least, as does Bishop Pearson (*Exposition of the Creed*), to refer it not to the Descent at all, but to the work of Christ by His Spirit before the Flood, in warning the antediluvians now "in prison." On the other hand many Christian thinkers, ancient and modern, have deduced from the words the doctrine that, either to the lost antediluvians, or to all the then departed, Christ disembodied offered His salvation; and inferences have been drawn to the effect that death does not, for man in general, end probation and evangelization.

Awful is the mystery of the questions involved. To God, not to us, it appertains to say absolutely and in detail what justice and mercy demand in the case, for instance, of man who has never heard the Gospel. But we earnestly commend the following *cautions* in speculation.[2]

1 Pet. iii. 18-20 is a passage practically unique,

---

[1] Not to speak of such Old Testament indications as the ascensions of Enoch and Elijah, and Psal. lxxiii. 24, and the appearance of Moses with Elijah "in glory" (Luke ix. 31).

[2] See Dr R. Anderson, *Human Destiny*.

THE DOCTRINE OF THE SON.

unless indeed, which is doubtful, 1 Pet. iv. 6 is to be grouped with it.

It occurs in a context, not of hope, but of exhortation and warning.

It mentions the antediluvians only, and distinctively, and without any hint that it has a wider application.

It does not reveal *what* our Lord "proclaimed" (ἐκήρυξε), nor does it indicate with certainty that His hearers, supposing them to be departed spirits, had actually died impenitent.[1]

The warnings of Scripture as to the mysterious connexion of probation and judgment with our *embodied*, that is our complete and natural condition, lie in the opposite direction to that of a "larger hope." See 2 Cor. v. 10. And see below, p. 160.

So does the urgency of Scripture language about the necessity of the human messenger in order to the "salvation" of those who have not heard the Gospel. See Rom. x. 13-15; and cp. Acts xi. 14; 1 Thess. ii. 16. (See further, p. 116.)

And, in general, the subject should be approached with a watchful, reverent remembrance, to be secured only by the convincing grace of God, of the "exceeding sinfulness" of sin and the immovable, eternal claims of the divine holiness.

HISTORY OF BELIEF ABOUT THE "DESCENT."

In the Commentary of *Rufinus of Aquileia* (cent. iv.-v.)

[1] It is to be observed that by some "the spirits" of 1 Pet. iii. have been explained to be not antediluvian men, but non-human beings, whose rebellious action in the Old World is (it is contended) indicated Gen. vi. 2, 4. To them, in their "prison," the crucified Lord (on this view) proclaimed His final defeat (Col. ii. 15) of all such efforts to thwart the work of redemption.

on the "Apostles' Creed," the article, "He descended into hell" (*inferna*), appears as part of the Creed. But Rufinus observes that it was absent from the then *Roman* creed, and from the creeds of the East. Nor does it appear, as far as can be gathered, in the Western creeds as known to St Augustine.

However, the belief of a mysteriously special "Descent appears already developed (cent. ii.-iii.) in, e.g., Irenæus, Tertullian, and Clement of Alexandria. With some variety in detail, these three Fathers (Pearson, *On the Creed*, pp. 237, 241, and notes) held that the Lord descended to impart His Gospel and salvation, in the unseen world, to those who looked for Him before His coming, or perhaps (Clement) to the dead in general.

In the early "apocryphal" literature the Descent appears in a luxuriance of strange and awful detail. Under the common name of the *Gospel of Nicodemus* several documents are included, among them the *Descensus ad Inferos*. In it the Lord appears in the Underworld, the realm of Hades (*Inferus*, Latin Version), and sets free Adam and the old saints, bringing them to "the glory of Paradise." This document has been assigned to the second century, but its present form is probably not older than the fourth.

In the belief of *a Descent* the Fathers are unanimous. But as to its purpose and work there was very various speculation. Some held that the lost souls themselves were all delivered; others, that some only of them : the former view was commonly held heretical. Some held that the souls of the old saints were translated to blessedness in Paradise, some that they were only illuminated where they were, and not locally removed. See Pearson, and Ussher's *Answer to a Jesuit*, for ample detail.

Later, discussions arose as to the nature of the Descent; whether it were local and literal, or virtual—an action of the Lord's will in the depths of the Unseen.

THE DOCTRINE OF THE SON.

It is instructive to turn from the detail and certainty of even the earliest ecclesiastical statements, to the extreme reserve of Scripture. Between the date of the main body of the New Testament and the earliest extant patristic teaching on the subject two generations at least intervened; and this, on a topic so alluring to human curiosity, is time enough for a great growth of unauthorized belief.

One fact transpires from the enquiry; namely, the absence from early belief of the conception of the Intermediate State as a *Purgatory*. This nowhere appears, certainly not within the first three centuries. Augustine speaks of some such possibility with great hesitation. As a rule, the Fathers of the first four hundred years speak of the faithful as going to a condition not pitiable but bright and blessed, under angelic escort, into eternal rest, into the kingdom of God, into the company of saints and angels. It is remarkable that the custom of *Prayer for the Departed* should nevertheless appear (certainly as early as the end of cent. ii.). But such prayers met with evidently frequent criticism; and it was alleged in explanation that they asked only for a continuance of blessing, and that this continuance was certain, yet, like other certainties, might be prayed for; or that the prayer referred to the prospect of the Last Day, and the eternal open acquittal then—which again was a certainty for the true believer departed, yet to be prayed for. These defences are inadequate, against the total silence of Scripture. But they are significant as against purgatorial theory in any of its forms. See Ussher, *Answer*, vi., vii., viii.

Returning to the divine simplicity of Scripture, we find:—

(*a*) No evidence for a change of place and condition of the old saints at the Lord's death, but rather allusions to their rest and glory from the first:

(*b*) No evidence for a "going down" of the departing Christian, but full and joyful reference to his immediate presence with the glorified and ascended Christ at death. This hope, as it seems to us, stands in a place faint and secondary in patristic teaching as compared with the Scriptural view:

(c) Full recognition of a vast accession of power and bliss when the "redemption of the body" (Rom. viii. 23) comes. Holy Scripture fully recognizes an intermediate *state*, while it maintains great reserve, to say the least, about an intermediate *place*. "Paradise," in Scripture, far from being locally distinguished from Heaven, the upper world, appears as in it and of it. See 2 Cor. xii. 2-4; Rev. ii. 7, with xxii. 2-5. And cp. e.g. Acts vii. 55, 56, with 59; and Phil. i. 23 with Col. iii. 1-3.

CHAPTER VI.

THE DOCTRINE OF GOD (CONTINUED).

THE DOCTRINE OF CHRIST (CONTINUED).

III. THE WORK OF CHRIST (CONTINUED).

THE RESURRECTION, ASCENSION, SESSION, AND RETURN.

WE do not state here the proof of the fact of our Lord's Resurrection. That all-important question falls under Christian Evidence. We assume here the convergence of manifold demonstrations on the belief that the buried Lord reappeared, in bodily identity, "on the third day;" blessed His followers; taught them; and before their eyes rose upwards out of sight. Our concern is with the Scripture doctrine of these facts.

Christ rose as the supreme attestation of His own truth, and victory, and of the certainty of His eternal triumph. See e.g. Joh. ii. 19; Acts ii. 24, 35, v. 31, xiii. 30-9, xvii. 31; Rom. i. 4, iv. 24, 25, vi. 9, viii. 34, xiv. 9; 1 Cor. xv. 3-22; Eph. i. 20, 21; Col. i. 18; 1 Thess. iv. 14; Heb. xiii. 20, 21; 1 Pet. i. 3, 21; Rev. i. 17, 18.

He rose, identical, yet with differences. His body risen was the same as His body buried. But we need not insist on an identity of particles, which certainly is not necessary to our own continuous bodily identity. That identity appears to rest on personal spiritual identity. The sameness of a hand at two times of life lies, not in its consisting of the same matter, but in its holding the same relation to the same spirit. What the Gospels make clear on the one hand is the reality and permanence of Jesus Christ's resurrection body, under tests of sense, to which the all-truthful Lord Himself appeals. On the other hand it is plain that the body's mode of being and action was new. It appears that it was capable of transitions, inconceivable to us, through material mass. It was in some new way under the control of His spirit. He could[1] manipulate it, so to speak, as He pleased. Some interpreters have seen in this the meaning of the words, "the last Adam (became) a quickening ('alive-making') spirit" (1 Cor. xv. 45). They explain this to mean that He rose in a condition in which His spirit was now no longer only "living soul." It no longer animated only, but as it were perpetually caused, its holy bodily vehicle.

This at least reminds us of what is implied by the context of 1 Cor. xv. 45; namely, that our Lord "became" *the Second Adam* at Resurrection. Historically, He was constituted then, and not before, the Source of the regenerating and sanctifying Spirit (see Joh. vii. 39) which effectually makes Him the Life-Head of the New Race.[2] True, there are other points of view. From the beginning the Son of God has been always the true secret of the spiritual life of all the saints (above, p. 41, and below, p. 191, etc.). But this fact was vitally related

---

[1] We say "could" with reference, of course, not to His omnipotence *in itself*, as to which He always "all things can," but to the order of His work, regulating the exercise of power.

[2] See C. H. Waller, *Doctrine of Christ as the Last Adam*.

THE DOCTRINE OF THE SON. 101

always to His Incarnation and Work, which were always present to the Divine Mind. And when historical realization was added to the eternal purpose the spiritual results were so developed in human experience as to make, as it were, a new beginning. In any case, it is important in Christian doctrine to remember that not Incarnation alone, but Incarnation as conditioned by the Death and Resurrection of the Incarnate, fully constitutes Him the Second Man; the Origin and Cause, for the New Race, of life and peace.

Organically connected with the Resurrection is the *Ascension*. The two are indeed one in essence. Scripture does not reveal any decisive change at Ascension in our Lord's resurrection state. "Flesh *and blood* cannot inherit the kingdom of God" (1 Cor. xv. 50); and Luke xxiv. 39 suggests that the Resurrection Body was already without blood. On the other hand Ascension did not annul its literal corporeity.[1] At the conversion of St Paul, Jesus was seen, not in "vision," but so that Paul was a witness of His *bodily* Resurrection (1 Cor. ix. 1, xv. 8). We are soon lost in the effort to follow the Ascension in detail. But to this we are not called. Our part is to grasp the certainty of revealed facts, and to appropriate them in their form of manifestations of the work of the Redeemer.

The Ascension was His actual entrance on His work as *Head of His Church*. He became this at Resurrection; but He was now fully inducted into His action as such. Then He sent forth from the

---

[1] The glorification of the Body does not appear to have lifted it above the laws of place. As true human Body, it is not *ubiquitous;* it is "in heaven, *and not here*" (last Rubric of the Communion).

Father the Spirit, as being also His Spirit, by virtue of ineffable connexion with His Person and Work (below, p. 125). Then He entered historically on His work as enthroned Mediator and Intercessor. See especially the Epistles to the Ephesians and Hebrews, and the Revelation; but also a large range of detached Scriptures, e.g. Joh. vii. 39; Acts ii. 33-6; Rom. viii. 34.

As incarnate, sacrificed, and risen, He is now *Mediator*. This word bears a general and a particular sense. The general appears, e.g. 1 Tim. ii. 5, where "Christ Jesus, Man," is presented as "the one Mediator ($\mu\epsilon\sigma\iota\tau\eta\varsigma$) between God and man"; the one way of true approach to God, with special reference (ver. 6) to His Atonement. The more particular sense appears, e.g. Heb. ix. 15, "the Mediator of the new covenant" (and cp. Heb. vii. 22, "the Surety of a better covenant"; see also viii. 6). Here the Mediator is not only the glorious Person one both with God and man, and dying for man, but specially that Person as undertaking relations to a *covenant*, to secure and convey its benefits. That Covenant (above, pp. 40, 41) is between God and His true Israel, the true Church. Its two main blessings are full acceptance of the sinner, and a new heart, inscribed with the law of God. This Covenant lies, directly, between God and (not man, or men, anyhow, but) Christ for Man; or, otherwise, Man in Christ. The Epistle to the Hebrews, the great treasury of covenant doctrine, leads us, along with the rest of the New Testament, to the conclusion that the covenant blessings were so won by the perfect work of the Lord Christ as to be lodged in Him for His Church, and to become actually theirs on their becoming His. He, for them, both "re-

THE DOCTRINE OF THE SON. 103

deemed transgressions" (ix. 15), and "received of the Father" the promised Spirit (Acts ii. 33), the Bond between Christ and His people (see Rom. viii. 9, 11; 1 Cor. vi. 17), and, as such, the Maker of their new nature. Thus the glorified Lord holds as Surety and conveys as Mediator the fulness of blessing for man.

The ascended Lord is the *Intercessor* (see Rom. viii. 34; Heb. vii. 25. Cp. Isai. liii. 12). Scripture represents Him as interceding, not as a suppliant, but with the majesty of the accepted and glorified Son once slain. He does not *stand before* the throne, but is *seated on* it (see especially Rom. viii. 34.; Heb. i. 3, iv. 14-16, viii. 1, x. 11-13.) "With authority He asks, enthroned in glory now." It is vain, of course, to ask *how* in detail He thus acts for us. The essence of the matter is His union with His people, and His perpetual presence, in that union, with the Father, as the once slain Lamb. As to the *scope* of the Intercession, Scripture appears to limit it to the Church. We must not for a moment limit within the Church our Lord's compassion.. But the special work of the Intercession appears thus limited.

A truth closely kindred to this last is that of the *High Priesthood* of Christ. For this the Epistle to the Hebrews is by far the chief authority. Guided by it, we see in Jesus Christ, true God and true Man, and sanctified and glorified, the fulfilment of the types embodied in the royal and unsuccessive Priesthood of Melchisedec, and in the atoning work of the Aaronic High Priest on the Atonement Day (Lev. xvi.).[1]

[1] Observe that this special and pre-eminent occasion of Aaronic High-Priestly work is almost alone in view in the Epistle. The type is not the Priests, but the High Priest, and the High Priest not anyhow, but as on the Atonement Day.

According to the Epistle, He is now as the High Priest was on the Atonement Day, when, having slain the victim out of doors, he had entered the Holiest Place, bearing and offering the blood as evidence of sacrifice. But one significant difference appears. The "great High Priest," in the true Sanctuary, *mounts the throne*. (Heb. viii. 1, x. 11, 12; cp. Zech. vi. 13.) The true Aaron merges into the true Melchisedec. When "the throne of grace" (iv. 16) is approached, upon it the eternal Priest is found seated, like the Shechinah above the ark, to dispense the blessings of His once offered and for ever perfect sacrifice. The Epistle insists (i. 3, ix. 25, 26, x. 10, 12, 13, 14) on the fact that not only the sacrifice, but also the *offering*, or presentation, of it is over for ever; while the royal, high-priestly intercession and benediction, based upon it, are present and continuous.[1]

Does Scripture represent the Lord as ministering *at an altar* in heaven? The Holiest of the Tabernacle contained *no altar*. Only the blood of victims slain outside entered it, as evidence of finished sacrifice. In the Epistle to the Hebrews no mention occurs of an altar in the Presence of God. In xiii. 13 the context fixes the reference to His "suffering without the gate" on earth. In the Revelation, indeed, we twice find an altar in the mystical scenery. But in vi. 9 the word is part of

[1] From Heb. viii. 3 it has been argued that our Lord must be *now* "*offering* somewhat," or He would not now be a Priest. But a Priest is a Priest (as to the altar-part of his function) not as always offering but as always being an Offerer. Our Lord is for ever *characterized* as an Offerer by His unique and ever-efficacious sacrifice *once offered*. He is "a Priest for ever," not as offering for ever but as ever carrying out, on the ground of His finished offering, His regal, sacerdotal intercession and benediction.

THE DOCTRINE OF THE SON. 105

the imagery of martyr-sacrifice; *the souls of martyrs*, as if poured out, blood-like, on an altar, are seen at its foot. And in viii. 3, 5, the altar is the *golden* altar; not of blood but of incense, and the ministrant is "an angel."

Nor is the presentation of His sacred Blood in the Presence regarded in Scripture as continuous, or as literal. In the type, the carrying of the blood into the Holiest was an act single and decisive, the accomplished security for continuous blessing. The passages which speak of the Antitype accordingly connect the presentation of the Blood of Christ with His decisive "entering in" at Ascension (Heb. ix. 12). His "entering in" as the Crucified One Risen *is* the presentation.

A cognate question is, does "*the Victim-state*" *continue* in heaven? Such a thought is quite absent from the Epistle to the Hebrews. In the Revelation, indeed, the Lord appears as "a Lamb as it had been slain." But the whole context, and book, explain this to mean that as the once Crucified He now, not continues a Victim, but wields royal mediatorial power in heaven and earth. See ch. v. throughout, vi. 16, vii. 9, 17, xiv. 1, 4, 10, xvii. 14, xxi. 22, 23, xxii. 3.

In brief, the Lord is a High Priest for ever; a High Priest upon His throne; eternally characterized as atoning Sacrificer and Sacrificed, once for ever; now and always doing the high-priestly work no longer of offering but of intercession related to it.[1]

Meanwhile He is *King*, in a respect separable in thought from Priesthood. The Risen One has "all authority given Him in heaven and in earth"

[1] Cp. Archd. Perowne, *Our High Priest in Heaven*.

(Matt. xxviii. 18). This royalty is not for a moment a supersession of the Eternal Father's action. But in it the Incarnate Son, One with the Father, is the divine Agent of the Father's will for the great special purpose of carrying into its eternal issues the plan of Redemption, to the glory of the Father in the Son. It has respect to God's final triumph over sin and death, and to the glorification in it of His Church. When sin and death shall be "put under the feet" of the Son, this royalty will have done its glorious work. *In respect of it,* "the Son Himself shall be subject unto Him that put all things under Him" (1 Cor. xv. 20-8). Whatever that supreme crisis means, it will be no eclipse of the glory of the Son. The eternal kingdom is "the kingdom of Christ and of God" (Eph. v. 5); the throne is "of God and of the Lamb" (Rev. xxii. 3).

Scripture reveals very fully a present personal action of the glorified Christ in the ingathering of His Church, and the sanctification of its members. But this subject will be best treated below, under the Doctrine of the Holy Spirit (p. 132).

Of the RETURN of the glorified Redeemer we speak on purpose in outline only, and without conclusions in detail. Unfulfilled prophecy is a vast field of study. And there is this difference between it and the study of "the way of salvation," that an interpretation of general history enters necessarily into it. The questions of Reconciliation, Regeneration, Sanctification, and the like, lie in the field of eternal principle and truth. Those of the time and mode of the Lord's Return, of the events conditional to it, and of the sequel to it, lie in part in a different field. Answers to them have to be

THE DOCTRINE OF THE SON. 107

sought (in many important details) not in Scripture simply, but in Scripture interpreted by history.

Scripture solemnly enjoins a reverent and earnest study of the things "not seen as yet," truly and miraculously foreshown in prophecy. Yet this is a region of enquiry quite *sui generis* and calling for constant recollection of the cautions just given. What we are content to do here is to collect specimens of Scripture testimony on some main points separately, rather to aid the reader's inferences than to give our own; and then to summarize the history of opinion.

(*a*) Scripture evidence for a Second Coming of the Lord, *not mystical but literal* :—See, among the wealth of testimonies, Acts i. 11 ; 1 Cor. xv. 23, 47, 52 ; Phil. iii. 20, 21 ; 1 Thess. i. 10, iv. 14-16 ; 2 Thess. i. 7, 8 ; 2 Tim. ii. 18 (with e.g. 1 Cor. xv.) ; 1 Pet. v. 4 ; 1 Joh. ii. 28 ; iii. 2 (with 1 Pet. i. 8).

Evidence from the Revelation is not here adduced, because the symbolism of the Book makes it difficult to bring it in without careful discussion. But the evidence above will of course make for a literal interpretation in many places (both in Gospels and Revelation) where there might otherwise be doubt. This principle is kept in view in the following groups of references.

(*b*) Scripture evidence for its connexion with *the glorification of the Church* :—Matt. xxv. 10, 19, 21, 23, 46 ; Joh. v. 28, 29 (with vi. 39, etc.), xiv. 3 ; Acts iii. 21 ; Rom. viii. 18-23, xiii. 11 ; 1 Cor. xv. 23, 35-7 ; Phil. iii. 21 ; Col. iii. 4 ; 1 Thess. iii. 13, iv. 16, 17, v. 9, 10 ; 2 Thess. i. 7, 10 ; 2 Tim. iv. 8 ; Jas v. 8 ; 1 Pet. i. 7, iv. 13, v. 4 ; 2 Pet. iii. 12, 13 ; 1 Joh. iii. 2 ; Jude 24 ; Rev. iii. 11.

(*c*) Scripture evidence for its connexion with

judgment on the wicked:—Matt. xiii. 41, 42, 49, 50, xxv. 11-13, 30, 46; Luke xiii. 27; Joh. v. 28, 29; Acts xxiv. 15 (with Joh. v. 29); Rom. ii. 16; 1 Thess. v. 2, 3; 2 Thess. i. 7-9; 2 Pet. iii. 7; Jude 14, 15; Rev. i. 7, vi. 16, 17, xx. 15, xxii. 12.

(*d*) Scripture evidence, apparent, for its connexion with *the close of the present order of nature:*—Rom. viii. 21; 1 Cor. xv. 50 (with 23), 53; 2 Cor. iv. 18 (with 14); Phil. iii. 21; Col. iii. 2, 4; Heb. xii. 25-8; 1 Pet. i. 4; 2 Pet. iii. 10-13; Rev. xx. 11, xxi. 1.

(*e*) Scripture evidence, apparent, for its connexion with *the beginning of a period of felicity on earth:*—A large tract of Old Testament prophecy comes under this head; e.g. Psal. lxvii.; Isai. xxv., xxxiii., xxxv., lx., lxv.; Jer. xxxiii. In interpretation of such prophecies, meanwhile, the student, devoutly believing the reality of Old Testament predictions, will remember that these prophecies, by their failure to indicate a decline or end to the promised bliss, may seem to point to the eternal Age under terrestrial imagery rather than to a terminable period, however long, under terrestrial conditions. In the New Testament, see, under this head, Rev. xx. 2-7.

(*f*) Scripture evidence, apparent, for its connexion with *the close of such a period:*—Rev. xx. 7-11.

(*g*) Scripture evidence, apparent, for its connexion with the (1) temporal, (2) spiritual *restoration of the Israelite race:*—Under (1), the Old Testament prophecies, of which examples were given under (*e*), are of course in point. And see Luke xxi. 24; Acts i. 6. Under (*b*), see Rom. xi. at large, and cp. Rev. vii. 4-8, xxi. 12.

(*h*) Scripture evidence, apparent, in *qualification of this expectation:*—As regards the expectation of

THE DOCTRINE OF THE SON. 109

a spiritual restoration of Israel, on a great and phenomenal scale, Rom. xi. appears to be decisive, by the nature of the passage, in which the symbolic element is practically absent. It is difficult, however, even there to say that the crisis in view is revealed as concurrent with the literal Return of Jesus Christ. Ver. 26 is not decisive; its possible reference is to the first Advent in its developed results.

As regards the expectation of a temporal restoration, while nothing in the nature of the Gospel creates a difficulty against it, and the present aspect of events is even suggestive of it, it is remarkable that the New Testament is extremely reserved on the subject, and that on the other hand it applies to spiritual events some predictions which in the Old Testament read like a temporal restoration of Israel. See e.g. Joh. vi. 45 and Rev. xxi.[1]

SUPPLEMENTARY.

HISTORY OF OPINION ON THE SUBJECT OF THE LORD'S RETURN.

(1) FROM the New Testament it is plain that the expectation of a literal Return ($\pi\alpha\rho o \upsilon \sigma i a, \epsilon \pi \iota \phi \acute{a} \nu \epsilon \iota a$) was universal. And there was a persuasion, at least in some Churches,

[1] Many of the Old Testament prophecies, taken literally, foretell a great restitution of the Temple and sacrificial Ritual, under the favour of God. See Jer. xxxiii. 18-21; Ezek. xl.-xlviii. But this is difficult to reconcile with statements of primary spiritual principle in the New Testament. See Joh. iv. 21-4; Acts vii. 48, 49, and the whole argument of the Epistle to the Hebrews, especially vii.-x., xiii. Is it not probable that this range of Old Testament prediction has its fulfilment in realities of the spiritual order, which is the highest? And if so, the question arises whether the same principle does not rule other Old Testament predictions of the future of Israel.

that it would be soon (2 Thess. ii. 1). Did the Apostles share this persuasion? Many passages (e.g. 1 Thess. iv. 17) look that way. But the language always falls short of a distinct statement, and along with it appears the same person's distinct anticipation of death in the Lord (Phil. i. 23; 2 Tim. iv. 8; and see 1 Cor. vi. 14; 2 Cor. iv. 14; Phil. iii. 11). The Lord Himself had implied that His absence would be prolonged (Matt. xxv. 19), and that death would be the practically universal experience of Christians (John vi. 39, 40, 44, 54).

(2) In cent. ii. we find the expectation that the Coming would be attended by the general Resurrection (Justin, *Dialogue*, 45). Justin (*Dial.*, 81, 82) looks forward to a Millennium of splendour for the saints, living and raised, in and around the (rebuilt) earthly Jerusalem, to be followed by the glorious Coming, general Resurrection, and Judgment. He says, however, that this was not the universal tenet of orthodox Christians. Irenæus (especially v. 33, etc.) holds like expectations, but seems to place the Coming before the Millennium, general Resurrection, and Judgment. He notices a difference of opinion on the subject among orthodox Christians.

(3) In cent. iii., Origen, and the Alexandrians generally, took an opposite line of interpretation, wholly idealizing and spiritualizing. Dionysius of Alexandria (255), finding "Chiliasm," the belief of a terrestrial Millennium, widely spread in his district, brought about a general reversal of opinion, after a conference (Euseb., *Eccl. Hist.*, vii. 24).

(4) In cent. iv., St Augustine advocated a view of prophecy in which the "binding of Satan" dated from the beginning of the Gospel, and his "loosing" was to be looked for at the close of the sixth millennium of the world. This view found wide acceptance.

(5) Throughout the *Middle Ages* the belief on the whole was that the Millennium was in progress, and was not far from its close. The *Reformers* in general held this view,

THE DOCTRINE OF THE SON. 111

and regarded their own epoch as the beginning of that "little season" which should precede the end.

(6) In cent. xvii., the expectation of a future Millennium of bliss and spiritual triumph on earth, preceded by the Lord's Return, was revived, mainly by the learned Joseph Mede (1586—1638). Particularly within the last half-century this expectation has attracted the deepest attention of Christian students.

A summary of the main views on this subject is subjoined, inevitably brief and imperfect.

It must be premised that the interpretation of the Revelation enters of course very largely into the formation of views. And among those who cordially agree in accepting that book as divine and infallible, there are two main divisions of interpretations. For some, the book is a prophetic history, which has been working out ever since the Ascension, so that much of its fulfilment is already to be recognized in history. For others, its predictions (e.g. chapters xvii., xviii.) concern very mainly a series of events still wholly in the future.

Under the first type of interpretation differences again occur. For some, as we have seen, the Millennium (ch. xx.) is already past; a thousand years of comparative freedom from unbelief and fundamental heresy in Christendom. The present time falls accordingly within the "little season" (Rev. xx. 3) of temptation and tribulation which is to precede the final Coming and the eternal order of things.

For others, the Millennium is yet to be, and perhaps ere long. It is to be a period of great blessedness on earth, under divine power and rule, in a new manner. Interpreters differ in detail as to the character of the period. But on the whole it is to be a blessed age, only with such a survival of elements of evil as that they shall revive in great force at its close. Then the "little season" will come in, before the End.

Under this interpretation again there are two important

divisions. For some, this great period is brought in and maintained by the exercise indeed of divine power, whether or not in modes openly miraculous, but not by a visible Personal Return of the Lord. For others, His visible pre-millennial Return is the central point of hope. It is the return predicted 1 Thess. iv., and will bring with it the resurrection of the buried saints, and the transfiguration of the living, to meet the Lord in the air, and to reign with Him either upon, or however over, the beatified earth.

With the interpreters of this latter school, in particular, but not with them only, the Millennium is to be a time of well-nigh universal triumph for the cause of God on earth, in the sense of general conversion. Whether by means of the great tribulations, or by the immediate power of the manifested Lord, no longer individuals here and there, but the nations, are to come to Him. Israel, converted as a nation, will occupy a pre-eminent place in the life of the blessed earth, the Lord Himself perhaps reigning in Jerusalem below; while new modes and degrees of intercourse may bind, as it were, heaven and earth together. In the belief of many, the risen saints of the Old Testament will then inherit their portion of the earthly Canaan.

Whether human birth and death will still take place is a point of difference. The glorious scene will, however, wane at last. The enemy will be released for his last "short time," and the last conflict of good and evil will be fought on earth. It will close with the final manifestation of the Judge, the collapse and transfiguration of the present order of things, and the coming in of the eternal state, with its endless issues of glory and perdition. Then shall be seen "new heavens and a new earth," and therein "righteousness shall dwell."[1]

[1] With Mede and his followers the entire "burning up" of the earth (2 Pet. iii.) was to *precede* the Millennium.

THE DOCTRINE OF THE SON. 113

We have said enough to indicate the range and complexity of this sacred subject. We can only add here a very few of the reasons of most weight on the side of the chief theories.

(a) In favour of a future Millennium of more or less material, with spiritual, blessedness are—the large mention in Old Testament prophecy of a time when "nature" shall be renewed on the earth, and the state of Eden restored; the indications in the New Testament (see above, p. 108) of a restoration of Israel, and of a triumph of the Gospel vastly more extensive than any now seen, or (humanly speaking) on its way to be seen, on earth; promises of a reward "on earth" for the righteous (e.g. Matt. v. 5); and the great prediction in Rev. xx. 7, etc.

(b) In favour of the belief of a premillennial Advent of our Lord are—the language of the prophets concerning e.g. a divine reign in glory "in Mount Zion," language large in quantity and most impressive in manner; passages in the New Testament (e.g. 1 Cor. xv. 23, 24) which may be interpreted of a great double crisis, a twofoldness, in the one great fact of the Second Coming (such a passage is 1 Cor. xv. 23, 24); the predictions of the Revelation, especially xx. 4, 6; and, above all, the many passages which exhort the believer to be *on the watch for the sudden Coming* of his Lord.

(c) In favour of the post-millennial view are the passages which connect the Resurrection with both the Coming and the final Judgment; the language of 2 Pet. iii.; the solemnity with which, in the matter of the Coming, the "*second* time" is named, without any explicit similar mention of a third; and the complicated difficulties to thought when the idea of a terrestrial reign of the glorified Lord is considered carefully. These difficulties are not necessarily impossibilities, nor do they affect all pre-millennial views; but they are, of course, cautions.

(d) In favour of an interpretation of the Millennium

in a sense more mystical than literal is the fact of the isolated character and, when studied closely, very peculiar wording of the great passage in Rev. xx., and the manifest rightness of explaining, on the whole, in Scripture, the obscurer passages by the clearer, the more isolated by the more extended.

Observe, too, the fact, mentioned above (p. 109), that some of the amplest prophecies of coming blessedness on earth in the Old Testament are applied in the New Testament not to a future millennial age, but to the present age, that of the Gospel.

Amidst the divergency of interpretations it is an important and happy reflection, that all those we have sketched leave possible a profound agreement on those central truths which concern the Person of Christ, His sacrificial and sanctifying work, and the "blessed hope" of His personal glorious Coming and Triumph. They no doubt affect the views of their holders as to the purpose and efficacy of the present agencies and resources of the Church, and the scope of its work, as revealed in the Scriptures. On the whole, however, we leave this subject as we entered upon it, with a reverent avowal of the conditions of mystery and, in some respects, inevitable suspense which attend its study.[1] On no topic of revelation should believing students be more watchful against premature conclusions and unloving mutual criticisms than on that of the details of the prediction of our Blessed Lord's most certain, literal, glorious and desirable Return. Meanwhile, let the topic invite an ever deeper, more hallowed, and more submissive study, and kindle a more ardent longing, and animate to a holier walk.

EVEN SO, COME, LORD JESUS.

---

[1] For able presentations of the Pre-millennial view see the Rev. H. G. Guinness, *Approaching End of the Age*, and *Light for the Last Days*. For the contrasted view, see the Rev. David Brown, D.D., *The Second Advent*, and Bp Waldegrave, *New Testament Millennarianism*.

THE DOCTRINE OF THE SON. 115

THE JUDGMENT.

Scripture abounds in predictions of a future *Judgment*, closely connected with " the Last Day." As a central passage see Joh. v. 29 (where read, "resurrection of judgment"); and see Matt. x. 15, xii. 36, 41, xxv. 34-6; Joh. v. 22, 24, 27; Acts x. 42, xvii. 31, xxiv. 25; Rom. ii. 5-16, xiv. 10; 1 Cor. iv. 4, 5, xi. 32; 2 Cor. v. 10; 1 Tim. v. 24; 2 Tim. iv. 1; Heb. vi. 2, ix. 27, x. 27; 2 Pet. iii. 7; 1 Joh. iv. 17; Jude 6; Rev. xx. 11-15.

The Judge is "God Himself" (Psal. l. 6; Rom. ii. 16; Heb. xii. 23), All-knowing and All-just. But especially the Son, the Christ, appears as the Judge. This is explained Joh. v. 22 (and cp. Acts x. 42, xvii. 31) to be a matter of eternal inner fitness; " because He is the Son of Man." His gracious and mysterious one-ness with Man, while He is also the Eternal Son, designates Him as the fit Judge of the tribes of which He is, as it were, the Patriarch. In His human experience of temptation, " yet without sin," the heart of man is afforded a divine guarantee, if the word may be reverently used, of perfect mercy and perfect justice in the scrutiny of its sins.

The subjects of the Judgment are the race, in all its individuals. Such is the plain bearing of e.g. Matt. xxv. 32; Joh. v. 28; Rev. xx. 12; and cp. Gen. xviii. 25; Eccl. xii. 14. The question at once arises what the incidence of judgment will be in view of the incalculable varieties of capacity, character, and circumstance. The reply must be that we know too little to reply; too little of the mystery of hereditary sinfulness and of the responsibility involved in the lowest phase of conscience, and generally of the nature and secret history of the soul. It is well to remember that the judgment is not in our hands, that "God is both legislature and executive." In each one of the innumerable cases the "Judge of all the earth will" infallibly "do justly" (Gen. xviii. 25). Nothing will be decided roughly and in the mass. No one will be condemned for ignorance of what it was impossible for him to know. The sentence will always have respect to sin. And the sin, though real and condemning, of the man never reached by the divine message of salvation will not be as the sin of the man who has heard it (Matt. x. 15; Luke xii. 47, 48). On the other hand, the awfulness of the least disobedience to conscience, even where there has been no explicit revelation, will then appear (Rom. ii. 12).

But the whole problem of the sentence on those who have never received revelation is of the deepest mystery. He who entirely submits to the teaching of Scripture will leave it in solemn silence to the Judge, remembering on the one side His absolute mercy and justice, on the other side the insistence of Holy Scripture upon the urgent necessity that the Gospel should be carried to men everywhere in this world with a view to their salvation. And meanwhile his own heart's experience tells him of man's profound need to know that Gospel, in its fulness, in order to do the will of God. Whatever speculation may do, the Holy Scriptures do not *encourage* vague hopes of human salvation apart from that Gospel. See Rom. x. 14, 15; and cp. Acts xi. 14.

It is clearly revealed that the accepted, the saved, the true Church, will then be somehow judged. See Rom. xiv. 10; 2 Cor. v. 10; and cp. 1 Cor. iii. 15. And on the other hand it is revealed, in verbal conradiction to this prospect, that the believer in the

THE DOCTRINE OF THE SON. 117

Son of God "cometh not into judgment" (John v. 24; cp. Rom. viii. 33). If a reconciliation may be reverently sought, the saved shall be then seen, without a doubt or fear, to be indeed amply and eternally accepted, but for them too the book of conscience shall be solemnly and entirely opened, and results from the discipline of time shall be carried on into eternity, making differences related to the quality of their service of love on earth (Matt. xxv. 19-23).

Again we gather that the "saints," the "members" of Christ the Judge, shall mysteriously share in His action as Judge. See 1 Cor. vi. 2; and cp. Dan. vii. 22; Matt. xix. 28; Rev. xx. 4. Speculation in detail is vain. We may humbly think that this participation will be a solemn approval of the verdict of the Son of Man, in absolute harmony with His whole mind in giving it, and as by those whose union with Him will then be supremely seen. It is indicated that "angels" as well as men will be subjects of the judgment. See Jude 6; perhaps Matt. xxv. 41; and cp. Matt. viii. 29 (a passage of mournful significance); 1 Cor. vi. 3. This prospect seems to indicate close relations between these "angels" and mankind.

The whole revelation of the Judgment points to it as to *an event*, not merely, as has been sometimes suggested, an eternal fact figured under the imagery of crisis and time. Doubtless a figurative and pictorial element is present in the Scripture presentation, in which we read, for instance, of opened "books" on which the sentence is based. But this is wholly different from a solution of the prospect into a vision, so to speak, of things which are not themselves an event. This great adjudication by the Son of Man is firmly linked in prospect to the Resurrection of the Dead,[1] an *event* (whatever be its details) definite, and wholly future.

In brief, the Judgment is presented to us in Scripture as the close of the dealings of God with man in probation and redemption. As that process had historical points of beginning and development, so it is to have an historical point of conclusion. We say "point," of course, not in a needlessly narrow sense. It is no part of the Creed to believe that the "Last Day" shall contain just twenty-four hours, or twelve. It may be a decisive period rather than a common day; it may on the other hand indicate a crisis of inconceivable rapidity, to which a common day should be as a thousand years; so little can we know of the judgment-process. But we mean that it is presented in Scripture as an event. Every event of time has relations to God's eternity other than those it bears to us who "become." But this does not make it less truly an event of time. And this is as true of the coming Judgment as of the First Advent.

"*We believe that Thou shalt come to be our Judge: We therefore pray Thee, help Thy servants whom Thou hast redeemed with Thy precious blood.*"

[1] Some theologians have explained even the promise of "the resurrection of the body" as not foretelling a vast future event, but presenting in a single idea numberless events of all time; the liberation, at death, of a spiritual body supposed to be latent in the natural. But if such be the meaning of the New Testament it is consistently concealed by its words. See e.g. 1 Cor. xv. 51, 52; 1 Thess. iv. 14—v. 2; and cp. 2 Tim. ii. 18. To support such an interpretation it is surely necessary to go yet further, and to say that the Return of the Lord is not an event, but an ideal presentation of innumerable events. To the submissive student of Scripture, one passage is sufficient correction to this; Acts i. 11.

CHAPTER VII.

THE DOCTRINE OF GOD (CONTINUED).

THE DOCTRINE OF THE HOLY SPIRIT.

I. THE PERSONALITY OF THE HOLY SPIRIT.
II. THE WORK OF THE HOLY SPIRIT.
III. HISTORY OF THE DOCTRINE OF THE HOLY SPIRIT.

(1) WE have already (p. 22) touched on the revelation of a Third Person within the Divine Being, a Third Agent in the divine action on and in creation in general, and man in particular. This Third Person appears under several designations: "the Spirit," "the Spirit of God," "the Spirit of Christ," "the Spirit of the Son of God," "the Holy Spirit," or, in older English, "the Holy Ghost," "the Paraclete,"[1] παράκλητος, *Advocate*, i.e. the *invoked* Helper of the soul.

This holy Power plainly belongs to the *divine* sphere. Thus, the Spirit "searches the depths of God" (1 Cor. ii. 10): wholly comprehends God, an impossibility but to infinite Mind (cp. Matt. xi. 27); "dwells in" the saint as in "a temple" (1 Cor. vi. 19), a phrase pointing direct to Godhead, in view

[1] The word "Comforter," *Confortator*, "Strengthener," is not the strict equivalent of παράκλητος. But it is a true though not full paraphrase.

of the jealous Theism of Scripture. The Spirit is such that "blasphemy," railing, against the Spirit is irremissible sin (Matt. xii. 31, 32); a statement which clearly points towards the supreme order of being. The Spirit was at one time (p. 148) taken to be a *created Personality*. But this view is so palpably discrepant with Scripture that it has long been practically obsolete. The only controversy now is about, not the order, but the mode, of the Spirit's being. Is the Spirit a divine Faculty, or Mode of action, in brief, a divine *thing*,—or a divine *Person?* For the former view there is much colour. Πνεῦμα (*Pneuma*) is neuter, and means "Breath," and so cannot *of itself* indicate personality. And the analogy of the human spirit suggests rather an element, condition, or phase in the divine Personality than a constituent Personality within Godhead. And in studying the Scripture view of the Spirit's Work it is often hard to draw a line between Operant and Operation, Giver and Gift. May not this difficulty lie in the facts? May not "the Spirit" be but a phrase, or symbol, for God spiritually working and giving?

But against all this appear some great phenomena of Scripture.

The scriptural doctrine of the Spirit is best studied from the centre outwards, or, to put it otherwise, from the development to the embryo. That centre, that development, is found in our Lord's Paschal discourse, Joh. xiv.-xvi. There He, at a crisis of infinite solemnity, speaks emphatically of the Spirit as a Person. In the Greek this emphasis is even stronger than in the English; the *masculine* pronouns ὅς, ἐκεῖνος, αὐτός, and noun παράκλητος, are freely used, though the noun πνεῦμα is *neuter*. (See esp. xiv. 16, 17, xv. 26,

THE DOCTRINE OF THE SPIRIT. 121

xvi. 7, 8.) Fully to appreciate this central testimony, the whole discourse must be read.[1]

In connexion, we next take the large group of passages which attribute consciousness and personal action to the Spirit. First among them stands the warning already referred to, Matt. xii. 31, 32. Then, throughout the *Acts*, the Spirit appears as personal; see v. 3, 9, vii. 51, viii. 29, 39, x. 19, xiii. 2, 4, xv. 28, xvi. 6, xx. 23, 28, xxi. 11, xxviii. 25. In the *Epistles* and *Revelation* a similar chain of statements and allusions occurs: see Rom. viii. 14, 16, 26, 27, xv. 30; 1 Cor. ii. 10, iii. 16, vi. 19, xii. 11; Eph. iv. 30; 1 Tim. iv. 1; Heb. iii. 7, ix. 8, x. 15; Jas iv. 5 (?); 2 Pet. i. 21; Rev. i. 4, ii. 7, 11, 17, 29; iii. 6, 13, 22, xiv. 13, xxii. 17.

The above are a few out of a multitude of mentions of the Spirit; they are those only in which the wording points more or less distinctly to personality and its action. They are enough to show the deep harmony between the Paschal discourse and the teaching of the Apostles; and meanwhile there is nothing in the mass of remaining mentions to negative the idea of personality.

Here again, as with the Godhead of the Son, the "Unitarianism" of Scripture (p. 20) secures the fulness of its Trinitarianism. Jealous for the glory of the One God, Scripture would not even seem to indicate to us the personality of the Spirit, the Spirit presented as knowing and doing divine things, if the Spirit were not both a Person, and of the Eternal Being.

[1] The question whether our Lord used Aramaic or Greek may seem to be material. But it is not so for those who see in Scripture as it stands the authenticated Word of God. For them, the discourses as we have them are, so to speak, revised by the true Author.

As we go back from the New Testament to the Old Testament we find, undoubtedly, a much less explicit revelation. "The Spirit of God," or "of the LORD," (רוּחַ יְהוָה, רוּחַ אֱלֹהִים) appears very frequently, from Genesis to the later Prophets; acting in Creation (Gen. i. 2; Job xxvi. 13; cp. Psal. civ. 30); and in particular in the gift of personal human life (Job xxvii. 3; cp. Gen. ii. 7); giving men special force (Judg. iii. 10) and skill (Exod. xxxi. 3) for the purposes of the kingdom of God; "poured out" for man's enlightenment and sanctification (Prov. i. 23), and remaining with them for such ends (Psal. li. 11; Isai. lxiii. 11); and, particularly, giving supernatural insight and foresight, and true utterance of it (2 Sam. xxiii. 2; 1 Chron. xxviii. 12; 2 Chron. xv. 1; etc.). But it is hard to say that any of these passages reveals of itself, and apart from the New Testament, the Personality of the Spirit. Not that therefore this truth was unknown to the ancient Church. That Church had a living line of prophetical teachers during the whole formation of the Old Testament, which thus was less exclusively the channel (though always the test) of Revelation then than the completed Scripture is for the universal Church now. Certainly the belief in the Spirit's Personality seems to be assumed by the Lord and the Apostles. As we have seen, they treat the Personality as a fact, but they never give it as a new truth.

But, returning, and viewing the whole revelation from its centre, we find in these Old Testament passages precious contributions to the doctrine of the Spirit, bearing, however, rather on the Work than on the Person.

Under the head of the divine Personality of the

THE DOCTRINE OF THE SPIRIT. 123

Paraclete falls the enquiry into His designation as THE SPIRIT.

Why should the Third Person be specially "The Spirit," when, altogether, "God is Spirit" (Joh. iv. 24)? The answer is to be humbly sought both in the inner relations of the Persons and in Their outgoing redeeming work. "The Spirit," "the Breath," is the fit designation of the Third Person if, in the ineffable intercourse of Godhead, He is the eternal *Nexus* of the Father and the Son, the eternal Resultant and Vehicle, if we may venture on such words, of Their infinite mutual Love in its yearning and breathing.[1] Again, He is fitly designated "the Spirit," "the Breath," if in Redemption His work is to apply subjectively the holy objectivity of the Father's Will and Love and the Son's Work and Life; penetrating with awakening whispers and new-creating *afflatus* into the subjects of the work of grace, and becoming their "breath of (new) life." We recall in this connexion His revealed work in the material creation. The Old Testament, in deep and suggestive intimations, shows us the Spirit as the immediate Cause of material things, as e.g. Psal. civ. 30.[2] His intimate impalpable Presence and Virtue finds here also its verbal counterpart in the word "Breath," "Spirit." And we may observe further that in Nature, as in Grace, it is the Son,

---

[1] See Augustine, *On the Trinity*, vi. 20.
[2] Such phrases, to the believer in the divine character of Scripture, are far more than "poetical." They are poetical, in a high degree, but they are also, and mainly, revelations of the inner ways of God's working, of the supernatural and divine everywhere at the basis of the natural. This applies also to the many Old Testament passages where "the Spirit of God" is said to work in matters of courage, artistic skill, and the like.

the Word, who is, through the Spirit, the immediate divine *secret* of Life.

As we pass from this enquiry about the Holy Spirit's Personality, let us reflect on the sacred practical moment of the subject. A clear view of His Personality will indefinitely deepen, solemnize, and soften, all our belief and all our action in regard of the work of grace. A mysterious and living glory is thrown upon the revelation and experience of the New Birth and Life, upon Regeneration, Sanctification, Union with Christ, when the soul remembers that indeed a Person is the Influence at work, that its Life is the Life Giver, its Comfort the Comforter; no impersonal force, itself incapable of loving and being loved, but One who is Himself archetypal Kindness and Tenderness.

The *Procession of the Holy Spirit* is a phrase sadly associated with theological strife (see below, p. 149). Let us view it here, if possible, in a different light. It has to do with revelations of the mysterious inner blessedness of the "Blissful God" (1 Tim. i. 11).

(*a*) The word *Procession* has its origin, for this subject, in Joh. xv. 26, "the Spirit of Truth, which *proceedeth* from the Father" (ὃ παρὰ τοῦ πατρὸς ἐκπορεύεται). The precise Greek verb is not employed of either the Generation or the Mission of the Son; and it, and its Latin equivalent, have been adopted to denote the eternal Origination of the Spirit from the Fount of Godhead, the Father (above, p. 23). That Origination must be eternal, supernatural, necessary, or there would have been at some time a great change developed within God. It must on the other hand be Origination; the Spirit, as a Person, is not His own Cause, or He

THE DOCTRINE OF THE SPIRIT. 125

would be an independent God. As regards mode, the Procession is wholly inscrutable. Only, it is not Filiation. But every word touched in such an enquiry is a divine secret.

(*b*) The Procession is from the Father *and the Son*. The history of this doctrine comes below (p. 149); let us here look at the truth in itself.

What this says is, in effect, that while the Father is the eternal Origin of the Spirit, the Son is concurrently His eternal Origin; Deity is in the Spirit, eternally, because of the Son as well as because of the Father. The Scripture evidence for this is briefly as follows. The Spirit is repeatedly called "the Spirit of Christ," "the Spirit of the Son" (e.g. Rom. viii. 9; Gal. iv. 6; 1 Pet. i. 11), just as He is called "the Spirit of God," "the Spirit of the Father." And the work of the Spirit is subordinate (in a reverent sense of that word) to that of Christ; He "testifies of Christ," "glorifies Christ" (below, p. 132). Now the "economical" relations and works of the Blessed Persons appear to rest upon their "immanent" relations (above, pp. 24, 25). Thus, He who is "sent by" Christ (Joh. xv. 26), and is "the Spirit of Christ" (1 Pet. i. 11, etc.), in the work of Redemption, is to be believed to be ineffably connected with the Eternal Son, in the inner relations of Godhead, in some way akin to emission. Not, again, that the Son is an Origin independent of the Father. All that He is in the Godhead, He is "of the Father," and of Him alone. But *inter alia* He is, of the Father, *this*—the concurrent Origin of the Blessed and Eternal Spirit. Does not the view (see above, p. 123) of the Spirit as the eternal *Nexus* between the Father and the Son, the Effect and Channel of Their inner Love, combine these revealed mysteries into one deep harmony?

And does not the work of the Spirit for us, in connexion with the work of Christ, gain indefinitely in our view as we contemplate the dual Procession? He who testifies of Christ, and glorifies Him, and imparts Him, does this not only as His holy Messenger and Co-operator, but as the Stream of love and life from Him the Fountain. Strong is the concord of such co-operation.

(2) We proceed to the *Work* of the Holy Spirit; and first to His work *in material Nature*. We have already seen (p. 123) indications of His work in the creation of the world, and in its renewal and sustentation—a work as divine as the initial act, for the momently permanence of things rests ultimately only on the will of God (Rev. iv. 11). We reverently infer from Scripture that the *immediate* divine cause of things is the Spirit (e.g. Gen. i. 2), while yet "all things came to be *through* the Son" (Joh. i. 3), and "hold together *in* the Son" (Col. i. 17). It is remarkable that things material (Job xxvi. 13), as well as conscious existences, should thus be seen to have "the Spirit" for their immediate true cause.

As regards His work *in Mankind at large*, the Spirit appears as man's Maker, in a special sense (Job xxxiii. 4). In Job xxvii. 3, the Spirit's *sustaining* power in man is vividly expressed: "the Spirit of God is in my nostrils;" and cp. Gen. ii. 7. But His revealed work for man goes mainly towards the moral and spiritual (Gen. vi. 3; whatever be the translation of the verb), and the supernatural in knowledge and action.

The Scripture indications, however, of His work

THE DOCTRINE OF THE SPIRIT. 127

outside the region of revelation and covenant are very sparing. Moses indeed freely quotes a Pharaoh speaking of "the Spirit of God" (Gen. xli. 38). But such words from such a speaker are quite exceptional, whatever their value. Gen. vi. 3 possibly indicates that a certain original universality of His work on men ceased afterwards in the order of dispensations. Yet no positive revelation *forbids* the thought that the Spirit has somehow dealt, and deals, with every human spirit, morally and spiritually, besides His work as Creator and Sustainer.

As the Messianic Age approaches, the prophecies indicate a coming universal "effusion" of the Spirit ("upon *all flesh*"; Joel ii. 28). The universality seems to refer to an extension to all races and ranks of men. The New Testament (Acts ii. 16-21) finds this fulfilled at Pentecost, when representatives of the race received the Gospel, and the universal believing Church definitely began to be, under the power of the Spirit. True, that beginning has a future in which "all the ends of the world shall remember and turn unto the Lord" (Psal. xxii. 27). Limits upon the work of grace at one period are no proof that it will be always limited. But the passages here in question indicate not so much a work in every individual, certainly not an " effusion upon" every individual, as a world-wide extension of the Spirit's full action upon individuals, resulting in union with Christ in His Church universal.

So of the great passage, Joh. xvi. 8-11. The Spirit when He "comes," "will convict the world concerning sin, and righteousness, and judgment," in connexion with Jesus Christ. We must not here infer a new and developed action of the Spirit, in the Christian Age, upon every human conscience, for the work spoken of is connected with knowledge of Christ, and belief or unbelief in Him; things practically limited within the range of the work of the Church. "The world" here means *man* rather than *men*, the race in the mass; man, irrespective of individual time, place, and character.

It is not ours to prescribe how and where the Holy Spirit shall or shall not work upon men. Ours is to "gather up the fragments" of things revealed. Among these fragments is not found such a universality of the Spirit's higher work as to indicate, as a revealed truth, that grace, in a special sense of the word, is universal.

Does the Holy Spirit do a work of conviction and conversion, in the Intermediate State? Many conjecture this, or affirm it. Who would not humbly welcome any real relief under the awful mysteries of the future of the impenitent? But Christian enquirers must beware of alleged relieving discoveries which are not in true proportion with the great outlines of the Gospel. Such a discovery we believe this to be. Its one apparently definite suggestion is 1 Pet. iii. 19, 20 (with possibly, iv. 6). That passage, on which we have already spoken (p. 94), warns us by its very isolation not to build on it any large inference not amply supported by Scripture. But the inference demanded is not only large but vast, practically modifying the whole aspect of the warnings of Scripture. Such a line of exegesis is an inversion of true principles. Never, for a moment, must we exaggerate the threatenings of the Word of God. In this as in all things we must be jealous of divine

THE DOCTRINE OF THE SPIRIT. 129

proportion. We must cherish the profoundest confidence in the equity, pity, and love of God. But on the other hand, and this in the direction where fallen man needs most to watch himself, we must cherish a sense of the awfulness of Sin, wherever it is, and of the dread sanctities of the Law, written or unwritten (Rom. ii. 14, 15, iii. 19). Above all, let the student cherish this sense, in humble and prayerful study of the Scripture, *with regard to himself*.

In studying the Spirit's work *in the Church*, we assume some results approached in more detail below (pp. 202, etc.). We assume a distinction between the conception of the visible Church and that of the invisible; the Church from the viewpoint of registration and organization, a body ascertainable by man, and the Church from the view-point of true life in Christ, of genuine faith and love, a body ascertainable (as to its limits) only by God.[1]

As regards *the Visible Church*, the registered and ordered Christian community, the work of the Spirit is deeply connected with the use within it of the Holy Scriptures and of the Christian Ministry. As we shall explain below (pp. 252, etc.), there does not seem to be evidence, either in revelation or experience, for holding that initiation into the visible Community secures *ipso facto* the regenerating presence and power of the Spirit in the *individual*. But as regards the *community* it is certain that the power of the Spirit works normally within the Church Visible as it does not without; acting along the lines of the Word read and preached, the Sacraments duly ministered,

[1] Cp. Hooker, *Eccl. Polity*, iii. 1, quoted p. 202.

discipline maintained, and, more generally, conscience quickened and informed by the diffused presence of Christian ideas, whether or not the individual has the New Life. Meanwhile it is to be remembered earnestly that this His action, inestimable in its own sphere, is not His highest and deepest; is not different *in kind* from action which He continually exercises outside the Church Visible, excepting the particular benefits of Sacraments.

As regards the *Invisible Church*, the Community in which every member is in God's view true, and whose total is the true "mystical Body of Christ, the blessed Company of all faithful people," we can speak much more definitely of the Spirit's work. Here again we must anticipate much that will be explained below.

The Work of the Spirit in *the Individual* first claims attention. The individual believer as one of the fallen race, invariably *begins fallen;* alienated from God; spiritually "dead." See further, p. 182. This is as true within as without visible Christendom. (See this implied Rom. viii. 1-11 ; and cp. 1 Joh. ii. 19.) Accordingly, in order to the gift of new life, wherever it is given the Spirit works ; the man is "born of the Spirit" (Joh. iii. 8). The *normal order* of the life-giving process is Conviction, Faith, Union.

(1) *Conviction*, of sin, righteousness, and judgment, is the first work of the Spirit, for Christ, upon "the world" (Joh. xvi. 8, 9); and all men begin as members of "the world."[1] When conscience sees not only in general the fact of personal moral

---

[1] So the English Church testifies, in the Baptismal Service.

THE DOCTRINE OF THE SPIRIT. 131

disorder and the certainty of retribution, which things can be seen without grace,[1] but also the relation of sin to the holiness of God, and the relation of condemnation to His infinitely sacred justice; when in fact it sees sin in the light of God and Christ, in some true measure; this is (Joh. xvi. 8, 9) the Spirit's personal and special work. The signs of that work may vary indefinitely with the character, age, training, of the man. And the conviction in question may occur not always at the same point of the process. And it is a consciousness certainly intended not to be once felt and over, but to underlie all after experiences. But the words of Joh. xvi. 8, 9 indicate that in the order of the divine thought it comes first.

In passing, let us point out the extreme importance of the doctrine of the Spirit's convictions. Shallowness, and passingness, of religious experience are often due to inadequate attention to this side of truth, and to a consequent weakness of hold on the revealed facts of acceptance and life. It is the parable of the Sower realized. The crop "dureth for a while" (Matt. xiii. 20, 21) because the stratum of rock ($\pi\epsilon\tau\rho\acute{a}$) beneath the thin soil has not been broken; there is no "contrition," no bruising.

(2) Conviction of sin does not itself secure the man's part in salvation. Conceivably, it may be deeply felt and yet leave him devoid of " life eternal." Scripture indeed indicates, in our view, that where it *does* fully take place it is, as a fact, followed by

---

[1] Not that the Holy Spirit may not normally act in and with all workings of conscience. But this may be fully true without a presence and working of the kind commonly called in Scripture "grace."

the new life. To be really "awake" is an idea always *associated with* the new "life" (e.g. Eph. v. 14). But it is not identical with new life, and conceivably might come and go without it, but for the mercy of the Worker. Accordingly, the work must proceed, and proceeds, to the point of *Union with Christ* "who is our Life" (Col. iii. 4; 1 Joh. v. 11, 12). The convinced man "sees the Son, and believes on Him" (Joh. vi. 40). He "hears the voice of the Son of God" (Joh. v. 25). He confides himself, convinced of sin, righteousness, and judgment, to a discovered Redeemer and Lord, capable of meeting his great need (e.g. Matt. xi. 28; Joh. iii. 36, vi. 37, ix. 35, 38, xx. 31; 2 Tim. i. 12). Now it is revealed to us as a divine fact that the man so doing enters indeed into a position of *forgiveness*, and more than forgiveness—*acceptance with God*. (e.g. Rom. iv. 23, 25, v. 1). But the deepest of all truths about the fact of "coming to Christ," the truth which carries all others with it, is that the man is *united to Christ*, as to the Head of a spiritual organism, as to which He stands in a connexion altogether unique. The contact of *faith* is perfectly simple in itself; it is no less and no more than the personal confidence of the awakened soul, on the ground of divine truth and promise. But it carries with it profound and incalculable results, because of the Object which it touches, Jesus Christ, Son of God and Son of Man, Second Man, Mediator and Surety of the New Covenant (above, p. 102). The man, awakened by the Spirit, and confiding in the Son, not only approaches Christ; he is joined to Him, one Spirit (1 Cor. vi. 17), he is "IN Him" (1 Joh. v. 20, etc.; cp. Joh. vi. 37; 1 Cor. i. 30), partaker of His life (2 Cor. iv. 10, 11; cp. Joh. xiv.

THE DOCTRINE OF THE SPIRIT. 133

19) in a sense illustrated in Scripture by the union of limb with Head, branch with Vine, etc. (Eph. iv. 15, 16; Joh. xv. 1-5). He is not only forgiven, but spiritually new-created (2 Cor. v. 17).

This mysterious but most real contact is the basis of all the man's spiritual gains and possessions. One with Christ, he possesses, and is enjoined to use, all that Christ has for His true member. The acceptance of the Head, the Second Adam, in His perfect merits, is for the member. (See further, p. 189.) The virtues of the glorified Manhood of the Head, the Second Adam, are for the member; he has " put on the New Man " (Eph. iv. 24, with Gal. iii. 27). The simple but magnetic contact of faith is the way to all this range and depth of result; or more truly still, is the reception of it. (See further, p. 182.)

But now all this is the work of the Holy Spirit, and from more than one point of view. First, He is the direct Author of faith; He is "the Spirit of faith" (2 Cor. iv. 13). That the man sees Christ and acts upon the sight, is due to the Spirit's skill and power (Eph. ii. 8; Phil. i. 29; 2 Pet. i. 2). Nor is this all. The Spirit acts in all this not merely as an instructor, external to his pupil, or an artificer, external to his work. True to His divine Name, He penetrates the man's being as the vehicle of the New Birth, the breath of the New Life (John iii. 8 ; Gal. v. 25, etc.). He enters into a deep, tender harmony with the human spirit (e.g. Rom. viii. 26, 27), not creating it, for it is already there (p. 163), but re-creating it into restored unison with Himself; not abolishing, or absorbing, but possessing. Thus the man becomes "spiritual" (1 Cor. ii. 14, 15). And again, the Spirit does all this to the member while being also the Spirit who abides in supreme fulness in the Head. He is thus a bond of divine strength and tenderness between member and Head.

For we have to carry into all thoughts of the relation between the Spirit and the Christian, the mysterious relation between the Spirit and Christ. We have seen above (p. 124) how the Procession from the Son throws a secret glory over the inner relations of the Eternal Persons, and over the work of the Spirit as the Witness of and Worker for Christ in the Gospel Age. To this must now be added the truth that all through the historical process of Incarnation and Redemption the Spirit has intense relations with the Incarnate Son. He is the immediate Agent in the holy Conception (Luke i. 35). He "descends," in ineffable speciality, upon the Son at Baptism (Matt. iii. 16, etc.), so that He goes to Temptation (Matt. iv. 1), and Ministry (Luke iv. 14, 18), "in the power of the Spirit." The Spirit secures for the Son of Man that He shall "speak the words of God" (Joh. iii. 34). It is "by means of the eternal Spirit" that the Lord "offers Himself without spot to God" (Heb. ix. 14). He is profoundly concerned in the Resurrection (Rom. viii. 11). After Resurrection, it is "by the Holy Spirit" that the Lord "gives commands to the Apostles" (Acts i. 2). And when the glorified Christ speaks to the Churches, as the Slain One risen, His voice is also the voice of the Spirit (Rev. ii. and iii.).

Thus the Regenerator of the Christian is He who was Agent in the Generation of Christ; the Strengthener of the Christian for spiritual conflict, service, sacrifice and witness, is He who did this work supremely in the Second Adam Himself, and

THE DOCTRINE OF THE SPIRIT.

that in quite the same reality, and with the same necessity, as in our case. For the passages just recited, amongst others, indicate that the Human Nature of our Lord was produced, and *maintained*, in its absolute and indefectible moral and spiritual perfection, not by His own action as God, but by that of the Spirit as God. Not after the manner of Fatherhood, but yet with true causation, the Spirit wrought the Manhood of the Incarnate.[1]

These considerations, taken along with the truths that the true Christian is "born of the Spirit" and "has life, having the Son" (1 Joh. v. 12), lead us to the conclusion that the believer's union with his Head is altogether by the Holy Spirit. It is not material, or quasi-material, or materially infused. It is spiritual, while perfectly real and unfigurative. The details are, at most, very partially revealed, and are quite beyond our independent speculation. But the general inference is that the life of the Second Adam is in the new man, because by the Spirit's grace he believes, and because the Spirit of Grace is at once in the Head and in the member. The man has the new nature, the re-created nature, now, and will enjoy its results through his whole being hereafter, "because (Rom. viii. 11) of the Spirit that dwelleth in him" (see further below, p. 251).

As we leave the inexhaustible topic of the Spirit's work in regard of our Union with Christ, we

---

[1] This is a truth quite separable in thought from the other divine truths, that the Manhood was, in eternal purpose and historic fact, never for a moment dissociated from, personally independent of, the Godhead of the Son, and that the Person in which it inhered was never for a moment other than the Person of the Divine Son. The Son assumed it; the Spirit caused it. See Owen, *Concerning the Holy Spirit*, bk ii., ch. iii.

observe that one result of the Scripture testimony is that while the Blessed Spirit is τὸ ζωοποιόν, "the Giver of Life," in respect of His immediate impartation of Life eternal to the man, He is not Himself the Life. In the last analysis, this Life is the Son of God, Jesus Christ, the incarnate, sacrificed, and glorified Head of His true Church (Eph. i. 20-23) and of every true member (1 Cor. vi. 17, xi. 3). The Spirit is the eternal and divine personal Vehicle; Jesus Christ, "who is our Life" (Col. iii. 4), is the Thing conveyed, given, united to the regenerate man. The eternal Life is not only from Christ; not only even in Christ; it is Christ. On the other hand the impartation of Christ is such as to leave absolutely intact the reality and freedom of the personality of the Christian. The personality of the member is not absorbed into, but annexed to, and adjusted under, that of the Head.

Thus, from different points of view, the believer "lives by the Spirit" (Gal. v. 25), and "lives by faith in the Son of God," who "lives in him" (Gal. ii. 20). The Spirit "dwells in Him" (1 Cor. iii. 16), and "Christ dwells in his heart, by faith" (Eph. iii. 16, 17; cp. Rom. viii. 9-11). The Spirit "sanctifies" him (1 Pet. i. 2), and Christ "is made unto him sanctification" (1 Cor. i. 30). To borrow an imperfect analogy from physical science, Christ is as the Sun of the soul, the Spirit is as the luminiferous Ether by whose vibration we have the Sun's light and heat.

(3) In the study of the life-giving work of the Spirit, as He unites the man to Jesus Christ, we must not forget His concurrent and related work of *illumination* and *witness*. The connexion is deep and necessary. Putting aside (see further below, p. 181)

THE DOCTRINE OF THE SPIRIT. 137

the abnormal case, for in the light of Scripture it is abnormal, of human life *closed* in infancy, we see in our enquiry thus far that the Spirit's decisive life-giving takes effect in the man in and through his coming to believe, to commit himself to Jesus Christ. The Spirit is distinctively "the Spirit of faith" (2 Cor. iv. 13). And He produces faith, of the unifying sort, that is the man's entrustment of himself in spiritual reality to the Saviour of sinners, by "revealing the Son in him" (Gal. i. 16); by bringing the man to "see the Son and believe on Him" (Joh. vi. 40). Under this head falls accordingly all we read of the Spirit's "testifying of Christ," "glorifying Christ," by "taking of Christ's things and showing them" (Joh. xv. 26, xvi. 14); bringing man to "say that Jesus is Lord" (1 Cor. xii. 3); "opening the heart to attend to "the things of Christ" (Acts xvi. 14).[1]

(4) In connexion with the whole subject, let us remark on the revealed *freedom and sovereignty* of the Spirit's work. "The wind bloweth where it listeth" (Joh. iii. 8). "The Spirit divideth to every man severally as He will." (1 Cor. xii. 11). This indeed is a general characteristic, in Scripture, of divine action in the things of grace (see e.g. Joh. v. 21; Jas i. 18), whether or no the Holy Spirit is in immediate view. But here, as elsewhere, it needs special and reverent remembrance. In particular, it reminds us here of what we shall see more in detail below (p. 252), the impossibility of restricting, even normally, much less universally, the Spirit's action, in the vital union of the man to Christ, to a

[1] Here, and in Gal. i. 15 quoted above, the Spirit is not explicitly mentioned. But the analogy of Scripture is altogether in favour of a reference to Him.

sacramental ordinance, or to any ordinance at all. Such ordinances have a most sacred work to do; but not to be the normal vehicles of the Spirit's vital operation. For, as we are seeing, a characteristic of that operation is its incalculable freedom; and the practical limitation of that operation, in a normal way, to a system (though divinely instituted) of external ordinance, capable of being worked and registered as to its material side by human agents, is a contradiction to that characteristic. *Deus non alligatur sacramentis* is a dictum which, in the light of Scripture, is not a concession in detail but a leading and ruling principle. Perfectly true it is that, in the deepest analysis, the free will of God has a sovereign place in all facts. But this leaves where it was the assertion in Scripture of a special phase of freedom in the Spirit's life-giving work. That work, to be *characteristically* free, must be, not capricious or arbitrary, which nothing divine can be, but incalculable as regards conditions and tests capable of reduction to, or correspondence to, a system of material operations falling within man's power. In the nature of things, a register of baptisms cannot with certainty tabulate a series of sovereignly wrought new births.

All the while, the sovereignty of the Spirit's operation, whatever mysteries may surround it, is a sovereignty of perfect wisdom working with the tenderness of eternal love.

And throughout the whole life of faith, as at its beginning in the new birth, He maintains the soul in faith by keeping and developing in its view the glorious Object of faith and by inwardly drawing its confidence in that divinely reasonable direction. (For faith in Christ is indeed on the one hand a

THE DOCTRINE OF THE SPIRIT. 139

supernatural grace, because the fallen heart, apart from grace, shrinks from self-entrustment to the Holy One. But on the other hand, viewed as the action of the soul, it is the most reasonable and natural movement and direction of personal trust that can be named.)

The Spirit's manner of action and influence as Guide and Friend, in this blessed life, must, of course, be beyond our analysis in countless details. Only some salient facts about it are given in Scripture. Among them we gather that the Spirit exercises a most real, while mysterious, personal influence on the subjects of His work (Rom. viii. 14); that He gives them intuitions, not to be explained by natural emotion or imagination, into eternal realities (1 Cor. ii. 9, 10); that He directs the judgment in things spiritual so that the believer, as such, has an instinct for the true and against the false in such things (1 Joh. ii. 27). "He witnesses with" the believer's human "spirit, that we are the children of God" (Rom. viii. 16); that is, He meets their filial faith and love with the supernatural assurance of divine paternal faithfulness and tenderness.

As "the Spirit of Christ in the Prophets" (1 Pet. i. 11), the Third Person is the true Author of the Scriptures. See especially Acts i. 16, xxviii. 25; Heb. iii. 7, x. 15, and cp. ix. 8. See also 2 Pet. i. 21, and cp. 2 Tim. iii. 16. It is interesting and important to observe the great prominence of this truth in the belief of the primitive Church. Thus Clement of Rome (cent. i.) quotes Isai. liii. in full (*Ep. ad. Cor.*, c. xvi.) as "spoken by the Holy Spirit about" Christ, and bids Christians study the Scriptures as "the true, the (Scriptures) of the

Holy Spirit" (c. xlv.). And by the way he speaks of St Paul, as of the Old Testament prophets, as "writing by inspiration" (πνευματικῶς, c. xlvii.). Justin (cent. ii.) uses the strongest language about the function of the Spirit in the production of Hebrew prophecy. The prophets' part was to yield themselves to His operation, in purity, that the divine power, descending from heaven, might "deal with just men as the plectrum deals with harp or lyre" (*Cohortatio*, c. viii.). Theophilus of Antioch (cent. ii.) calls the Scripture-writers "vehicles of the Holy Spirit . . . so that in things to come the fulfilment will be as they say" (*ad Autolycum*, ii. 9). Irenæus (cent. ii.) calls them men "accustomed to carry (*portare*) God's Spirit" (*Adv. Hæreses*, v. 14). Tertullian (cent. ii.-iii.) speaks of them as "*inundated* with the Holy Spirit" (*Apologeticum*, c. xviii.); and of their writings as the "writings (*litteræ*) of God." Cyprian (cent. iii.) speaks repeatedly of the Holy Spirit as speaking in Law and Gospel. Clement of Alexandria (cent. iii.) speaks of those who "reject the Scriptures, that is, the Holy Spirit" (*Stromata*, vii. 16, 98). Origen (cent. iii.) gives it as a point in the teaching of the universal Church, that "the Scriptures were written by the Spirit of God."[1]

The catena might be indefinitely extended and enriched. See above, p. 7.

The submissive recognition of the Holy Spirit's authorship of the Scriptures leaves quite free our conceptions of the *consciousness of Inspiration in the*

---

[1] See Westcott, *Introduction to the Study of the Gospels*, Appendix ix. B. See also Goode, as referred to p. 7, above. On the general subject cp. Smeaton, *Doctrine of the Holy Spirit*, pp. 136, etc.

THE DOCTRINE OF THE SPIRIT. 141

inspired writers.[1] But it fixes for us the all-important fact that the "divine Scriptures" (to use a favourite patristic term), whatever the external circumstances of their production, are His Word, and carry His authority. It leaves us free to trace to the full each writer's individuality. But it sees in these individualities the intention of the Inspirer, who divinely moulded the instrument for His infallible use; that instrument being not the voice only, or the pen, but the whole personality, and its adjustment in time and place. We are amply free to see the genuine human character of a Moses, or a Jeremiah, or a Paul in their inspired writings. But surely we are *not* free to believe that a fabricated writing under their names, used with a view to false prestige, could, by moral possibility, be one of the "writings of God."

We proceed to the Spirit's work for *the community* of the true Church. Thus far we have studied His action for the individual, in new birth and new life. This is the just and scriptural order of thought from man's point of view. From the point of view of the plan of God the true Church precedes the true believer; the holy Organism is in its measure the "final cause" for which the personal regeneration takes place. But in the history of the individual, and of the Church, personal regeneration brings the man into the true spiritual Organism, and contributes to the realization of its idea. The man is not in the true Church, and so of course does not contribute to it, till he is personally regenerated.

But on the other hand this regeneration is

---

[1] And observe that e.g. 2 Tim. iii. 16 calls the *writing*, not the *writer*, inspired. See Waller, *Authoritative Inspiration*, p. 89, and generally.

always related to the Organism of the regenerate company. Accordingly the Spirit's work appears prominently in Scripture as in and for the whole Body. See e.g. 1 Cor. xii. 4-13; Eph. iv. 3, 4; and perhaps 1 Cor. vi. 19. And cp. 2 Cor. xiii. 14; Phil. ii. 1; "the communion of the Holy Spirit." The truth of such Scriptures is that the divine Worker, residing at once in the Head and the members of the mystical Body, works always in each member with regard to all, and with supreme and all-including regard to the Head. To this end He directs His working always, alike in its multiplicity of mode, and in its unity of character. Meanwhile, in His infinite thought and skill the true interests of the member never suffer for those of the Body, nor those of the Body for those of the member. He maintains each individual in a union with the Head as direct, as vivifying, and as sanctifying, as if the one member were all. He maintains the Body in its union with an adjustment as delicate and perfect as if there were no complexity in the Body.[1]

On some special points.

(1) "*Spiritual gifts*" ($\chi\alpha\rho\acute{\iota}\sigma\mu\alpha\tau\alpha$). In the New Testament Church we find the manifestation, in Christians, of supernatural powers in the material sphere; "tongues," "gifts of healing," besides prediction and specially illuminated instruction. These "gifts" are always attributed to the Holy Spirit as the immediate Giver (see 1 Cor. xii. etc.). Were they a grant to the Church for its initial work only, or so as to be always present at the call of faith? The answer is not easy. And it is not ours to be decisive where Scripture is reticent.

[1] See the second Collect for Good Friday.

THE DOCTRINE OF THE SPIRIT. 143

But on the whole Scripture points to a cessation of *charismata* (as distinguished from χάρις in its larger and deeper sense) in the normal life of the Church. In the Acts, while the exercise of the *charismata* was distributed widely, though not universally (1 Cor. xii. 28-30), the power thus exercised was very rarely given (see Acts x. 44-6, for the one clear exception) without a human medium, and this medium was the imposition of the hands of *an Apostle* (see Acts viii. 14-15). At least, no clear contrary case occurs. With this fact compare the intimation (1 Cor. xiii. 8) of a certain transiency in these manifestations, in contrast to the permanency of "grace."

(2) On the meaning of Grace (χάρις). This all-important word presents a large field for Scriptural study. We can only summarize results.

The word habitually implies the *gratuitous freeness* of the gift, or act, denoted. Thus it means sometimes the *free pardon* and *acceptance* of the sinner, under the Gospel covenant, in contrast to an acceptance earned (Rom. xi. 6; Eph. ii. 8, 9, etc). Or, again, unbought divine kindness in general (2 Cor. viii. 9). But it often specially denotes a gift and blessing working in the soul and will (e.g. 2 Cor. viii. 7). Here the characteristic of gratuitousness is still as present as ever, but the action is different. What is saving grace, thus present *in* the Christian? The answer lies not in any analysis of the word, nor in any explicit Scripture, for there is none, but in the harmony of revealed truths. "Grace" manifested, for example, in regenerate love, or patience, is a distributed and specialized phase of the central gift, "eternal life." And what is that life? Nothing less than the possession (expressed

Joh. xvii. 3 as the "knowledge") of God in Christ; the "having the Son of God" (1 Joh. v. 12). It is participation of the divine Nature (2 Pet. i. 4), which is holiness and love.[1]

Grace, in its highest sense, is nothing less than "God working in us, to will and to do, for His good pleasure's sake" (Phil. ii. 13). It is not a separate or separable entity, projected, as it were, from God into man. It is God Himself, "in-working" in special ways for special ends; above all, for His glory in the salvation of His Church from condemnation and from sin, and in its conformation to the likeness of His Son. In the light of our view of the Spirit's work, grace may thus be described as the freely given presence of the Holy Spirit in the man, applying Christ to him, and manifesting Christ in and through him.

(3) The work of the Holy Spirit in *the Old Testament saints*. What is the essential difference between the work of the Spirit in believing individuals before and after the First Advent? Like many other Scripture problems, this is far easier to state than to answer.

The indications are somewhat thus:—

The Spirit was not only with, but in, the true believers of the old time. The New Testament believer has "*the same* Spirit of faith as they" (2 Cor. iv. 13). The New Testament writers quote them as illustrious examples of faith, without any suggestion that their faith was inferior in kind. The terms used in the Old Testament, especially in

---

[1] Cp. 2 Pet. i. 5-7 (in the Greek, or Revised Version) for a suggestion that the whole chain of Christian "graces" is in effect the distributed manifestation of the possession of this "divine Nature."

THE DOCTRINE OF THE SPIRIT. 145

the Psalms, about spiritual life, are highly evangelical (e.g. Psal. li. 10-12, xci. 1, 9 ; Isai. lxiii. 11); indeed, the Christian believer everywhere finds in the language of the elder saints the expression of his own deepest experiences. And the effect of Old Testament faith was essentially the same as that of faith now; the God-given reliance carried with it spiritual union with God, the God of Covenant and of the great Promise, the God of the coming Christ. Thus the blessed Spirit's work was, in kind, always the same in the saints. The "old fathers" were, as truly as we are, united by Him to Him in whom is Life; to Christ who is our Life. They were, as truly as we are, made by Him partakers of the divine Nature; regenerated to be true followers of God (see e.g. Isai. lxiii. 16, lxvi. 8 ; and cp. p. 240, below). There was thus a sense in which the Spirit, long before the effusion of Pentecost, had "come," and was doing His sacred work in the world; convincing, transforming, giving life.

On the other hand it is equally plain from the New Testament that the "coming" of the Spirit, on the glorification of Christ, was in a sense new; a "new departure," if the phrase may be reverently used. Perhaps the reconciliation of these phenomena lies in a very simple statement. The newness of the presence and the work was not of kind but of degree. The Spirit, having now to deal with men in connexion with the historically manifested, perfected, and glorified Son of God, was (if we may venture to put it so) able now to deal in a vastly developed manner with men ; in fuller and more intense convictions; in a larger impartation to faith of the glories and virtues of its Object, and, to the renewed will, of its Example ; in a far brighter

146 OUTLINES OF CHRISTIAN DOCTRINE.

illumination of the regenerate mind as to the full purposes of Redemption. It is remarkable that the great work of the Spirit at Pentecost was to enable the saints for a totally new energy of testimony to Christ; a fact which leaves it abundantly credible that His visitation was new rather in degree than in kind. Meantime, so profound is the development in degree that in effect it is, in many respects, a quite new manifestation. See the language of Joh. vii. 39, and cp. Joh. xiv. 17.[1]

This question is an example of many others in Scripture, where the *dealings of God with man in time* are in view, and particularly where the difference between the circumstances before and after the Incarnation is in view. We have to remember on the one hand the equal relation to God always of all times; on the other hand the mystery of His dealing with men after the conditions of successive time. From the first point of view the Incarnate Head is and was ever present to be the life of His members. From the second point of view the fulness of the promise waited for "the fulness of the times."

SUPPLEMENTARY.

HISTORY OF THE DOCTRINE OF THE HOLY SPIRIT

Our Lord, in the baptismal formula, had associated the Holy Spirit with the Father and the Son, under the One Name. And we have seen above how decisive was Christ's testimony (Joh. xiv.-xvi.) to the truth that the Spirit is not only principle but Person. Just outside the Canon,

---

[1] In this last passage, however, "He shall be in you" does not logically imply that in no degree was the Spirit "in them" as yet.

THE DOCTRINE OF THE SPIRIT. 147

Clement of Rome (*Ep. ad Cor.*, c. 58 [1]) recognizes both the power and personality of the Spirit in the words, "God liveth, and the Lord Jesus Christ liveth, and the Holy Spirit." *Ignatius* (*Magn.*, c. 13) speaks of Christians as "in the Son and the Father, and in the Spirit." A curious testimony to the early belief in His Personality is given by the appearance of a "Holy Spirit" in the Gnostic systems. Their theory is indeed wholly distorted from the Scripture view, but yet their "Holy Spirit" is as personal as their "Christ." Meanwhile the language of some of the early Church teachers is undoubtedly sometimes wavering, sometimes plainly unscriptural. *The Shepherd of Hermas* identifies the Spirit with the pre-existent Son (*Simil.*, 5, 9); so does the primitive homily called the *Second Epistle of Clement of Rome* (c. 14). *Justin Martyr* speaks varyingly on the point (see *Apolog.* I., c. 33). And, on the other hand, the works scripturally assigned to the Spirit are by some assigned to the Eternal Word,—a fact capable, however, of scriptural explanation.

A little later, in *Irenæus*, *Tertullian*, and *Origen*, clearer views are more prominent. The relation of the Spirit to the Father and the Son, not only in work but in being, in "immanence" (p. 24), is discerned and stated. Before all creation (*constitutio*) the Spirit (identified with the Wisdom of Prov. viii.) was, like the Son, with the Father (*Iren.*, iv. 34, 3). He is one of the two "Hands" of the Father (iv. *præf.*). He is eternal. He is the *communicatio Christi*. He is the great Teacher of the Church, through prophets and apostles, and her abiding Enlightener. *Tertullian's* teaching is closely akin to this. He discerns and teaches the Personality, and the divine Essence, of the Spirit. He is the first who distinctly calls the Spirit "God." On the other hand, he emphasizes His subordination to and derivation from the Son "as fruit from branch, stream from river" (*adv. Prax.*, 2, 8). Tertullian

[1] See Lightfoot, *Clem. of Rome*, Appendix Volume, p. 284, for the recently recovered text of this chapter.

is one of the first writers to use the word *Trinitas*.[1] *Origen* does not definitely call the Spirit "God," but clearly holds His Deity, and His distinct "hypostasis," which with Origen means, usually, "person" (Bigg's *Bampton Lectures*, pp. 163, 172). He uses the word Triad (Trinity). The Spirit is, *through* the Son, *of* the Father, who is "Fountain of Deity." As to His work, Origen taught that its speciality was confined within the circle of believers; He works life in them that believe. All men have being from the Father, and "reason" from the Word; but not all share in the Spirit. Meanwhile, however inconsistently, he speaks of the Spirit as "*coming into being*" (ἐγένετο) by the Son; and even as a Creature. But He is before time.

The Arians regarded the Spirit as a quasi-divine Person, but lower than, and created by, the Son.

At Nicæa (325) the controversy scarcely touched the doctrine of the Spirit. Later (360 and onwards), *Athanasius* took the question up earnestly, and discerned and stated the full Scripture truth of His Person, as distinct, and as uncreated; fully and eternally within the blessed Trinity, "which is all One God." He is less distinct on the doctrine of the Spirit's Work. The semi-Arians, or Macedonians, confessing the Deity of Christ, denied that of the Spirit. For some time, it is evident, popular religious opinion hesitated and wavered over a full confession. Very much by the labours of *Gregory of Nazianzus*, *Basil*, and *Gregory of Nyssa* (late cent. iv.), the view which alone harmonizes all the facts of Scripture won its way to full prevalence; the Spirit, with the Father and the Son, is a not separated but distinct Bearer, Subject, of the divine Essence; one with the Two in nature, and in operation; so that the divine

[1] Bishop Kaye, *Tertullian*, p. 561 (ed. 1829), says: "The occasional ambiguity of his language respecting the Holy Ghost is in part to be traced to the variety of senses in which the word *Spiritus* is used. . . . The Son is frequently called [by Tertullian] the Spirit of God." This remark is of wide application.

THE DOCTRINE OF THE SPIRIT. 149

action is of the Father, through the Son, by the Spirit The *differentia* of the Spirit is His eternal and mysterious· (not Generation, but) Procession, Forthcoming.

The Dual Procession. Was the eternal Forthcoming from the *Son* as well as from the Father ? The teaching of *St Augustine* made the affirmative view prevalent in the West ; for he insisted to the utmost on the eternal inner unities of the Holy Trinity. In particular, he brought out the thought that the Spirit is the eternal Bond and Vehicle of the mutual Love of the Father and the Son (*de Trin.,* vi. 20 : above, p. 123). · In the East, without at first any formal denial, the tendency was to a negative ; though Athanasius approaches very near to the Dual Procession. The Spirit, in his teaching, is by (διὰ τοῦ) the Son, but His " Cause " is the ·Father only. In the next century this view was largely repudiated in the East, in favour of a wholly single Procession. The question did not come up at Chalcedon (451).

In cent. v., in Spain, heretical attacks led to a ·special emphasis on the belief, long current in the West, of the Forthcoming from Both; and cent. vi. (589) saw the words "*and from the Son*" inserted in the Spanish version of the "Nicene " Creed, apparently without any intention of innovation. Not till more than a century later was the divergence of East and West a subject of *Church* debate. It was discussed at· a council at Gentilly in 767. Just later, *Charlemagne* advocated with great energy the Dual doctrine, and sought,· but in vain, to· secure the Pope's consent to the insertion of the words "*and from the Son* " into the Roman Creed. The issue of the doctrinal struggle was the Great Schism of cent. xi., in which East and West excommunicated each other.

The last effort for reconciliation was made at the Council of Florence (1439), when the Greek Empire was tottering to its fall. An unreal compromise was the only result. As lately as 1863 a Greek encyclical denounced as heretical the doctrine of the words "*and from the Son.*"

Of modern views of the doctrine of the Person of the Spirit we notice only one, widely prevalent in Germany, and within the vast sphere of German theological influence. It is that which scarcely, if at all, recognizes the Personality of the Blessed Spirit; but takes "the Spirit" to be rather the God-taught *Geist* of the Christian community—a mysterious "Christian consciousness;" to be described from another side as the manifestation of God in the Church, God acting in the Church, the Union of God with the Church. The view is essentially Sabellian. It needs little but a careful comparison with Scripture to bring out its discrepancy with apostolic views.

It is observable that a lax view of the authority of the Holy Scriptures ordinarily accompanies this doctrine. The "Christian consciousness" is the judge and touchstone of Scripture. And another characteristic is an inadequate conviction of sin as transgression of the Law.[1]

To trace fully the history of the doctrine of the Holy Spirit's *Work* is quite beyond our limits. On the whole, in the patristic period, the doctrine of His new-creating work, in regeneration and sanctification, is less fully dealt with in the Eastern than in the Western theology. The *Montanist* movement (cent. ii.), joined by Tertullian, in which a revival of the gift of prophecy was asserted, did not at first, perhaps, connect itself doctrinally with the Holy Spirit, but more generally with "the Lord God Almighty." But inevitably it drew both its followers and opponents to a deeper reflection on the promises of Joh. xiv.-xvi., and so was overruled to bring home anew to the Church the abiding and most real personal action of the Spirit, as (in Tertullian's phrase) the true *Vicarius Christi* (see Smith's *Dict. Christian Biography and Doctrines*, iii., p. 116). *St Augustine*, next after St Paul, is the chief expositor of this truth, of which he had learnt much in his own experience. His great successor

[1] Cp. generally Smeaton, *Doctrine of the Holy Spirit*, Div. iii., pp. 358-364.

THE DOCTRINE OF THE SPIRIT. 151

was *St Bernard* (cent. xii.), who wrote on *Grace and Free Will*, on Augustine's lines, and with deep personal realization. The *Mystic* theology of the middle ages, as of later times, was greatly occupied with the doctrine of the Holy Ghost, as the means of the soul's fellowship with God in Christ. At and after the period of *the Reformation* a great revival and development of the doctrine of the Spirit came in; bringing, alas, tares with its wheat, and an inevitable sequel of controversy, above all on the relations between the Holy Spirit and the human will in the work of salvation (p. 174. And see Smeaton as quoted just above).

At the present moment the minds of innumerable Christians are powerfully directed towards the truth of the Holy Spirit's Personality, Power, and living Presence with the believing soul and the true Church. Not only in the important way of doctrinal accuracy, but in that, yet more important, of living realization, it is owned more and more that the Eternal Paraclete is the supreme need of the soul, and of the Church, as regards saving faith in Christ, entirety of obedience to Him, and powerful witness for Him. This is a happy and holy omen. All Church history bears witness to the fact that with the greater or less recognition of His reality and glory, and of our need of Him, flows or ebbs the life and witness of the Body and Bride of Christ.

CHAPTER VIII.

THE DOCTRINE OF MAN.

I. Man as Created.   II. Man as Fallen.

III. Man as Restored.

I. Man as Created.

SCRIPTURE gives no formulated Anthropology. But in its representation of man, as in its revelation of God, it gives facts and principles, inviting reverent formulation. It implies meanwhile two provisos; first, that it considers man from the divine view-point, above all as the subject of redemption; secondly, that the theory which it suggests must be tempered by the remembrance that about ourselves, as truly as about God, "we know in part."

Man appears, on the first page of the Scriptures, as the last work of the Sixth Day. Gen. i. 26, 27 gives the creation of man in the abstract, so to speak; Gen. ii. 7-25, the creation of the first man in the concrete; not different events, but different views. From the *first* passage we gather that man is a result of specially deliberate and direct creative will. Neither "the earth" "brings him forth" (vers. 11, 24), nor "the waters" (vers. 20, 21); Elôhim

THE DOCTRINE OF MAN. 153

(above, p. 24) consults within Himself, and makes him.

Further we gather that man in his creation was related to God in a way quite peculiar, among the works of the Six Days. He was made "in the image, after the likeness," of God. And he was made to be head of the orders of terrestrial creation.

From the *second* passage we gather that the First Man was produced from the existing "dust of the ground," that the Maker "breathed into his nostrils a breath (*neshâmah*) of life;" that he thus became "living soul;" and that his spouse was "builded," by the direct will of the Maker, out of the man's own body.

We attempt here no detailed enquiry how far these narratives are to be read "literally." We only remark, first, that they are assumed in the New Testament to be historical (e.g. Matt. xix. 4-6; 1 Tim. ii. 13, 14), and not only so, but fundamental to after revelation (see Rom. v. 12-19; 1 Cor. xv. 45-9). For the New Testament writers, beyond doubt, Adam was as real a personage as Christ. The minute account of the locality of the garden (Gen. ii. 8-14), an account on which recent research throws clear light,[1] looks in the same direction. On the other hand the narrative, by its manner and subject matter, as a very brief account of natural and spiritual "origins," allows us to read beyond the letter as regards details. We are free to explain "the dust" not narrowly, but as probably meaning existing matter, proper for the end; and the "breathing into the nostrils" as a pictorial phrase for the divine act of will by which the lifeless frame became the seat of

[1] See Sir J. W. Dawson, *Modern Science in Bible Lands*, ch. ii.

life and personality. So with the making of Woman; the same creative will which long after worked the multiplication of the loaves, willed the origin of the human female from "the side" of the male; but we need not figure to ourselves a mechanical operation.

It is impossible to avoid all mention of the modern evolutionary philosophy. We only point out, modestly but firmly, what that philosophy cannot lawfully say against the Scripture account of man's origin; an account endorsed by One whom Christians believe to be man's Maker (Matt. xix. 4-6).

It cannot, *from observed phenomena*, pronounce it proved that man was not a properly "new departure." No strictly scientific evidence to that effect has yet appeared. It is difficult even to imagine the future appearance of any, even should the present manifold deficiencies in the physical links between man and the most nearly related beasts[1] be yet much reduced. For Scripture allows, or rather asserts, a plan, progression, harmony in Nature. Not one word makes it unlikely that, when man was to be willed into being, he should prove to be moulded of the same matter as that of predecessors and coevals, and on a similar plan. What Scripture does none the less assert is a mysterious new departure when the first human pair was produced. There was not a dislocation of immaterial design, but a break of mere material continuity, when there was to appear the creature, at once spiritual and material, who should resemble, know, and love the Creator.

No discoveries in material nature can properly disprove this. One thing is certain, that the earliest discovered human skulls are even finely developed, and on a plan, in some respects, divergent (as now)

[1] See Mivart, *Lessons from Nature*, ch. vi.

from that of the skulls of the highest "anthropoid" beasts. Another and far more significant certainty is that man, amidst his many variations, is found to be everywhere, even at his lowest, capable of loving and obeying God; a gulph between him and the highest lower animals which has neither bottom nor bridge. The exceptional origin of such a creature is the reverse of an anomaly.

We may here briefly remark on the general prevalence of an evolutionary *philosophy*, claiming more or less distinctly to explain the universe by matter and impersonal force. Such a philosophy gets a high prestige from its present adoption by a host of eminently skilled students of material nature. Their proper studies are concerned with phenomena, capable of precise observation and verification as such; and from this an impression arises that all inferences of such observers carry a peculiar weight of accuracy and certainty. But as soon as these observers pass from physical observation, and from inferences of the nature of mathematical reasoning on proper subject matter, to philosophize on the nature and origin of things, they are on the open ground of universal human thought. The physical observer, as such, has no more *knowledge* than his neighbour about things which are not physical phenomenon, and has no peculiar mental apparatus. If, because of his knowledge of the phenomena of the body, he claims a right to say that the brain originates thought, or that the beast can be true ancestor of the man, he is off his ground. Wrong or right, he no longer speaks as the observer of verifiable phenomena.

More particularly, the word "evolution," now irrevocably familiarized, needs careful usage if we would avoid confusion. It means "unrolling" of something already there. If what is unrolled is an ascending and all-including plan and progress, already in the eternal Mind and Will, Scripture is evolutionary. If what is unrolled is all organic life from primary inorganic material, excluding the factor of creative purpose, (which must be free to act as uniformly or as acutely as eternal Mind shall order, now modifying by degrees, now effecting "new departures," by its own at once sovereign and immanent action,) Scripture is anti-evolutionary. Most decisively it is so when "evolution" is taken to mean that it is proved that *man* is merely the result of insensible variations from below; that *human nature as a whole* is continuous with animal.

And if Scripture is, in this sense, non-evolutionary, so is the vast phenomenon of man as he is, amidst the lower races as they are, and as the rocks show "animals" to have been in the remotest past. Too often we fail, in this matter, "to see the forest for the trees."

As regards the *Antiquity of Man*, it is allowed that the chronology of the early chapters of Scripture must be handled with great reserve. Not that it is therefore loose and mythical. But it lies in a narrative presented, so to speak, enigmatically, by its very brevity, and it goes very probably on principles of enumeration not yet fully understood. Still, Scripture represents man as originating in a past quite recent, compared with what it allows for nature in general. On the other hand it has been asserted by naturalists that the origin of man must be put back hundreds of millenniums into past time. This belief rests partly on *à priori* reasoning on "origins," partly on the occurrence of human relics in certain geological surroundings. But the believing Scripture student need not

THE DOCTRINE OF MAN.

"make haste in this matter," while yet he takes care not to assert hastily on his own side. An eminent geologist, Sir J. W. Dawson, recently President of the British Association, has just (1888) published his conviction that the origin of man is to be fixed, geologically, within a moderate number of millenniums, say seven or eight.[1] To him, on the whole, geological evidence and the comparatively brief chronology of Scripture appear to be converging. He regards "palæolithic man" as the antediluvian of Scripture, and finds geological indications of a general, if not universal, deluge within the human period.

As regards the *Unity of Mankind*, clearly asserted by Scripture (Acts xvii. 26, with Gen. i., ii., ix. 19), naturalists have often asserted, or conjectured, many centres of origin. But their researches now strongly favour the proper unity of the race.

THE IMAGE AND LIKENESS OF GOD.

Of the mysterious and much-discussed words of Gen. i. 26, we offer no minute exegesis here. Even to examine the different references of *Image* (*Tselem, Shadow*) and *Likeness* (*D'mûth*) is beyond our scope; we only notice one suggestive interpretation, that God *made* man, as to constitution, in His *Image*, to be *brought out*, as to development, into His *Likeness*. Our more possible enquiry here is, What is the Image? Is it reason, in its highest sense? Or power to know God? Or actual holiness, positive sanctifying knowledge of God? Or immortality? Or sovereignty over the creatures? We reject the last as inadequate. And as to the theory of positive holiness, it is a fact against it that *fallen men* are

[1] *Modern Science*, cc. i., iii. Cp. at large Southall, *Recent Origin of Man*.

viewed in Scripture as "made in the image of God" (Gen. ix. 6; Jas iii. 9); the original making of man in that image is a fact permanent for all men.

The solution which to us seems most comprehensive is that the Image lies in the mysterious gift of Personality, bringing not only mental but, much more, moral capacity, and true free-will and free-agency, such that man within his sphere becomes a true self-guiding Cause, as God is in His sphere.

The beasts are not so. They are not moral, not responsible, not disengaged from material circumstance; not true causes. Man is all this; and so can know God as like knows like. God, the Archetype of all Personality, supremely self-conscious, self-acting, moral, has made man to be, in the remarkable words of the Apocrypha, "the image of His own peculiar nature" (Wisd. ii. 23: εἰκόνα τῆς ἰδίας ἰδιότητος).

Such is Man, as Man, as possessing "the abysmal deeps of personality,"[1] that the individual, profound as are his relations to the race, and particularly to his immediate ancestry, still is never their irresponsible effect, but always a responsible moral cause amidst and above them. We know it, in our inmost self-knowledge. Be "heredity" what it may, the man is so *himself* that he, not his ancestry in him, has each moment to face, for himself, the mysteries of right and wrong, as truly as if he had waked up, at the first touch of the Creator, in an immaterial environment. Our individual personality, and our generic continuity, are "antinomies"; truths equally certain always, however impossible fully to reconcile while "we know in part."

Thus interpreted, the Image stands, in a sense,

[1] Tennyson, *Palace of Art*.

apart from man's "Original Righteousness." The Righteousness he could and did lose. The Image he retains, whatever fatal disorder may have touched it; he is for ever personal, moral, responsible. And in this view it is the Image which makes him capable of redemption and regeneration, while yet it gives no contradiction to his "death in trespasses and sins." Nay, it is this possession which makes that "death" possible. Only a true personality can be "alienated" from God.

Here too seems to lie the deepest indication in Scripture of man's *natural immortality*. We believe that immortality to be a revealed fact, taken for granted in some awful passages, where the "second death," the hopeless retribution on the impenitent, is seen to have no necessary tendency to cessation of being (see, e.g., Matt. xxv. 46; Joh. iii. 36; Rev. xiv. 11, xx. 10, 15). It seems to be indicated, not precisely that "the substance of the soul is indissoluble, and therefore indestructible," but that moral personality is mysteriously permanent, as God has constituted things. This seems to underlie our Lord's reasoning for the Resurrection of the dead (Matt. xxii. 31, 32). He assumes, for one thing, the necessary ultimate coherence, so to speak, of body and spirit in man, so that if man lives for ever his body must ultimately share that life. But He assumes also, and first, the *natural permanence* of the creature constitutionally capable of knowing God, of having God for "his God."[1]

The enquiry about the Image of God suggests that about man's constitution, according to Scripture,

[1] The question, observe, was of the resurrection, not of the saints, but of "*the dead*." Our Lord uses words spoken of the saints as also intimating universal human facts which they presuppose.

as *Body, Soul, and Spirit*. Here first observe the peculiar language of Scripture about the Body. It puts an honour on the body found nowhere else. The formation of the body, in Scripture, is not an accident of man's creation, but the first step to his becoming "living soul." Scripture nowhere makes the body, *apart from the awful accident of sin*, the prison, or clog, of the spirit,[1] so that the *summum bonum* should be to quit it. It is the spirit's congenial home, and its true normal vehicle of experience and action. We do not read that it was created immortal, so that had man not sinned his body, *apart from the special will of God*, would not have died. But it is implied that such was that will that had man not sinned his entire constitution, body and "breath of life," would have known no dislocation. Somehow, through whatever transfiguration, the whole being would have "lived for ever" (Gen. iii. 22). Accordingly redemption, salvation, sanctification, glorification, is for body as well as soul (Luke xxiv. 39; Joh. ii. 21; Rom. viii. 23; 1 Cor. vi. 13-20; Phil. iii. 20, 21); and so is retribution also (Matt. xviii. 8, 9; Joh. v. 28, 29; 1 Cor. vi. 18). There awaits man, as an essential for his vast final future, a re-embodiment, most mysterious, but not figurative. The "spiritual body" (1 Cor. xv. 44) will not be made of spirit.

With this agrees the consistent indication of Scripture (especially 2 Cor. v. 10) that the final judgment of man, as a responsible personality, will proceed upon his embodied life, "the things by means of the body" (2 Cor. v. 10, lit.), the things done through it as the vehicle of formation of habit and

---

[1] Contrast Wisdom ix. 15. But even this may refer mainly to the *fallen* condition of man.

THE DOCTRINE OF MAN. 161

registration of result. This is a solemn intimation of a fallacy in the hope of repetitions, in the Intermediate State, of the offers and graces of the Gospel. (See above, p. 95.)

Finally, in this sacred importance of the body, resting upon relations of matter and spirit inscrutable to us, we read some of the reasons of our blessed Lord's Incarnation. Only by taking both the immaterial and material sides of our nature could He become entire Man, and so entirely man's Representative and Head. Thus too " the body of His glory" (Phil. iii. 21) is now an everlasting fact in His blessed Life.

The words *Spirit* (*Ruach*, *Pneuma*) and *Soul* (*Nephesh*, *Psyché*) suggest a host of doctrines, Christian and non-Christian. We can only ask what, on the whole, they mean in Scripture. Are they two separable immaterial elements, so that man can have one and not the other; can lose the one, while keeping the other? Or two departments of consciousness, such that one denotes emotions, the other the pure reason which guides them? Or again, such that *soul* is our point of contact with the world and man, *spirit* with God?

None of the above distinctions seem fully to satisfy the Scripture *data*. The two words, in Scripture, perpetually cross each other, while again they are certainly not mere synonyms. The explanation which best includes all facts seems to be this. Both words denote man's being as immaterial, the "inner man;" but from different aspects. "Spirit" is man's being considered as God's gift; "Soul" is that being considered as the individual's possession in life and experience. Put somewhat otherwise, Soul may be described as Spirit organized; Spirit viewed in the workings of human personality, inseparably linked, for its development, with the body. But they are not separate elements of existence, and many experiences may be described in terms of either. It will thus be further seen how natural, on the other hand, is the occasional reference of higher aspects of experience to the human Spirit, and that the action of the Eternal Spirit is specially connected with it; while lower aspects of experience, such as vehement emotions, are often assigned to the Soul. If Spirit is man's inner being viewed as given from God, and Soul man's inner being viewed as his own, that fact is at least partially explained; while yet it is constantly crossed by other facts.

Here too is a suggestion why the human person disembodied is called a *spirit* rather than a *soul* (e.g. Luke xxiv. 37, 39; Heb. xii. 23),[1] and why personal existences other than human, and about which we read nothing analogous to man's corporeity, are called spirits, never souls.

All this indicates that while man's being is in one aspect threefold it is more essentially twofold. Some modern Christian thinkers[2] have held that the human *spirit* was lost, or at least thrown into abeyance, at the Fall; that it was not infected by the Fall; that it alone is immortal; that salvation consists in its restoration, or awakening, without which the whole being ends at length in the annihilation of personality.

---

[1] In Rev. vi. 9 (cp. xx. 4) we have disembodied "souls." But the reference is peculiar. The case is of those who have, in self-devotion, yielded up their lives in bodily death. The more *self-related* word is in point. Cp. Isa. liii. 10-12.

[2] As Dodwell (cent. xviii.). In our own time the Rev. J. B. Heard, and the Rev. E. White, have taken similar lines of teaching.

THE DOCTRINE OF MAN. 163

This theory falls if Scripture attests the ultimate identity of soul and spirit.[1] Most certainly Scripture indicates the possession of "spirit" by "all flesh" (Numb. xvi. 22); and, on the other hand, the share of the "spirit" in the Fall; its sinful defilement and disorder (2 Cor. vii. 1).

Thus, on the one hand, Man is *dual*. The familiar (but not scriptural) distinction between *matter* and *spirit* may indeed be pressed too far, till it suggests the anti-Christian idea of the necessary evil of matter. But Scripture freely presents "*body and soul*" as distinct and separable constituents of man's normal state (Matt. x. 28). And it always assumes the actual existence of man's spirit, without the body, after death (e.g., Luke xxiv. 37, 39; 2 Cor. v. 8; Heb. xii. 23). On the other hand, it views Man as yet more essentially *single* and homogeneous; "living soul," embodied spirit. It knows no theory that matter is evil, or again that in man's inner world, by original constitution, there is a necessarily rebel element, held more or less in check by a higher and purer; the psychology of Plato. Not nature, but its invasion by sin, has produced an inner discord. Man, as man, is the homogeneous and good work of God; body, soul, and spirit. He is a true unity, alike in creation, in fall, and in grace.

Scripture says much about man's *heart*. The word is large; its possible reference embraces understanding, conscience, affections, will. It is thus "the organ, rather than the seat, of personality."

---
[1] The remarkable words of Heb. iv. 12 may be explained not of separation so much as penetration; man's being as spirit is found and searched by the Word through and under man's being as soul; his relations to God through his knowledge of himself. See Prof. Laidlaw's *Bible Doctrine of Man*, p. 63, note. To this book we are greatly indebted here.

Man has, and is, "a *soul*;" man has, not is, "a *heart*."

Scripture speaks of *the inner man* (Rom. vii. 22; 2 Cor. iv. 16; Eph. iii. 16). In itself the phrase is morally neutral; it means the inner world of consciousness. But by usage it refers to the regenerate state.

Man has, in Scripture, *mind* (νοῦς), in the sense of both mental and moral perception (Rom. vii. 23, 25; Eph. iv. 23). By usage, the word seems to denote man's highest faculties viewed out of special relation to God and grace.

Man has *conscience* (συνείδησις); the knowledge in himself of moral differences. The word sometimes refers specially to the *sense of guilt* before God (Heb. ix. 9, 14, x. 2, 22).

Man has free *will*. He is not the product of circumstances; he is responsible amongst them for moral choice (see above, p. 158). This is always assumed in Scripture, especially in divine reasonings and appeals (e.g., Jer. xxvii. 13; Joh. v. 40). True, Scripture is always jealous for the supremacy and sovereignty of the Will of God (e.g., Dan. iv. 35; Luke xxii. 22; Joh. i. 13; Acts ii. 23, iv. 27, 28; Rom. ix. 19; Eph. i. 11; Rev. xvii. 17). This is one of its great and conspicuous characteristics. His will has sovereign relations to all events, such that all things somehow contribute to the perfect realization of its purposes. But among these "all things" is the reality of the will of the created personality, such that man is a true though secondary cause. We fail, by the necessary limits of our view-point, to see mentally the harmony of the absolute sovereignty of the will of the Holy Creator, and the true freedom, and so true respon-

THE DOCTRINE OF MAN. 165

sibility, of the will of the personal creature. But the two facts are equally plain in revelation, and equally important in a true theology.[1]

MAN'S ORIGINAL STATE.

"The Man whom the Lord God had formed" is seen in Scripture as "put" into (not created in) a scene of outward safety and beauty, with occupation, and with the dominion of a true personality over the unpersonal animals (Gen. ii. 8-15). The primal narrative, and the later Scriptures (e.g., Eccl. vii. 29), imply that his moral state was "very good;" particularly, that he held untroubled intercourse with God, as friend with friend. We are not to assume that his moral state, or his mental, was of *developed* excellence. But it was nobly innocent; childlike in some respects, but also infinitely higher, as it, unlike the child-life now, contained no germ of sinfulness waiting only the development of faculty. Adam "walked with God," in holy simplicity, in inner harmony; "upright" with his eternal Friend and Father (Luke iii. 38). No "lower element" of his constitution wrestled with a "higher" for primacy; nothing in his nature resisted his blessed concord with the divine Nature.

We give thus the account of Man unfallen which seems to us clearly scriptural. Very different views have been taken of man's first state.

---

[1] Is the individual "soul" (in the common meaning of the word) *derived from the parents* (the "*traducianist*" view), or divinely *originated* (the "*creationist*" view)? The former seems to throw some faint light on the mystery of Original Sin; the latter, to accord better with the fact of individual personality, and on the whole with Scripture. Origen held the *pre-existence* of all souls "from the beginning," and their fall in a previous state; a view certainly without definite support in Scripture. Cp. Shedd, *Hist. of Doctrine*, Bk iv., ch. i.

Non-scriptural theories usually assume that man, however originated, began at a low level, one remove above the brutes, and was slowly disciplined into something higher. Great difficulties of common reason attend this view. Man's muscular inferiority to the beasts, and other physical characteristics, e.g., the unclad human skin, make his early survival and propagation a mystery, unless under exceptional original conditions. But to the believer it is enough that Scripture assumes all along the primeval goodness and greatness of human nature. Adam was simple, but not savage; undeveloped, but noble; inexperienced, but conversant with God.

The Roman Catholic theology, as worked out by the Schoolmen, holds an elaborate theory of Original Man. He was created morally neutral, and with conflicting elements in his nature. Then, perhaps after a first probation, he received a supernatural gift, by which he became positively holy and immortal. This gift, and only this, is lost in the Fall, which thus has left man as he was at first, only somewhat weakened morally. (See further below, p. 169.)

This view minimizes, in a way alien from Scripture, both the glory of our nature and the awfulness of its fall. Everywhere in Scripture Man is, from one point of view, kept profoundly low before God; not only as sinner, but as creature. Man owes everything to God; creation to begin with. He is no necessary outcome of the Divine Nature. He is not such that God, being God, need, or must, have made him. He is, in these respects, "the potter's clay" —which the Potter has first freely willed into existence. But, on the other hand, he is the most glorious work of the Creator; "the image *and glory* of God" (1 Cor. xi. 7). No theology true to Scripture must

THE DOCTRINE OF MAN.

decry Human Nature. Not man the creature, but man the sinner, is to be criticized and censured. And again, everywhere Scripture assumes that *sin* is an incalculably discordant and *unnatural* thing in man ; not a mere gravitation of his nature as created and finite, inevitable but for an abnormal intervention. It is a terrible distortion, anomaly, and discord. He ought never to have been, and never to be, a sinner. No theology true to Scripture must venture to minimize the mystery and horror of the Fall, which is correlative to the essential glory of Human Nature.[1]

Thus as we now approach the revelation of the Fall, we emphasize again the height that went before it. Man was "made upright;" spiritually harmonious with God ; so formed that his moral "habit" (*habitus*), the cast and condition of his being, the source of actions, was "very good." All this was by the Holy Spirit ; but by Him in normal action, not abnormal.

Man thus appeared on earth, the crown of God's works, made in His image, knowing and enjoying Him as a kindred Nature. He was not divine ; not God in disguise. He was as entirely a subject product of creative will as the beasts, or the plants. To this all Scripture bears witness. But he was "the son of God" (Luke iii. 38). Not that he was so yet in that deeper and loftier sense, the ultimately true sense, reached through redemption and regeneration in Christ. (See above, p. 34.) No hint in Scripture (above, p. 72) indicates that man is *by creation* "in" the Only-Begotten Son. But as a direct production, "in Image and after Likeness," Adam was "son of God" as truly as Seth was Son of Adam (Gen. v. 3). And the son

[1] See Pascal, *Pensées*, partie i., ch. iv. (ed. Faugère).

walked with his Eternal Father, in peace and light, and in conscious intercourse.[1]

One great mystery and fact about Primal Man remains to be spoken of. It comes out explicitly in the later Scriptures (Rom. v.; 1 Cor. xv., especially; and cf. Eph. iv. 22-4; Col. iii. 9, 10). But the whole revelation prepares for this, in its manifold witness to the spiritual as well as physical unity of the race; not least in its one word for Adam, the individual, and for Man, the race. It is, the position of the First Man as Head and Representative of Man. Adam was a true individual, as truly as Abel. But, unlike his son, he was, what only one other Being ever has been, the moral intelligent Head of a moral intelligent race; not only the first specimen of a newly created Nature, but in such a sense the Spring of that nature to his after-kind that in him not only the individual but the race could, in some all-important respects, be dealt with. His incalculable advantages were theirs; his gentle probation was theirs. This, certainly nothing less, is the mystery taken for granted in Rom. v. (see below, p. 175).

No revelation of Scripture leads us more abruptly, so to speak, to the edge of the unknown. And the strongest efforts of thinking have been spent in the search for a complete theory of it. We believe that its *rationale* rests upon unrevealed

[1] On this last point it appears to be impossible to avoid the testimony of Scripture to the gift of speech, in however simple a form and vocabulary, to primal man. That deeply mysterious gift, our power to formulate (not only to express) general and particular thought in words, such that it is certainly now at least *difficult*, in idea, to dissociate thought from words, was not, according to Scripture, a result of countless experiences. It was, as it were, a sound struck on the harp of primal human nature by the touch of God in supernatural intercourse.

THE DOCTRINE OF MAN. 169

relations between Race and Head. Our safest course, till eternal light is cast upon it, is to keep strictly to what "is written;" to be quite sure that nothing capricious, nothing not purely good, entered into the sovereign divine appointment; and to study it, not in the abstract, but in the glory of its counterpart, the Headship of Christ.

II. MAN FALLEN.

The record of the Fall, in its stern yet pathetic simplicity, must be read at once as fact[1] and as mystery (above, p. 153). The story of the Garden is given as a fact, without a hint of discontinuity in kind between it and the record, for instance, of the Flood. On the other hand, its position, its brevity, and the later expositions of its significance, all prepare us both to forbear asserting a mere literality in all details, and to see in every detail a revelation.

Man, originally holy, was invaded by a personal Intelligence hating God.[2] Man, in the female, suspects a lack of love in God; and, in the male, prefers the creature's will to His (1 Tim. ii. 14). God's will, in its one known prohibition, is violated. Thereupon, by a law quite mysterious in some aspects, but almost self-evident in others, the personal creature not only loses the bliss of intercourse with God, but suffers moral revolution in his being. There is no change in the nature, or constitution, of

[1] See Dawson, *Modern Science*, ch. iv.
[2] On any view of Scripture inspiration, "the Serpent" is not a mere serpent. No hint appears in Scripture that the beasts can rebel against God. A rebel intelligence, such as long after invaded, and as it were animated, bestial bodies (Matt. viii. 30, 31), "possessed" and used such a body in the Temptation. And cp. Rev. xii. 9, etc.

man, which retains all its noble parts and faculties. Man is still " living soul;" spirit, soul, and body; still has conscience and will. But the "habit" (*habitus*) of the personality, the state of the "subject" of all these parts and faculties, is distorted (*depravatus*). Man no longer loves and obeys God as the law of his life. Moral discord is there. Knowledge and choice no longer delightfully converge upon right, upon the will of God. Man "knows good *and evil*" (Gen. iii. 5, 22). The very idea of discord with God apparently had as yet been absent from his happy being; now it is awfully present. He is now "like God," in knowing that such a thing is; but with what a difference! God knows it as the infinite Observer and Judge; man, as the guilty subject of its experience.

Was this a growth, an enrichment, of man's consciousness? Some have ventured to call it "*a fall upward*," as if the incoming of moral discord were a normal condition of human development. But this is the precise contrary to the witness of Scripture. It contains a fragment of truth; for supernatural, abnormal grace overruled the Fall to glorious ends.[1] The eternal plan mysteriously included the fact of the Fall, in its vast progression towards the final glorification of God in Christ. But all this leaves untouched the awfulness, ruin, loss, guilt of the Fall, as it was man's free act. For it *was* wholly free. No faintest force was put on man's will by God. Man's personality, and it alone, chose and caused the disobedience. And so actual evil, sin, had its "origin" for man.

Scripture nowhere reveals the *absolute* "origin

---

[1] A truth boldly expressed in the medieval sentence, *O beata culpa, quæ talem meruisti Redemptorem.*

THE DOCTRINE OF MAN. 171

of evil," that dark nucleus of all distressing mysteries. It does not even state the (to us) insoluble problem, why one moment's wrong was permitted in the sovereignly created universe of an all-holy God. Thought has laboured at the problem. An approach to its answer lies in St Augustine's teaching, that evil *has no origin*, inasmuch as it is negative, not positive; defect, failure; illustrated by the discordant state of a damaged harp. And plainly the abstract possibility of such defect lies in the conception of a *probation*. But, on the other hand, we cannot say that free and willing holiness is impossible without a moral precariousness, an actual liability to fall. God is holy, with infinite willingness and yet with eternal inner necessity. Is it inconceivable, on any abstract principle, that He should will a finite nature into being in a truly kindred state?

No; the solution of the problem of permitted evil lies beyond our sight. What we know is that sin is a fact, a fact in our own inmost personality; and that wherever it is, there, by its idea, it is condemnable—that is, by its very idea it makes the subject of it, the person, condemnable; and that the all-holy God not only is not its cause, but "hates" it with infinite repulsion. That "hatred" is wholly unlike the bitterness and gloom of fallen man's hatred, but it is none the less an absolute personal aversion. And in graciously dealing with its presence in us God has shown His estimate of its formidable, incalculable greatness (above, p. 80) by "giving up His own Son" (Rom. viii. 32).

We cannot thus examine the Scripture estimate of sin without a grave appeal once more to the student. It has been said that every heresy shows some subtle connexion with inadequate views of the "exceeding sinfulness of sin" (Rom. vii. 13). Great differences, affecting whole systems of theology, are traceable to deeper or shallower views of the extent of the Fall; of the malign power of the infection of sin in man; and, not least, of the awful reality of its guilt (*reatus*), its essential liability to condemnation; the profound fact that the sinner, *as such*, has no claim on God, no title to grace, whether in remission or amelioration.

Meanwhile, Scripture, as we have seen, plainly indicates that man's nature, as a constitution, remained intact. Fallen, he was just as much man as before; a true Ego, possessing understanding, affections, will. No force *ab extra* upon his will compelled him now, any more than before, to rebel against God despite himself. In sorrowful truth his will was *bound* towards God; he was *unable* to choose God as his All. But the bondage was from within; not in circumstances, or fate, but in himself; analogous to God's holy *inability to choose evil.* Conscience still spoke of moral difference. Reason still tended to affirm the claim and glory of God, the beauty and duty of virtue. Emotions could still be stirred about God and goodness. But the ultimate decision of the Ego now ran in the line of the Fall, away from God's full rights, and towards self and the creatures. God, as not merely a glorious Object of thought, but the absolute and holy Possessor, End, and All, was now not loved but dreaded by the very centre, so to speak, of the personality. No better response was to be found by awakening, or discovering, some deeper and "better self." The fall was thus "total." The central and ultimate choice was wrong.

THE DOCTRINE OF MAN. 173

What man thus became, men are. Scripture bears witness, with the vast experience of mankind, to the "depravity" of men, to their *distortion* (*depravatio*) universally (e.g., 1 Kings viii. 46; Psal. li. 5, cxliii. 2; Jer. xvii. 9; Matt. vii. 11; Rom. iii. 19, 20; Eph. ii. 1-3). One implied testimony is the universal necessity of a "new birth;" "except a man (a person, τίς) be born again, he cannot see the kingdom of God" (Joh. iii. 3. In Rom. viii. 5-8, under different imagery, the same truth is put with solemn decisiveness). Sinful tendency, underlying sinful action, is co-extensive with mankind. In terms of conscience, no man, of himself, does all the right he knows. In terms of divine right, no man, of himself, fully loves the true God, beheld in all the truth of His holy claims. Here is the deepest of mysteries; but it is also one of the surest of facts. The phenomenon of strictly universal sinfulness is remarkably attested, not only by Scripture, but by universal human thought.[1] One distant instance may serve for many. The ancient Chinese moralists, who moulded national thought to a high degree, take a lofty theoretical view of the goodness of man. Confusing, probably, conscience with will, the approbation with the love of right, they teach that "*man is born good.*" Yet an ancient Chinese proverb speaks of "two good men; one dead, the other unborn."

The fact of *universal* sin points direct to a mystery below it; to a "law," in the naturalist's sense; to a normal tendency correlative to the uniform phenomenon. This leads to the statement of the doctrine of *Original Sin*.

"If all the individuals who come under the head

[1] See, by all means, Prof. J. B. Mozley, *Lectures, etc.*, No. x.

of a certain nature have sin in them, then one mode of expressing this law is, to say that it *belongs to the Nature*, the nature being the common property and ground in which all meet" (Mozley, *Lectures, etc.*, No. ix.).

"It is the fundamental article of Christianity that I am a fallen creature. . . that an evil ground existed in my will, previously to any given act, or assignable moment of time, in my consciousness; I am born a child of wrath. This fearful mystery I pretend not to understand. I cannot even conceive the possibility of it; but I know that it is so . . . and what is real must be possible" (S. T. Coleridge, *Omniana*, at the end). The Christian, with a true insight into himself, and with the Scriptures before him, owns and affirms this. "He knows that it is so." He is himself a sinner. He did not at any point in his individual life choose to leave unbroken personal goodness for sin. He was sinful before he sinned. He also knows that this antecedent sinfulness cannot be rightly conceived as mere misfortune; it was implicit rebellion, real guilt. It was the free attitude of his true personality. When it came to expression, that expression was not due to a mastering fate, wrong while the victim-self was right, though weak. It was the due to—himself.

As of man fallen (above, p. 172), so of the individual, Scripture attests the "totality" of this "depravity," or distortion. That is, it has not only touched every region of the individual's constitution; it is lodged at its centre, so that there is nothing deeper in the Ego with which the Ego can reverse it, or lead up to a reversal of it. A more than reversal, great and full, is possible. But this is due altogether, in its true causation, not to the Ego, but to God.

THE DOCTRINE OF MAN. 175

Meanwhile, as with man so with the individual, the nature is complete, though the being is fallen. Every faculty and aspect of the nature is there. The man is a free moral personality, the Creator's image. No fatalism has invaded him. But in one direction, that of the blessed Maker and His holy will, he is held fast—not from without, but from within. He wills freely, choosing truly, but always, in the ultimate, crucial choice, choosing not to be "subject to the law of God" (Rom. viii. 7), *bonâ fide, toto corde*. Conscience must protest; the affections may kindle and waver; the mind may assent to truth; but the man ultimately wills *not* for God.

All this leaves wide room for differences of character, and of inter-human morality. And these differences are not nothing in themselves, or in the sight of God. But they do not touch the central fact of sin—that men, as fallen, are of themselves alienated from the true God, and of themselves cannot, because they will not, reverse that alienation.

These statements, supported as we hold by Scripture, and by the inmost voice of Christian experience,[1] are connected in one remarkable passage, Rom. v. 12-21 (cp. 1 Cor. xv. 21, 22, 45-9), with Adam and the Fall (see above, p. 168). There we gather that (*a*) our normal sinfulness has a profound connexion with Adam's sin; and (*b*), a mystery even deeper still, that the connexion is such that we have from him not only an infected nature but an inherited exposure to condemnation, antecedent to our acts (vers. 12, 14, 16, 18). Indeed, this is the point of the Apostle's argument. Not "infection," primarily, but "condemnation," lies on the race, and

[1] Far beyond the circle of doctrinal agreement on the *theory*.

on the individual, "for that all sinned" (ver. 12) in "the offence of the one" (ver. 15).

The greatest force of thought has been spent in the study and discussion of this mystery for fifteen centuries. And in the study of the thoughts of an Augustine, an Anselm, a Bernard, or a Calvin, the student will surely gain spiritual as well as mental benefit. But after all they leave us in face of the mystery as a mystery still. We need less to analyse than to adore and act. We return to the Scripture, and to the awakened soul, and there, as we believe, are found affirmed and confessed the universality of sinfulness, the solidarity of the race in guilt (*reatus pœnæ*) and in pollution (*macula*), the totality of the distortion of the fallen being from the holy will of the true God as such, and so the absolute need of a mercy which man cannot claim, and of a power not his own, for his recovery. We read in Scripture, and in awakened consciousness, the unresolved "antinomy" of our true responsibility yet guilty impotency. We read another contradiction too, less of speculation than of practice, in the facts that (*a*) we are unable, without special grace, even to "prepare ourselves to faith and calling upon God" (Art. X.), yet that (*b*) every hearer of the Gospel is invited with the sincerity of eternal goodness. "As I live, I have no pleasure in the death of him that dieth. Turn ye; why will ye die?" (Ezek. xxxiii. 11).

For the practical needs of the heart, the doctrines of the Fall are meant wholly for mercy; meant to drive the last vestige of self-trust and self-esteem from the mind, shutting us up into "the confidence of self-despair" as we turn to the glorious opposite pole of truth, the revelation of love and grace in Jesus Christ

THE DOCTRINE OF MAN.

III. MAN RESTORED.

Much has been anticipated here under the doctrine of the Work of the Eternal Persons. There we saw the Father's holy love for the fallen world, His provision for the call and salvation of the Church in His beloved Son, the covenant of eternal grace, in which the Church was "blessed with all spiritual blessing" by the Father in the Son. We saw the Son's undertaking to be the Mediator and Surety of the Covenant, providing in Himself for His members all things needful for acceptance and holiness—in His sacred incarnation, atoning death, and resurrection-life and headship. We saw the Holy Spirit's office and efficacy in dealing with the soul for its new birth and life in union with the Son by faith, that union of which the Spirit is Bond and Channel. It remains to consider the Scripture revelation of man, of man, thus restored, regarded as the effect of these divine Causes.

One or two points call for brief remark first.

We shall here again recognize those apparent contradictions (antinomies) which always appear when we deal with the relations of eternity and time, God and man. Scripture richly assures us that God is Love, that His every act and purpose is of transcendent moral goodness, that He is to be loved and trusted by His creatures without reserve. Accordingly, it represents Him as meeting the Fall with a gift of redemption immeasurably great and sincere; and as purposing to bring out from the facts of evil, in the end, only a nobler victory of goodness and love. (See esp. Rom. v. 20, 21.) But, on the other side, Scripture makes it solemnly plain (certainly, from the first, to the vast majority of submissive students) that there will not be an actual salvation of all men. From the first Scriptures to literally the last runs the doctrine of Two Ways, and Two Ends. (See, e.g., Gen. iv. 1-16; Deut. xxx. 15; Psal. lxxiii. 27, 28; Prov. xv. 24; Dan. xii. 2; Hos. xiv. 9; Mal. iii. 17, 18; Matt. vii. 13-27, xxv.; Joh. iii. 16, 19-21, 36, v. 28, 29, ix. 39; Acts xiii. 38-41; Rom. ii. 2-11.; 1 Cor. xi. 32; Gal. vi. 7, 8; Eph. v. 6; Phil. iii. 18, 19; Heb. vi. 4-8; 1 Pet. iv. 17, 18; 1 Joh. v. 16; Rev. ii. 11, xxi. 1-8, 27, xxii. 14, 15.) Efforts are made (and who can wonder, that has really *felt* the mystery?) to read a *universal hope* between these dark lines. The phrase (Acts iii. 21), "the restitution of all things," and the words of Eph. i. 10, Col. i. 20, are earnestly adduced as witnessing to an ulterior future in which the two ends shall, as it were, result in one—the good and peace of every individual man. But is the awful weight of the main drift of Scriptural warnings meant to be thus ultimately neutralized? Acts iii. 21 expressly refers to "the *things which God spake by* the prophets;" i.e., the final triumph of His cause after such seeming defeats as the rejection of Israel (cp. Matt. xvii. 11). The language of Eph. i. and Col. i. significantly refers to heaven and earth, without inclusion of "things under the earth." But the great alternative appears not only in explicit passages. It is present, in its most tender and solemn form, in the divine entreaties to the Christian to watch and pray against powers of ruthless evil; in the tears of the Lord and the Apostles over the impenitent (Luke xix. 41; Acts xx. 31; Phil. iii. 18). Below all articulate statements there lies in such facts the

THE DOCTRINE OF MAN.

infinitely grave assurance of an alternative which knows no compromise, no solution.

When, on our knees, we ask the account of this, the one reply, as we believe, is, that it lies with the account of the origin of sin, and of the full wrong and malignity of sin; that is, it lies out of our sight. Sin is both an insoluble riddle, and a terrible fact, in the freely created universe of the Holy God. It is impossible to reason *à priori* on the effects of an unknown cause.

If with deep reverence we may figure the action of the Eternal Mind in terms of the action of a finite mind, as Scripture does, we may put the case somewhat thus [1]:—The Blessed God, in absolute wisdom and goodness, willing to create, chose of all possible orders of things the best. For ultimate ends of pure good that system involved the moral probation of finite moral beings, and this involved the certainty that some of these would, of themselves, depart from God. In the case of man, a race having a Head in whom the nature was tried, it involved the result that the race, in the Head, would so fall as quite to lose, by moral judicial sequel, the power of self-recovery, and that some of that race would never be recovered, from within or from without. Yet He who is Love, knowing the whole of things, saw it best, truly best, that thus it should be. And He bids us, looking on His face, in His Son, be sure that for the most magnificent possible "bringing" of human "sons unto glory," the order chosen was the best. As a fact, it shall result in a redeemed host incalculably great (Rev. vii. 9). And we know absolutely nothing of

[1] See A. A. Hodge, *Lectures on Theological Themes*, p. 157.

180 OUTLINES OF CHRISTIAN DOCTRINE.

its *extra-human* effects, except that "the whole creation" (Rom. viii. 22) longs for its issue, and "angels desire to look into" its process (1 Pet. i. 12).

Here we confessedly present a conception of divine and eternal thought in terms of human thought. But this is not to limit God. Scripture and our being alike witness to the necessary and eternal absoluteness of God in every attribute, or characteristic. But in every revelation of the relations of God to the world, of the Eternal to time, we come by strict necessity to seeming inconsistencies of thought (p. 37). We have to view the Absolute as under relations; to observe the Almighty Creator as using means, working through design. The limits thus induced are real; but they lie not in the Nature of God, but in that of finite being and its thought.

It remains to add that those who hold what we may call the Augustinian doctrine of grace, as read in Scripture (where they see it revealed, but also on every hand balanced, and limited, by the unrevealed), hold that He who chose that order chose it as both the most righteous and most benignant of all, for His dealings with man. They will bow to His doings, confessing them to be "past finding out" (Rom. xi. 33). But they will also work for God and man with the simplicity and energy of faith in the Almighty. And they will look for the day when, though our minds will never be infinite, we shall yet no longer "know in part," but "as we were known" (1 Cor. xiii. 12). Then we shall praise the infinitely Wise, Mighty, and Loving, in a song free from all undernotes of sadness, sung above the clouds of time.

To resume;—on "Man Restored" our statement, as we have said, has been largely anticipated;

THE DOCTRINE OF MAN. 181

especially under the heads of the work of the Son, and of the Spirit.

It is perhaps necessary to point out that the great restoration is not revealed as acting *apart from the knowledge*, more or less articulate, of the true God. It is not revealed as a process which silently and without known means penetrates Humanity, so that, for example, the Incarnation of the Son has affected the condition of body, soul, or spirit where no moral and spiritual means have been brought to bear on men or nations. The great and urgent missionary commission to the Church speaks clearly in this direction. (And see Rom. x. 12-15.) The gracious "Judge of all the earth will do right" with every human individual. We may trust Him with His own handiwork. But the Scripture is deeply silent as to any restoration of man, certainly normally, without the message of grace.

One great exception there is. The innumerable multitude of infants "dying before they commit actual sin" belongs, as we firmly believe, to "man restored," everywhere and always. Opinion on this has differed in the Church of Christ. The loss of the infant soul *without baptism* has been widely held.[1] To us the words of our Lord (Mark **x.** 14, 15) seem to carry us far beyond the baptismal limit, and to encourage the belief that where human life terminates here as infant-life, though the very fact of that death is (Rom. v. 14) a testimony to the extension over humanity of the liability of its fallen Head, yet for the sake of the Second Adam there is such an application of His merits and His Spirit as

[1] It is nowhere now *affirmed* by the English Church, though it was otherwise in the early stages of the Reformation.

assures us of life eternal. The case, immensely common as to *numbers*, is quite abnormal in *idea*. Only the Creator knows the limits of it, and of *all the other cases which fall under its class*.

Normally, the individual restored was at once an instance of fallen human nature (a subject of original sin), and an actual transgressor (Eph. ii. 1-3). He now, from the point of view of God, has been regenerated, new-created. From his own point of view he has, with genuine willingness, "come to Christ" (Joh. vi. 35, 37), "received Christ, believing on His Name" (Joh. i. 12), coming to "obedience, and the sprinkling of His blood" (1 Pet. i. 2). To use a word familiarized by our version of Psal. li. 13, Matt. xviii. 3, etc., he has been "converted," "turned about," as to affections and will, from original inner alienation from God, so as to submit, believe, and love. The subjective experience of this conversion (μετάνοια) may, and does, widely vary. To consciousness, it may be gradual, and even imperceptible, or intensely otherwise. But it is essentially one thing in all cases; a forsaking of all else as the man's peace, strength, and aim, in favour of "Christ as the power and wisdom of God" (1 Cor. i. 24); for this He is to "the called," the apostolic term most closely akin to our "converted." The relations of *time* between regeneration and the consciousness of conversion are secret. The consciousness of conversion is not precisely of the essence of conversion It is conceivable (not natural, or probable) that a man truly regenerate may pass through mortal life to death not fully conscious of the divine life; not able to analyse and affirm it to himself. But it seems also to be clear that where true regeneration is, there, by a spiritual law, it always tends to come out in a new life

THE DOCTRINE OF MAN. 183

(Joh. iii. 8, an all-important verse), whether or no the man recognizes it as such. We infer that ordinarily no assignable interval separates actual (not ceremonial, see pp. 249, 255) new birth and its potential manifestation.

The man, then, thus restored, new-born, and turned to God, is a person who, once "alienated," is now *united* really to Jesus Christ by the indwelling of that Spirit who also dwells in his Head, and who has brought him to repentance (i.e., humble turning from sin to God) and to faith in Christ (Acts xx. 21). In this mysterious, but most true and vital, Union he (above, p. 133), possesses the two great covenant blessings (Heb. x. 16, 17), acceptance for his Redeemer's merits, and a regenerated state of nature, and particularly of will and affections, by His Spirit. Not to retrace old ground, we only deal here with certain main questions about the actual condition of the restored individual in Christ.

(1) *His justification.* The word "*justify*" is frequent in Scripture, not only in doctrinal connexions (see, e.g., Exod. xxiii. 7; Deut. xxv. 1; Prov. xvii. 15). The great passages for its doctrinal application are the first half of the Epistle to the Romans, part of the Epistle to the Galatians, and Jas ii. 14-26. It is clear everywhere that the essence of the idea is judicial acceptance; not pardon merely, but a verdict of the law's contentment with the person. The quality of such contentment will vary with that of the law. Human law, speaking broadly, demands a *minimum*; abstinence from positive and exterior disobedience. And its acquittal accordingly avouches this and no more. Divine spiritual law demands in its nature a *maximum*; supreme love of God and unselfish love of men. And so its "justi-

fication" avouches that the person examined contents it in these respects. But how can this actually be, when "in the sight of God no man living shall be justified" (Psal. cxliii. 2) on his own merits? Here comes in the mystery and fact of the application of the merits of Christ (see above, p. 81), the substituted Victim, valid Representative, and Covenant-Head, of "all who come to God by Him" (Heb. vii. 25). The great justification-argument of the Roman Epistle is in effect this: that such is Jesus Christ, the sacrificed Son of God, and such is the relation, to believing sinners, of the propitiation He wrought in death, that they for His sake, being personally guilty and de-meritorious, are accepted with unreserved contentment by the eternal law as its fulfillers. That this amazing but holy paradox is *meant* is shown by the fact that the truth did from the first suggest the perversion (meaningless, without a real counterpart in the thing perverted) that it *favoured moral licence* (Rom. iii. 8, vi. 1). And the Apostle meets this, not by modifying the paradox, but by placing it unmodified (ch. vi.) in organic connexion with the *other truth* of concurrent spiritual life. Pauline justification, isolated for study, is the acceptance of the sinful person, believing, *irrespective* (in this isolation) *of any consideration whatever* but the sacrifice of Jesus Christ accepted by faith.

This grandly simple and heart-moving view of justification has been impugned from many quarters. Thus, it has been held that by "*the works of the law*," or more simply by "*works*," is meant, not personal morality of practice, but either Judaist observances or morality practised in the definitely Pharisaic spirit. But that the phrase goes far

THE DOCTRINE OF MAN. 185

deeper is plain from Rom. iii. 19, 20, with the previous context. There "the works of the law" are defined by their contraries, enumerated vv. 9-18. And it thus appears that these "works of the law" are—seeking after God, fearing God, doing good, right use of the tongue, reverence for human life, and the like. The practical issue of the argument is, that the eternal standard in such things is such that personal obedience on the part of fallen man always and fatally falls short, by whatever intervals. And the eternal law, in its nature, knows no compromise; so that acceptance before it, in a saving sense, is hopeless for man on his merits, even if his merits are only a part of his plea. And the deep need is met, not partially, but wholly, by the sacrifice of Christ, by Christ the Propitiation, appropriated as such by faith.

Again, the simplicity and depth of the truth have been weakened by disturbing the simplicity of the idea of *faith*. It has been held that faith is a short expression for true Christianity; faith, or credence, along with its assumed results of obedience and piety. This was the view, in essence, of Bishop Bull, cent. xvii. And most other theories impugning the view above given as the Pauline view, run up ultimately into this. But a full study of the word "*faith*" in Scripture, and in common human speech, will, we think, be conclusive the other way. Particularly, our Lord's use of it (e.g. Matt. vi. 30, viii. 10) gives it an essential connexion with the idea of *personal reliance*. Such reliance, by the nature of the case, assumes an underlying credence of, or assent to, expressed or implicit statements. But its vital characteristic is an act of accepting reliance, not on immediate evidence, but in immediate trust. The woman of Canaan shows her faith by invincible trust in Jesus against all appearances.

St James' words (ii. 14-26) are undoubtedly a grave problem on the other side. But we believe the solution lies in the fact that by "*faith*" St James means orthodox credence (ii. 19), not personal reliance; and that in this meaning he does not give his own view of faith, but takes his opponents on their own ground. One thing is practically certain,—that St James is cautioning his readers, not against ultra-Paulinism, but against Rabbinism, with its tenet that the orthodox Jewish "confession of faith" (Deut. vi. 4) was a passport to life eternal.

The large *scale* of revelation on this subject in the Pauline Epistles warns us that, while both Apostles convey infallible truth, the bearing of St James' words should be inferred from St Paul's, rather than the other way.

Again, it has been held that while the simplest doctrine of Justification by Faith applies to the Christian's first entrance on the new life, a more complex doctrine applies to the sequel. The man is welcomed in for the mere sake of Christ the Propitiation. He is allowed to remain, he is held in acceptance, because of his regenerate obedience, or because of it concurrently with the first ground. The deepest answer to this, apart from explicit Scripture, lies, we think, in the inmost consciousness of all true believers, *of many varying types of thought*, when brought at any moment of their course face to face with the Eternal Holiness. At such moments of intuition it is seen, or rather felt and known, that something "not ourselves," absolute and perfect, availing in the legal sphere, must

THE DOCTRINE OF MAN.

stand between the man and the "fiery law." Psal. cxliii. 2, for the true Christian as for the true Israelite, alone expresses the soul's conviction then. From this point of view there is no room for a "first and second justification;" the first by faith in the Propitiation only, the second on the ground of our obedience too. "I know whom I have believed." (2 Tim. i. 12) is a word as fit for the latest as for the earliest conviction of the saint. See too, by all means, Phil. iii. 9, with its whole context.

The words of the dying Hooker are in point: "Though I have, by His grace, loved Him in my youth, and feared Him in my age, and laboured to have a conscience void of offence. . . yet if Thou, O Lord, be extreme to mark what is done amiss, who can abide it? And therefore, where I have failed, Lord, show mercy to me; for I plead not my righteousness, but the forgiveness of my unrighteousness, for His merits who died to purchase pardon for penitent sinners."[1]

Nothing is more essential to a full view and humble enjoyment of our salvation than a reverent hold on the divine paradox of Justification by Faith, as (speaking broadly) that paradox was brought into the foreground of Christian thought by Luther, and as it will be found in our Eleventh Article, illustrated (as the Article directs) by the "Homily of Justification," i.e., the third Homily of the First Book. See, too, Hooker's great sermon *On Justification*. That paradox is only the correlative of the glorious fundamental of the Gospel, "Christ is all." In the full view of what Scripture says of His all-precious Sacrifice, it will be less a tenet than an instinct to remit the whole weight of our acceptance to Him

[1] Walton's *Life*.

as our Propitiation, and to recognize faith, that is, a trustful acceptance, as deep as it is absolutely simple, as that which on our side puts us into contact with the Propitiator. Not our sufferings or sacrifices unite us savingly with His, for our acceptance. He is all, and we sinners accept Him as He is.

A few words may come in here on *the Imputed Righteousness of Christ*. This phrase, once widely accepted, and not least by such Anglicans as Andrewes and Beveridge (cent. xvii.), is now much disputed, and even repudiated. But it rests securely upon Rom iv. 6, with its context. There has been a tendency to over-refinement upon it; a too elaborate distinction between our Lord's active keeping of the moral law and His awful suffering beneath the penalty of our sins; the one considered as supplying our *defects*, the other as meeting our *violations*. But this is not the essential view of the phrase; and we see this all the more as we remember (above, p. 83) the profound connexion between the obedience of our Lord's life and the merit of His Passion. The essential of the phrase is just this, that the Son of God, as the supremely meritorious One, as infinitely *satisfactory to law*, is, before the law, and for the purposes of law, accepted, reckoned as the believing sinner's substitute. The man, incorporated in Him, is counted, reputed, as involved in His whole merit, as the Lord was counted, reputed, as involved in the man's sin. His merit is thus imputed, that is to say, set down, to the man.

Alike for his defects and his violations,—which ultimately run up into one idea of $\dot{a}\nu o\mu\acute{\iota}a$ (1 Joh. iii. 4), i.e., non-correspondence to the holy law,—the man involves himself, or rather consents that he should be involved, in that perfect merit. As thus

THE DOCTRINE OF MAN. 189

involved, he stands accepted. His *ground* of justification and peace is not only not his own "works," but not even (as some hold) the presence of Christ *in* him, taken along with its eternal development in prospect. It is Christ *for* him, in the quite different region of merit, of law.

We do not repeat here what we have said above (p. 132), on the connexion of this sacred paradox of free justification with our Union with Christ. But the subject is all-important, and calls for the devout attention of the Christian. To the last, the ultimate *rationale* of the Atonement of our Lord, and so of our acceptance through faith on its account, "goes off into mystery." But within the circle of light and revelation on the subject lies the fact that the effectual application of the Atonement is for the living members of the living Head of the mystical Body, one with their Lord in an unspeakable reality of conjunction; and that it is faith, the acceptance of Christ for salvation by the awakened soul, which from our side is the *nexus* of that union. Faith is *ipso facto* entrance into Christ. And in Christ, the Propitiation, resides perfect merit for acceptance before God, for all that are "found in Him" (Phil. iii. 9).

Meanwhile it is abundantly revealed that the justified man, while decisively and continuously accepted before God from this point of view, is, from other points of view, under paternal discipline, liable to paternal displeasure and correction (see, among the wealth of references, 1 Cor. xi. 29-32; Heb. xii. 5-11; and cp. Deut. viii. 5; Psal. xciv. 12). And not only so, but (p. 44) the justified man, if he is not only to stand accepted before God, but to enjoy the bliss of the fact, must, as a spiritual condition, " walk humbly with his God," in regenerate obedience. The act, and yet more the habit, of admitted and willing sin is fatal to personal assurance in that sense.

(2) We are led now, in considering the actual condition of man restored, to the direct view of his *Sanctification*, or personal and internal separation from sin to God. The connexion of this with his justification is close and manifold. Justification is, we may say, (*a*) his entrance on the possibility of Sanctification; for a true because willing and loving holiness has a necessary connexion, by way of resulting gladness, gratitude, and love, with an entrance into "peace with God through our Lord Jesus Christ, . . . by whom we have now received the atonement" (Rom. v. 1, 11). And Justification thus also, and as a yet deeper truth, has to do with Sanctification because (*b*) our entrance on acceptance is altogether *for the very purpose of* our holiness. This is manifest, and most important. Scripture nowhere forbids or condemns the profoundly natural and human gladness of our personal deliverance in Christ from " the wrath to come " (e.g. 1 Thess. i. 10). Scripture is not committed to the doctrine, rather unnatural than supernatural, that gratitude for the rescue of our personality from eternal woe, and unto eternal bliss, is an unworthy element among motives to obedience; that the Glory of God is the *one* possible element in true motive. But it does place that Glory in such supremacy over every other kind of motive, and adjusts every other so to it, as to make it spiritually impossible for the renewed man to rest short of it as the recognized goal of his being, his blessed *raison d'être*. From this point of view, sanctification is greater than justification somewhat as end

THE DOCTRINE OF MAN. 191

is greater than means. We are justified for an ulterior purpose. We are sanctified, we are subdued and transfigured, as the fulfilment in us of the will of God, for whom we exist; and the ulterior purpose is attained.

We do not deal here with Christian ethics, and therefore do not enter on the discussion of the holy precepts for renewed man in detail. We only observe that they amount, in their sum, to just this—a *total abstinence* in Christ's name from admitted sinning, of motive and act, and a *true and entire dedication* of " spirit, soul, and body " to the will of God.

What we have to say here concerns the restored man's personal equipment, in Christ, for this holy purpose.

The work of faith in Sanctification. This is manifold. As by faith we enter the justified state, we so far owe to faith all the holy motives that state brings to bear on our acts and habits. But also faith is exercised at whatever moment the Christian for any purpose definitely trusts his Lord's word and power. It is precisely the same faculty as that exercised in the act of receiving remission and acceptance, and its exercise is *quite as simple* as then; but it now takes another direction. And this direction of faith figures very largely in the Scriptures in the matter of the Christian's victory over sin, or deliverance from it (see e.g. Acts xv. 9, and probably xxvi. 18; Gal. ii. 20; Eph. vi. 16). It is clearly indicated that for the man in living contact with Christ the true secret for internal moral purity is Christ (1 Cor. i. 30), living and overcoming within, by the Holy Spirit who effects His presence there (see above, p. 136). And our part is to believe.

In one great passage (Eph. iii. 14-19) we reach the heart of the matter. The believer's practical experience of "all the fulness of God," i.e., of all that which, being in Him, is communicable as holiness to His regenerate creature, is there connected with the "coming of Christ to dwell in the heart." And this is connected on one hand with the work of the Spirit, "strengthening" the Christian "in the inner man;" and on the other hand, with the Christian's "faith," obviously as the result of that divine work. The Indwelling, with its sequel of blessings, is secured and retained on our side "by faith;" not by a process of discipline and labour, but by the same humble and reverent reliance on God in His word which is our entrance into justification. Thus the heart is "purified by faith," because faith is the admission into it of Jesus Christ, its indwelling Redeemer, Friend, and King, divinely able so to work on it and in it, along all its lines of spontaneity, as to conform it effectually, yet without force, to His most sacred will in all things.

This deep yet open secret of spiritual victory is largely illustrated in Scripture. The combat of the soul is seen portrayed, for all believing students, in the language of the Psalms about enemies and battle. And the Psalms bear inexhaustible witness to a secret of victory which is in fact the man's committal of himself, for victory, to Jehovah (see, out of many passages, Psal. xxv. 15, xxvii. 1-6, cxxxviii. 7, 8). His is the one really prevalent force; His people prevail by Him. So with the conflict of the Christian under temptation. His secret is to "put on the Lord Jesus Christ" (Rom. xiii. 14), who is, in effect, "the whole armour, the panoply, of God" (Eph. vi. 11). "In Him" alone, as vantage ground

THE DOCTRINE OF MAN. 193

and fortress, His follower is " strong " (Eph. vi. 10) against the powers of evil. " In Him, enabling," the Christian " has strength for all things " (Phil. iv. 13) which are to be borne or done in the will of God.

This divine principle needs an always large and glad, while an always guarded, recognition in the teaching of Sanctification, and above all in its practice. A full view of it is vitally connected with the doctrine of our Union with Christ as the Second Man, in whom Manhood, perfected and glorified, is personally united to Godhead, and who, thus constituted the Head of His people, is for them the fountain of all grace and virtue, to be derived from Him by faith in Him.[1] He in His blessed constitution is at once our new Life, the Basis, as it were, of our regenerate condition and action; and also, in His personal energy, through the Holy Comforter, our Conqueror, Ruler, and Keeper, in the exercise of that life. And our realization of Him as such is " according to our faith," our submissive and recipient reliance on Him as we are His members. From Him equally we derive both gifts of the New Covenant; acceptance, and spiritual power to do the will of God. And both, amidst many differences in the experience of their application, are alike in this, that each is the divine response to simple "faith in the Son of God."

Meanwhile, the Scripture doctrine of Sanctification teaches no effortless passivity. No will is so fully constituted for work as the regenerate and surrendered will. And in this matter of inner sanctification, which lies at the base of true and faithful outward service (2 Tim. ii. 21), the will has abundant work to do, in watching and prayer, in self-examination and confession of sin, in diligent study of the divine Word, in the spiritual use of sacred

[1] See Marshall (1690), *Gospel Mystery of Sanctification*.

ordinances, in holy contemplation of Christ, in attention to every whisper through the conscience. But these works will all be done with a view to maintaining and deepening that sacred practical contact with Christ by faith which is the one ultimate secret of spiritual success. They will be helps and guides to faith, not substitutes for its divine simplicity. The temptation of the hour will be met less by direct efforts of the will than by indirect; through, and "in, Him who enableth."

In connexion with this subject, the question arises, does the regenerate man actually attain, by this divine means, such a deliverance here from sinfulness in his constitution and from sinning in his acts (inward and outward) as to entitle him to say, "*I am devoid, in all respects, of sin*"?

Undoubtedly the promises and offers of Scripture are magnificently large (see, e.g., Eph. iii. 20, 21; Col. i. 10; 1 Joh. ii. 5, iii. 6, 9). And the New Testament obviously contemplates the Christian's life as a life meant to be, *not intermittently, but normally*, a "walk with God" in the deep peace of a loving obedience of motive and act, pleasing to Him in Christ. To speak for a moment of Christian ethics rather than doctrine, very many believing lives fall far below the divinely intended realization of this, in a "peace which passeth understanding, keeping the heart and thoughts, in Christ Jesus" (Phil. iv. 7); and are thus hindered not a little in the joy and also in the fruitfulness of service.

But then Scripture has another side, of limit and caution. While spreading before us the animating truth of the divine perfectness of grace, of God working in us, it intimates the humbling *imperfection of our receptivity*, while as yet the redemption of our being from the effects of the Fall awaits

THE DOCTRINE OF MAN

actual completion (Rom. viii. 23). Here seems to lie the root of the mystery, and fact, of the spiritual antitheses of Scripture as regards sanctification (see, e.g., Psal. xvii. 3, contrasted with cxliii. 2 ; Jas iii. 2 with Jude 24, in the Greek ; 1 Pet. iv. 18 with 2 Pet. i. 11 ; 1 Joh. i. 8 with iii. 6, 9). From the side of grace and gift, all is perfect, and the realization is to be indefinitely better and more delightful. From the side of the Christian there is imperfect receptivity, and accordingly imperfect holiness, to the end of his pilgrimage. So to the last he is to join, with profound sincerity, in the prayer, "Forgive us our trespasses," and to reflect on his abiding need (see above, p. 85) that " the (propitiatory) blood of Jesus Christ should cleanse him from all sin," in a process continuous and therefore not completed. He is divinely entitled to, and enabled for, a continuous spiritual emancipation from sin's " kingship " (Rom. vi. 12); for he has by the Cross become " dead to sin " (vi. 2), as he is " dead to the law " (vii. 4), in the sense of deliverance from arrest and doom, and entrance in his risen Lord into a new life (vi. 4) of power before and for God. But he is not yet exempted from sin's presence, in his (not yet wholly redeemed) complex being (viii. 23). He has still to *reckon with* " the flesh " (Gal. v. 16, 17), that mysterious element, or rather condition, of the once fallen and not yet wholly redeemed being whose " mind," or bias, even in its faintest vestige, " is not subject to the law of God, nor indeed can be" (Rom. viii. 7). He is not "*in it*" (viii. 9), for it is not his spiritual sphere, or atmosphere ; but it is *in him,* just so far as its " infection " is there, needing every moment the conquering counteraction of the Spirit (Rom. viii. 13 ; Gal. v. 17). It is " crucified " (Gal.

v. 24), a word of profound import as regards a deci-sive rejection by the regenerate will of the very idea of a self-life. But the imagery of the Cross, while it suggests a stern execution (not by our power), may suggest also the lingering death of the thing crucified. (See *Addenda*, p. 268, on "*the old man*.")

What is the bearing on this subject of the great passage Rom. vii. 7-25? Very various views have been taken of it. It has been explained of (*a*) the struggles of conscience against will in fallen man as such; (*b*) these struggles intensified and complicated by the first stages of spiritual recovery, in which the man, convinced and attracted by grace, but not yet actually regenerate, seems to himself a double self; (*c*) the inner experience of the fully regenerate man, in a normal and hourly balanced conflict between the Holy Spirit and the flesh; (*d*) the inner experience of the fully regenerate, but presented for study under peculiar conditions—isolated from the divine factor of the Holy Spirit's conquering work, and observed as in view of the absolute holiness of the law of God (ver. 12), and the constant presence (ver. 18) of "the flesh," and the insight of the renewed reason (vers. 22, 23, 25) into the glory of the will of God and the hatefulness of the least sin. Of these interpretations we believe (*a*) to be clearly untenable, and (*b*) only less clearly so; for the passage throughout deals with an experience in some sense "present" to a man who has learnt not merely to respond in conscience to the will of God, but sympathetically to "delight in it" (ver. 22)— the height of the work of grace. Again, (*c*) offers serious difficulties in view of the witness of Scripture to the joy and peace of the true Christian's life, and the provision for him, in the work of the Holy

THE DOCTRINE OF MAN. 197

Spirit, of an habitual deliverance from an internal captivity under the power of sin. In (*d*) appears to lie the true line of solution. Observe that throughout the passage no mention is made of the Holy Spirit. The highest words employed are "the inward man" (see above, p. 164) and more markedly "the mind" (νοῦς), the human spirit directed in recognition upon truth. The regenerate man, assailed by temptation through "the flesh" (in its moral, not material sense), meets the attack with his highest regenerate powers, but without actively calling in the divine force of the Comforter, by whom he is in Christ and Christ in him. And the conflict continues in partial but serious failure, at best. It is otherwise when (viii. 13) "we *through the Spirit* mortify the deeds of the body."

Rom. vii. thus describes a real element in the regenerate life, liable to be experienced at any stage or moment. And, in the mystery of the Fall, it *is* experienced, in the light of the absolute holiness of the law (ver. 12), brought home by the Spirit as enlightener. Rom. viii. 23 testifies, in the midst of a passage full of divine triumph, to the presence, potential if not actual, of a "groan" in the regenerate, during the pilgrimage. But the great aim of Rom. vii. is to bring out to the full the awful yet blessed holiness of the law of God, and so it contemplates the regenerate man at his very best, but isolated (as it were) from the activity of his divine Indweller. Every moment, however brief, in which the Christian yields to even the most refined temptation, is an instance in point of the passage; and at every such moment there is definite defect in the man's use, if we may say so, of the Spirit's power. And the more advanced his intimacy with the Holy

God, the deeper then will be his response to the language of that passage.

The question has been raised, whether the life of sanctification (as its deepest requisite, on our part, like that of justification, is faith) begins similarly with *one great initial step*, in which the man commits himself, in a crisis of entrustment, to his Lord, entering thus on a path of continuous peace and purity within. We think that no definite revelation of such a "law" is made, certainly not as in the matter of justification. But the case may reverently be stated thus. Every true entrance on acceptance is a true entrance on spiritual life and power, in its fulness, because it is an entrance into Christ (above, p. 133). The man decisively accepted in Christ is the man also fully endowed in Christ, and needing only to discover his wealth. And no man who, in believing so as to receive the remission of sins, has really seen at all "WHOM he has believed," can be quite in the dark both as to the immediate call to obey His Redeemer, and the immediately given new willingness and power to obey. But time inevitably discloses spiritual need and personal weakness, and there come in the man's life occasions, often very definite, of developed insight into and use of spiritual resources in Christ. And if, in the particular case, the easy mistake has been made at first of taking the emotion and motive of joy and gratitude on acceptance for the *basis and treasury* of strength, then the first discovery that nothing less and else than Christ in us by the Spirit is basis and treasury is likely to be a conscious crisis in life as deep and definite as possible. In the language of Eph. iii. 14-19, we think, there is reference to this; and see too Rom. vi. 13-19; Gal. v. 16-25;

THE DOCTRINE OF MAN. 199

Eph. i. 15-23; Col. i. 9-13, etc. Yet the analogy is not complete between the decision and crisis in the two cases. In that of justification the real crisis is an entrance, *from the law's point of view*, into acceptance of the person. In that of sanctification it is an entrance, *from the Christian's point of view*, on realization of inner peace and strength. The first case is in its nature one and single: an admission, an incorporation. The second is in its nature progressive and developing: the discovery, advancing with the occasion for it, of the greatness of the resources of Christ for life. The latter *may*, not *must*, thus include one great crisis in consciousness, one particular spiritual act. It is much more certain to include many starting-points, critical developments, marked advances. The act of self-surrendering faith in the power of Christ for inward cleansing of the will and affections may be, and often indeed it is, *as it were* a new conversion, a new "effectual calling." But it is sure, if the man knows himself in the light of Christ, to be followed by echoes and reiterations to the end; not mere returns to and beginnings from the old level (certainly it is not the plan of God that it should be so), but definite out-growths' due to new discovery of personal need and sin, and of more than corresponding " riches " in Christ.

With each such advance the sacred promise of the *Fulness of the Spirit* will be received with a holy and happy realization. The idea of the phrase (Eph. v. 18), " be ye filled *in the Spirit*," is that of a receptacle surrounded by air, or water, and filled with its environment in proportion to its receptive freedom. The more the regenerate man, in the way of humble reverent self-abnegation and believing surrender, presents himself to God, the more this sacred inflow into every faculty of the soul will take place. He shall be ever filling, and *ever flowing as a channel of good for other men* (Joh. vii. 38, 39).

Thus man restored stands and lives. Justified and new-born in Christ, to whom the Spirit has united him, as member to Head, in repentant faith, he by the same Spirit, working in and welcomed by his spontaneity, "mortifies the deeds of the body," in the life of watching and prayer, by faith. He is a "child of God by faith in Christ Jesus" (Gal. iii. 26). He is the brother,[1] in the regenerate life, of the Son of God (Rom. viii. 29); his body is the temple of the Holy Spirit of God (1 Cor. vi. 19). He "worships God by His Spirit, rejoices in Christ Jesus, and has no confidence in the flesh" (Phil. iii. 3); that is to say, in anything out of God which in any sense is his own. In his exalted Head he has, and uses, the true secret for holy serviceableness and the life of duty, in its highest or humblest forms. He recognizes in others and their needs the expression of his Master's will for him, that he should live "no longer to himself" (2 Cor. v. 15). Whether he lives or dies, it is "to the Lord," with reference to Him as Possessor (Rom. xiv. 7-9). "The world"—that is to say, unregenerate and unspiritual humanity—"knows him not" (1 Joh. iii. 1), cannot read his secret; whether that fact attracts it or repels it. And to himself "it does not yet appear what he shall be; but he knows that when his Lord shall appear, he shall be like Him, seeing Him as He is" (1 Joh. iii. 2).

He expects the mysterious future with the fear of

[1] Not "the child."

THE DOCTRINE OF MAN. 201

holy reverence and profound *self*-distrust, but in the joy of divine peace. For him to die is "to go home to be with the Lord" (2 Cor. v. 6, 8), to begin to "walk by sight" (*ibid.*, 7), "to be with Christ, which is far better" (Phil. i. 23) than even a life here which "is Christ" (*ibid.*, 21). If indeed his Redeemer shall return from the heavens before his own dissolution, he expects the instant transfiguration of his whole being (1 Cor. xv. 52; 1 Thess. iv. 17), and reunion in that being with "the children of the resurrection" in the presence of Christ. And if he himself is then one of "them who sleep in Jesus" he is well assured that "He who raised up the Lord Jesus will raise up him also, and present him with Him" (2 Cor. iv. 14). Because the Spirit of God "dwelt in his mortal body," the Father, who raised the Son, "shall also quicken his mortal body." It will have been "sown" as "not that body that shall be" (1 Cor. xv. 37); the link of continuity and identity is mysterious (see above, p. 100); but nevertheless that which is "sown" shall be "raised, in incorruption, in glory, in power, a spiritual body" (1 Cor. xv. 42-44) "in" "the Second Man, the Lord from heaven"; "with Him, in glory" (Col. iii. 4). So transfigured, into the final perfectness of his nature, restored man shall "serve God day and night in His temple" (Rev. vii. 15), in whatever ways—doubtless infinitely various, as they will be eternally important and efficacious—the everlasting life shall open up. Dimly but really revelation indicates that the saints, the Church, shall have immeasurably great things to do in the eternal realm of God, while they personally and together "enjoy HIM fully for ever."

CHAPTER IX.

THE DOCTRINE OF THE CHURCH.

"THAT Church of Christ which we properly term His body mystical, can be but one; neither can that one be sensibly discerned by any man, inasmuch as the parts thereof are some in heaven already with Christ, and the rest that are on earth (albeit their natural persons be visible) we do not discern under this property whereby they are truly and infallibly of that body. Only our minds by intellectual conceit are able to apprehend that such a real body there is, a body collective, because it containeth a huge multitude; a body mystical, because the mystery of their conjunction is removed altogether from sense. Whatsoever we read in Scripture concerning the endless love and the saving mercy which God sheweth towards His Church, the only proper subject thereof is this Church. Concerning this flock it is that our Lord and Saviour hath promised: 'I give unto them eternal life, and they shall never perish, neither shall any pluck them out of My hands.' They who are of this society have such marks and notes of distinction from all others as are not object unto our sense; only unto God, who seeth their hearts and understandeth all their secret thoughts and cogitations, unto Him they are clear and manifest. All men knew Nathanael to be an Israelite. But our Saviour, piercing deeper, giveth further testimony of him than men could have done with such certainty as He did, 'Behold indeed an Israelite, in whom there is no guile.' If we profess, as Peter did, that we love the Lord, and profess it in the hearing of men . . . charitable men are likely to think we do so, as long as they see no proof to the contrary. But that our love is sound and sincere . . . who can pronounce, saving only the Searcher of all men's hearts, who alone intuitively doth know in this kind who are His? And as those everlasting promises of love, mercy, and blessedness, belong to the mystical Church, even so on the other side when we read of any duty which the Church of God is bound unto, the Church whom this doth concern is a sensible known company. And this visible Church in like sort is but one. . . . Which company being divided into two moieties, the one before, the other since the coming of Christ, that part which since the coming of Christ partly hath embraced and partly shall hereafter embrace the Christian religion, we term as by a more proper name the Church of Christ. . . . The unity of which visible body and Church of Christ consisteth of that uniformity which all several persons thereunto belonging have, by reason of that one *Lord,* whose servants they all profess themselves; that one *faith*, which they all acknowledge; that one *baptism*, wherewith they are all initiated. . . . Entered we are not into the visible Church before our admittance by the door of baptism. . . . Christians by external profession they are all, whose mark of recognisance hath in it those things (one Lord, one faith, one baptism) which we have mentioned, yea, although they be impious idolaters, wicked heretics, persons excommunicable, yea and cast out for notorious improbity. . . . Is it then possible that the self-same men should belong both to the synagogue of Satan and to the Church of Jesus Christ? Unto that Church which is His mystical body, not possible; because that body consisteth of none but only . . . true servants and saints of God. Howbeit of the visible body and Church of Jesus Christ, those may be, and oftentimes are, in respect of the main parts of their outward profession. . . . For lack of diligent observing the difference, first between the Church of God mystical and visible, then between the visible sound and corrupted, sometimes more, sometimes less; the oversights are neither few nor light that have been committed." (Hooker, *Eccl. Polity*, iii. 1.)

We quote this classical passage as introductory to an outline of the doctrine of the Church, mainly because in it a singularly representative theologian states a distinction essential, as we believe, to just opinions on that doctrine. The Church as an organized society, open to human observation, is to be distinguished from the Church as a spiritual organism, living with a life whose secret and limits are fully known only to God, and whose manifestation is by faith, hope, and love (above, p. 129). The importance of the passage does not stop here. In respect of the Church as visible, it both describes it as *one*, so that its division by discordant polities is an accident, contrary to its ideal; and also it states with Scriptural moderation the essential marks (*notes*) of its oneness. (See further, p. 210.)

Now to examine the subject as presented in Scripture. The word *Ecclesia* (lit., company, or

THE DOCTRINE OF THE CHURCH.

assembly, *called out*) is common in Old Testament Greek. In the Pentateuch it is frequent for the Assembly of Israel, Israel as "called out" (from tents and work) to meet before God. Elsewhere it often means any assembly, more or less sacred. In the New Testament it occasionally means an assembly other than Christian (Acts xix. 32, 39, 41). Very often it means the Christians of a district, town, or even household, regarded as "called out" of the unbelieving world, associated, and organized (e.g., Acts viii. 1, xiii. 1, xv. 41; Rom. xvi. 1, 4, 5, 16; 1 Cor. i. 2, iv. 17; Gal. i 2, 22; Phil. iv. 15; Philem. 2; Rev. i.-iii. *passim*, xxii. 16). Less often it means Christians of every place, or rather irrespective of place; one ideal assembly or society, "called out" from the world to Christ (e.g. Matt. xvi. 18, xviii. 3; Acts xx. 28; 1 Cor. x. 32, xii. 28, xv. 9; Gal. i. 13; Eph. i. 22 and always, Phil. iii 6; Col. i. 18, 24; 1 Tim. iii. 15; and ? Heb. xii. 23) In many of these latter places the word seems to keep to the sphere of the visible and temporal; meaning the total of accredited Christians, irrespective of locality. In some places, and especially in Ephesians, it rises to a higher sphere, and means that *ideal* which is also in this matter the ultimate *real*; the company, society, organism, of which in full spiritual reality Christ is vital Head, and which shall be His Body and His Bride in glory. That a man may belong to a Church, or the Church, as organized within human observation, and not to the Church in the supreme sense, is plain from e.g. Acts. viii. 21; Rom. viii. 9; 2 Cor. xiii. 5.

The distinction thus noticed by Hooker lies in the nature of the case. Union with Christ, if union indeed, is by the Spirit (p. 132). But it is possible to be within Christian organization and yet to be devoid of the Spirit (see the texts last quoted); so it was with Simon at Samaria (Acts viii.). But no register at all dependent on human observation can infallibly exclude such names from the Christian roll. And if but one such name is upon it, the coincidence of the Church as visible with the Church as spiritually real is not perfect. On the other hand, the guardians of the register have no right normally to exercise such an excluding power as would even seem to claim supernatural insight into the man's inner union or disunion with Christ. Within limits, certainly, scrutiny must be applied to protect the privileges of membership from scandalous misuse. But no such scrutiny can ever claim to go infallibly, by its nature, to "the thoughts and intents of the heart."

This principle is illustrated by Rom. ii. 25-29, where a distinction is drawn between the "Jew" who is such by the register of (divinely ordered) circumcision and the "Jew" who is such "inwardly." This bears *à fortiori* on the case of the Christian Church. For the community of Israel had more to do, at least on the surface, with merely external tests of membership than the community of the Christian Church has. The Jewish Church was, from one point of view, *a nation*, as capable of census as any other; a society in which physical pedigree was highly important. Yet even in its case, with a view to ultimate realities, Scripture recognizes the difference of nominal and real, visible and not (humanly) visible; an Israel fully recognized by God, narrower than the Israel lawfully recognized by man. *À fortiori* the limits of a Community which is lifted above tests of pedigree and nationality, and whose watchwords are Christ, the Spirit, faith, saintship, must admit such differences. There must be Christians and Christians, Church and Church, Body and Body, Vine and Vine; not opposed camps, but gravely different aspects of one word.

This distinction was stated strongly by St Augustine. In his *De Doctrinâ Christianâ* (iii. 32) he discusses with general approval a book, by one Tichonius, *The Seven Rules* for clearing up Scripture mysteries, and writes: "The second rule is that 'Concerning the Lord's *twofold Body*.'. . . He should have said, 'Concerning the Lord's true and mingled Body' or 'true and feigned Body,' or the like. For not only eternally, but now, hypocrites are not to be described as being with Him, however they may seem to be in His Church. . . Often the Scripture, turning from one party to speak of another, seems to be still speaking of the first, as if the two made one Body, by reason of their temporal commingling and equal share in sacraments." The distinction thus drawn was strongly insisted upon in the Reformation theology. See, e.g., Bishop Ridley (*Works*, Parker Society, pp. 126-7):—"That Church which is His Body and of which Christ is the Head standeth (consisteth) only of living stones and true Christians, not only outwardly in name and title, but inwardly in heart and in truth. But forasmuch as this Church . . . as touching the outward fellowship, is contained within that great house [2 Tim. ii. 20], and hath, with the same, outward society of the sacraments and ministry of the Word, many things are spoken of that universal Church (which St Augustine calleth the mingled Church) which cannot be truly understood but only of that purer part of the Church."

If this is true,—and it lies in the nature of the case,—the greatest care is needed in the use of the sacred word Church, lest claims should be made for the outward organization, even in its original and truest form, which ought to be made only for the spiritually living organism.

On the other hand it is plain, both from Scripture and the reason of the case, that the external aspect of the Church is a thing of high sacredness and importance. If from one point of view the Christian community is (in the full truth of those terms) "the blessed company of all faithful people," known to their Lord and Head as truly "His" (Rom. viii. 9; 2 Tim. ii. 19), from another point it is meant to be a *visible Society*, combined for work and witness in the actual human world. As such, we find it from the very first (below, p. 217) possessing ordained officers, and external order however simple, and ordinances outward and visible connected with entrance on membership and maintenance of it (p. 236). And we find repeated warnings and appeals to the members to be loyal to the society; to avoid division, and all that leads to it—whether insubordination or arrogance (see, e.g., Heb. xiii. 17; 1 Pet. v. 1-5). All this leaves quite untouched the ruling truth of the purely spiritual secret and bond of the life of the true Church. But it does solemnly emphasize the claims of visible order. That order is a thing not indeed of the first rank, yet next to the first. Can it be doubted that the work of the Church for God in the world would have its "freest course" and influence if it were never forgotten on the one hand that "he is a Christian which is one inwardly," and on the other that the collision and friction of rival polities con-

THE DOCTRINE OF THE CHURCH.

tradicts the idea of the visible Church, and most gravely obstructs its mission? The Christian who recollects these principles amidst actual circumstances will never venture to unchurch a Christian community, confessing the truth of God in Christ, because it is not organized on what he thinks the ideal model, and so far diverges from or even collides with his own community. But he will not acquiesce in this state of things as right, as best. He will never put true order before true creed and true life; but he will never despise true order. He will revere it as an ordinance of God, while he remembers that an institution may be divinely sanctioned which yet in divine order and proportion may need, in a measure, or for a season, to give way to divine commandments of a yet higher kind. See in illustration the language of the prophets about the divine sacrificial ritual (e.g. 1 Sam. xv. 22); and cp. Mark ix. 38-40.

The Christian in this attitude of thought will pray and lawfully seek for a healthful re-union of visible Christendom, now so deplorably broken by discrepant and *competing* organizations. He will value highly the witness of history (p. 228) to the truth of any claims of apostolicity in an organization. Meantime he will be reasonably sure that, at this date, no re-union can hope to be not merely *feasible* but *just* where concessions are all on one side. And he will recognize in many organizations which he holds to be imperfect yet the presence of enough of the ideal often to command his reverence, and at least enough of the divine institution of *order* to be immeasurably better than anarchy. And he will always qualify his claims by remembering that the true unity of the true Church is in its inmost essence spiritual. Each true member is in direct and vital contact with the glorious Head, through faith, by the Spirit. The worst and deepest *schism* is after all that which slights that holy bond. And thus reverent loyalty to order, to the order held to be divinely sanctioned, will yet not lead down into definitions of the Church which contradict its inmost nature. Firm convictions about the rule will yet see the justness of even large exceptions. The man may be an Episcopalian, by the maturest results of thought and enquiry, and may consistently wish to see a genuine (not exaggerated) Episcopacy universal; yet he will heartily recognize and honour the Church position of his Presbyterian, or Independent, or Baptist, or Methodist, brethren. He will prize the divine blessings of Sacraments, and pray that they may be everywhere revered and used, and yet will see in the saintly " Friend " a true member of the eternal Head, and so of the true Body. He will love, and seek for, not only the precious unity of Christian love, but its lawful counterpart in a temperate uniformity of Christian order; yet he will never suffer the claims of the latter to break the antecedent and more sacred bond of the former.

"*Notes*" *of the* (*visible*) *Church.*—Article XIX., "*Of the Church*," states the "notes," or test-marks,[1] thus: "The visible Church of Christ is a congregation (*cœtus*) of faithful men, in the which the pure word of God is preached, and the Sacraments be duly (*rectè*) ministered, according to Christ's ordinance, in all things that of necessity are requisite to the same." The earliest comment

[1] A Church may possess all the " notes " of *reality* while not all the conditions of *ideality*.

THE DOCTRINE OF THE CHURCH. 211

on this (Rogers, 1586) runs: "The Lord . . . only knoweth them that are His. For to man the Church of Christ is partly invisible, and visible partly. The invisible are all the elect, who be or shall be either in heaven triumphing or on earth fighting . . . not because the men be not visible, but for that their faith . . . Godward is not perfectly known unto us." Hooker's " notes " of corporate visible unity have been given above (p. 203). Field (Dean of Gloucester *temp.* James I.), in his treatise *Of the Church* (ii. 2), gives the notes of the "true (visible[1]) Catholic Church" to be (*a*) "the entire profession of those supernatural verities which God hath revealed in Christ His Son ; (*b*) the use of such holy ceremonies and sacraments as He hath instituted . . . to serve as provocations to godliness, preservations from sin, memorials of the benefits of Christ, warrants for the greater security of our belief, and marks of distinction to separate His own from strangers; (*c*) an union or connexion of men in this profession and use of the sacraments, under lawful pastors and guides, appointed, authorized, and sanctified, to lead them in the happy ways of eternal salvation." Pearson (*Of the Creed*, pp. 339-350) cautiously but clearly distinguishes in the Church those who are "efficaciously called, justified, and sanctified," and says of others that they have "no true internal communion with the members and Head (of the Church)," "the congregation of those persons here on earth which shall hereafter meet in heaven;" and he finds the notes of the organized Church in (*a*) agreement in one faith; (*b*) observance of the

[1] He is careful to distinguish the visible and invisible aspects of the Church, as Hooker had done.

same sacraments; (c) expectation of one heaven; (d) sympathy in one mind and love; (e) use of one discipline and government. "As there is no Church where there is no order, no ministry, so where the same order and ministry is, there is the same Church."

It will be observed that none of the writers here quoted explicitly lays down episcopal government as a "note" of the Church, though Pearson seems to approach the position. It was certainly not made a "note" by the leading Anglicans of cent. xvii., as a class (see further below, p. 231). On the other hand, *all* the great leaders of Reformed Christendom, cent. xvi., xvii., set high and reverent value on Church order as a principle, whatever their views were about details of system.

The word *Catholic* (Universal) applied to the Church, appears first in Ignatius (early cent. ii.), in the famous sentence (*Ep. to Smyrna*, c. 8), "Wherever Jesus Christ is, there is the Catholic Church." A little later, the contemporary account of Polycarp's martyrdom speaks of "all the sojourning-bodies ($\pi\alpha\rho o\iota\kappa\acute{\iota}\alpha\iota$) in every place of the holy and Catholic Church." Later, the term is very frequent. Athanasius (cent. iv.), says that the Church is called Catholic "because it is diffused universally ($\kappa\alpha\theta\acute{o}\lambda ov$) in the world." The first notion of the word was plainly local diffusion; Christians combined in a way irrespective of territorial limits. It glided not unnaturally from this to mean also "orthodox" as against heretical; with regard to the central body of professing Christians, holding the primary revealed truths, as against numerous divergent or rival bodies. It certainly referred to consent about revealed truth more prominently than to uniformity of polity.

THE DOCTRINE OF THE CHURCH. 213

The claim of the Papal Church is to be, in her own words (*"Creed of Pius IV.,"* 1568), " the holy Catholic and Apostolic Roman Church, Mother and Mistress (*magistra*) of all Churches." Her Trent Confession of Faith, the "Creed of Pius IV.," is " the true Catholic faith, outside which no man can be saved." No assertions can be more completely met by historical and scriptural disproof than these.[1]

Before quitting the subject of Catholicity, we quote the following weighty words: " The early Christian fathers often urged the name and authority of the Church Catholic against heretics. The thoughtful student will, however, perceive a very important distinction between our position and theirs, which may materially affect, not the truth and point of their assertions, but their application to the changed circumstances of the Church. We have arrayed against us the bulk of the Western Church, which has overlaid, added to, and corrupted the ancient faith, and abandoned the rule of faith in Scripture. We are severed by almost as serious differences from the varied sections of the Eastern Church. And there have grown up amongst us communities of Christians differently organized, and often opposing our action, and yet for the most part readily acknowledging the same creeds and doctrinal articles. There is no parallel to this state of things in antiquity. . . . Ignatius might truly say (*Ep. ad Trall.*, c. 3), speaking of the three orders of bishops, presbyters, and deacons, 'Apart from these there is no Church.' . . . Apart from them there might be Jew, Heathen, or Gnostic, but not the Church.

---

[1] See the Rev. R. C. Jenkins, *Romanism, an Examination of the Creed of Pius IV.*, a mass of learning in a small compass; and Dr G. Salmon, *Infallibility of the Church*.

But to take these sayings of old, and to force their application dogmatically to a condition of the Church of which the venerable martyr had not the faintest glimpse, must surely be unjust to his memory, and untrue to the facts" (Boultbee, *Exposition of the Articles*, pp. 160, 161).

We may add that in almost every great instance of secession from the main organization it will be found that part of the cause was the neglect, or repression, of some great principle of life or order on the part of the main body or its representative authorities.

Meanwhile we reassert none the less earnestly that a temperate uniformity of polity is the true counterpart of the inner unity of the true Church. May He who is able "hasten it in its time," and in His way.

Authority of the (visible) Church. Two English Articles (XX., XXXIV.) are devoted to this subject. In them, and by the nature of the subject, the authority discussed takes two directions: doctrine, and order, including order of worship. The question of authority in doctrine is practically that of authority in interpretation of Scripture. This we have briefly discussed already (pp. 7, 8). It may be enough to repeat here that the authority of the Church as an Interpreter is (*a*) real, such that the individual should treat it with deep reverence; (*b*) not ultimate, so that it can silence the individual's appeal to Scripture by anything other than Scripture. This latter principle may of course be gravely misapplied, to excuse or assert the wildest claims of individual ignorance, folly, or pride. But the misapplication must be met, not by denial of the principle, but by adjustment of it to other principles. And undoubtedly the Church, as an organized community, has the right (which is also the most grave responsibility to God) of making terms of external communion, and of denying outward privileges of membership to persons refusing certain articles. This right must, however, be exercised under recollection of the overruling truths of the spiritual nature of the true Church (p. 202), and the immediate connexion of each of its true members with the Head, and the inalienable right of that Head to "know," in His own sense, "them that are His." The full recognition of the constitutional rights of the visible Church (in its total or in a substantive " branch ") is one thing; the assertion that those rights will always be rightly exercised is another. And history bears conclusive witness to the fact that the visible Church has no gift of inerrancy; certainly not until all its members are "ruled by the Spirit and Word of God." Christendom owes great blessings to the early ecumenical Councils, particularly to Nicæa and Chalcedon, where in God's providence the truth of Christ's Person, gathered from the Scripture, was affirmed and published with an authority which gave it in time universal currency. But ecumenical Councils have contradicted each other. And of none of them can it be said that it was, in its actual constitution, an *ideal* representation of the visible Church.

The Church of England (Art. XX.), while asserting the rights of the visible Church, is still more careful to limit their exercise constitutionally, under the divine supremacy of Scripture. She nowhere claims for herself, or the whole Church visible, the right of either interpreting Scripture by a mere *dictum*, or of adding anything to Scripture as *de fide.* Only that which is laid down *in Scripture*, or lawfully to be proved *by it* (Art. VI.), (not by even the Church's mere word *about it*), is to be believed as " of faith." Even a general Council must be overruled by this principle (Art. XXI.), if need be.

As regards *order of worship,* the exercise of authority is a manifest right (and responsibility) of the visible Church, within the limits (given in Articles XX., XXXIV.) that nothing be ordered " contrary to God's Word written," and that " all things be done to edifying." It is remarkable that the New Testament, as compared with the Old, is nearly silent as to the procedure of public worship. This fact, along with the great general principle of order, so amply recognized in the New Testament, indicates that rules of Christian worship are, as things sacred but secondary, committed in a large measure to the Church's discretion. Usages of worship are thus not necessarily unscriptural, anti-scriptural, merely because they are not prescribed or described in the holy Scriptures.

Some valuable statements on this subject will be found in those sections of the Introduction to the English Prayer Book headed "Concerning the Service of the Church" (1549), and "Of Ceremonies" (1552).

CHAPTER X.

THE DOCTRINE OF THE MINISTRY

THE New Testament contains numerous allusions to offices and officers in the visible Church, and to a special designation and ordination of men to Church functions, sufficient to justify the words of Art. XXIII. : " It is not lawful for any man to take upon him the office of public preaching, or ministering the sacraments in the congregation (*ecclesia*), before he be lawfully called and sent to execute the same. And those we ought to judge lawfully called and sent which be chosen and called to this work by men who have public authority given unto them in the congregation (*ecclesia*) to call and send ministers into the Lord's vineyard."

Cp. (besides references to the Apostles of Christ) Acts vi. 3-6, xi. 30, xiii. 1, xiv. 23, xv. 2, 4, ὁ, 23, xvi. 4, xx. 17-35, xxi. 18; Rom. xii. 6-8; 1 Cor. xii. 28; Eph. iv. 11, 12; Phil. i. 1; Col. iv. 17; 1 Thess (the earliest of St. Paul's Epistles) v. 12, 13; 1 Tim. iii. 1-13, iv. 14, v. 1 (?), 22 (?); 2 Tim. i. 6; Tit. i. 5-8; Heb. xiii. 7, 17; Jas v. 14; 1 Pet. v. 1-4; 3 Joh. 10 (an instance of misuse of apparently real authority); and perhaps Rev. i. 20, ii. 1, 8, 12, 18, iii. 1, 7, 14.

That office of some kind, a constitutional leadership and order, should appear in the Church visible arises from its nature as a Society, founded for work, extension, and cohesion (p. 208). The additional facts indicated by the notices in Scripture are about as follows. At first, after the Ascension, the ministry was lodged *in toto* with the Apostles, whose authority, used temperately and in full consultation with the community, was, however, derived, not from the community, but from Christ. Then, with growth of operations and numbers, began a "differentiation" of functions. Assistants, for practical work along with spiritual effort (the Church has called them "*deacons*," διάκονοι, from almost the first), were, by apostolic advice or order, chosen by the community and consecrated by the Apostles. Then, somewhat later, appear "*elders*" (Acts xi. 30, etc.), grouped, at Jerusalem, around a president, St James, and frequently mentioned as in fact the council and leaders of the Church. The same officers are otherwise called "*bishops*" (*episcopus*, "superintendent;" Anglo-Saxon *biscop*), overseers of the flock. And in the case of James at Jerusalem, and Timothy and Titus later, we see a pastor who is not an Apostle exercising a presidential pastorate, which in the latter cases is plainly one of some authority (whether permanent or not) over pastors, and with power to constitute or ordain new pastoral elders. We gather that, on the whole, this system of ministry was such that the "deacon," and "presbyter" or "overseer," was never (at least normally) constituted merely by the voice of the community. He was at least ratified in his function by a representative or representatives of the existing ministry. And 1 Cor. xii. and Eph. iv. in a remarkable way connect the origin of a ministry with the direct will of God, and particularly of Christ glorified.

Meanwhile there is much to indicate that the

THE DOCTRINE OF THE MINISTRY. 219

sacred rule had its considerable exceptions. Proclamation of Christ was certainly not restrained to the ministry (Phil. ii. 16). Apollos (Acts xviii. 24-28) preaches, without any hint that he was, or was to be, formally ordained. And the presence of the mysterious *charismata* (p. 142) in the primeval Church plainly modified to some degree the otherwise normal order of the ministerial work.

In the very earliest sub-apostolic writings we find the Christian ministry a most important factor in the life of the Church. In the *Teaching of the Twelve Apostles* (cent. i.) "bishops and deacons" appear as the stated ministry, just as at Philippi (Phil. i. 1). In *Clement of Rome* (cent. i.) "presbyters" (whose office is called an "episcopate") and "deacons" similarly appear. In *Ignatius* (early cent. ii.) bishop, presbyters, and deacons are conspicuous, and are for him a vital requisite in the Church. It would be needless to travel lower in illustration.

To recur for a moment to the origin. The apostolate (of the Twelve)[1] stands in many respects quite apart from ministerial "orders." For one thing, the Twelve are viewed often in the New Testament (e.g. Joh. xiv.) as rather *the Church by representation* than ministers or rulers of the Church; so that promises to them are often promises to all the faithful, who are all in this sense their successors. And as regards ministerial orders, the apostolate *as a ministry* is succeeded to, not by one order, but by all. All are "differentiated" out of it. The deacon (Acts vi.) succeeds the Apostle as table-server ; the presbyter as one of the local rulers

[1] We are much indebted here to an essay by the Rev. C. H. Waller, *The Harmony of the Bible and Prayer Book as regards the Christian Ministry.*

and pastors of the flock; the bishop (in the later sense) as presiding presbyter, competent in a special way to ordain or constitute others. But in the apostolate proper, with its immediate divine authority, and its witness-bearing, there is no *succession*. Matthias and Paul were not ordained by the Church to be Apostles, but designated by the Lord Himself, like Peter and John Paul *was* (with Barnabas) ordained (Acts xiii.), but not to be an Apostle. His Church commission, given by divine direction, was to be (may we say?) a missionary bishop, a travelling constitutor of churches. Thus the whole ministry succeeds the Apostles, but succeeds them so as not properly to claim their prophetic authority. And further, a ministry which does not contain all the offices in which they were succeeded, yet if it contains any, has apostolicity about it, though imperfectly.

SPECIAL POINTS IN THE DOCTRINE OF THE MINISTRY.

SUCCESSION.

The idea of a ministerial succession is clearly to be seen in the New Testament, as in the Pastoral Epistles, and is amply confirmed by the earliest sub-apostolic writings. As the idea of a ministry at all is implied in the fact that the Church as visible is an organized society, so the idea of a succession in the ministry is implied in the fact that it is a society with a continuous work to do and development to follow. What are the conditions of succession, and the powers it gives, are great questions quite separable from these facts. It is quite possible, by unjustified inference, to argue, e.g., that a developed episcopacy is of the very essence of the Church, from the fact that the presidential or mon-

THE DOCTRINE OF THE MINISTRY. 221

archic element is traceable in the New Testament, and appears in full growth two generations later. But this argument is not warranted by fact or reason. Church government is a great phenomenon of the New Testament. But it does not appear there as a thing of the vital order, in the sense of the above theory. It appears as a matter of the very highest rank of expediency and common benefit; certainly as a thing which cannot be despised and rejected without grievous sin. But it is not a thing of the rank of saving truth. Neither in scale nor solemnity of treatment does it stand with the truths of repentance, faith, acceptance, and holiness; with union and communion with Christ by faith. And while the New Testament, as we shall see, indicates a certain system of government originating in the apostolic age, it does not assign that system to the immediate commands of Christ, and it does not so develope its idea as to allow us to make it a test of communion or excommunication from the Church visible as a whole. On the other hand, a historical succession, rightly viewed, is an invaluable benefit, to be reverently guarded and used. A just estimate of it has much to do with the recollection that the ministry is a divine monumental institution, one thing ideally from age to age; not a mere aggregate of workers for God dispersed through time, but an ordinance once appointed as a means of salvation, a lasting witness to divine truths, and a divinely intended guardian of religious order.

SACERDOTALISM.

The word is difficult to define. But perhaps it is fair to say that it marks an idea of the ministry in which the minister is the mediator between God and the individual Christian, particularly as an offerer of sacrifice, a guardian of sacraments, and a conveyer of pardon by special absolution. Here first it is important to distinguish between *mediator* and *medium*. A medium of communication is not necessarily mediatorial. A friend sends me a gift by a messenger; here is a medium. I can approach God only through Christ; here is the Mediator. The medium may be highly convenient and useful, and in an ordinary way needful. A mediator is, for the purpose, indispensable.

Now the deepest principles of Christianity preclude the idea of an ultimately *indispensable* ministry. The primary and ruling idea of the Church is that of a body whose every member, by the Spirit, lives directly by his Head (above, p. 132); and a ministerial theory which really crosses that idea is untenable.[1] The ministry may be, and in the immemorial order of the Church is, the guardian and dispenser of sacraments; though Tertullian (*Exhort. Castit.*, c. 7) held that under real exigency the Church (of laymen) has full right to supplement this in its inherent character as "a royal priesthood" (cp. Hooker, *Eccl. Polity*, vii., c. 14). But the ministry is not so the guardian of sacraments that it can withhold for a moment the grace and fulness of the blessed Head from the true receptive faith of the individual, by withholding "the sacrament of so great a Thing." The ministry is a medium, not a mediator. If it wrongly withholds the holy sealing ordinance, or if that ordinance is on any account inaccessible, the true idea of the Church assures us that the benefit will come some other way to the believing man. The guilt and loss will be with the minister, not with the believer.

It is remarkable that the Christian minister as such is *never* in the New Testament called ἱερεύς

[1] See Lightfoot, *Philippians*, pp. 181-3.

(*hiēreus*), *sacerdos*.[1] (See *Addenda*, p. 268.) As one of the true Israel, he is " a king and priest to God" (1 Pet. ii. 9 ; Rev. i. 6, v. 9, 10), but on a footing precisely that of his lay brethren. It has been reasoned, indeed, that he may in a guarded and secondary sense be called, officially, a *sacerdos*, as he is in some respects the representative of the congregation to God, and of God to the congregation. But such reasoning and usage is absent from the New Testament, in which the pastoral aspect of the ministry is (to say the least) very far more conspicuous than the representative.

On this whole subject the reader should, if possible, consult Bishop Lightfoot's *Dissertation on the Christian Ministry* (*Philippians*, pp. 181-269, especially pp. 244, etc.). The Bishop cautiously defends the secondary use of the word *sacerdos*. But he dwells on the fact that " an exclusive sacerdotalism (as the word is commonly understood) contradicts the general tenour of the Gospel ; " and that the sacerdotal idea, under which the threefold Christian ministry is held to be the counterpart and analogue of the Aaronic orders, is fallacious. He traces the entrance of the sacerdotal idea of the ministry into the Church to the pagan sacerdotalism to which vast numbers of converts had been used, and sees in the Aaronic analogy an *ex post facto* justification of the idea thus once introduced. As a fact, it is an idea scarcely traceable before the age of Tertullian (late cent. ii.), and even then largely controlled by the strong parallel assertion of the priesthood of all Christians. Not till cent. iii., the age of Cyprian, do we find it fully developed.

[1] So also, by the way, in the practically authorized Latin Prayer Book (Durel's) of 1670. There *presbyterus* always, and rightly, represents the "*priest*" of the English.

CONFESSION AND ABSOLUTION.

The New Testament is extremely reticent on this great matter. In general terms the duty of confession to man, as well as to God, is plainly stated (Jas v. 16; cp. Josh. vii. 19; 2 Sam. xii. 13; Matt. iii. 6, xviii. 15-17; Acts xix. 18). But nothing explicit in the New Testament makes the minister the special recipient of confession. An obvious fitness and reasonableness suggests that he must, within careful limits, be the trusted friend and adviser in the Lord of each member of his flock—a principle which fully authorizes private consultation in cases of need. But the Scriptures give no hint of the reduction of this sacred and important branch of pastoral work to a system, certainly not to a system considered as vital to the individual Christian's maintenance of Church communion. Such a systematization did however at length come in, and in the Church of Rome is one of the most powerful factors in Church life. In order to reception of the holy Eucharist, the *sine quâ non* is a secret and particular confession, followed by a judicial allotment of penance, and the utterance of an *absolvo te* conceived to convey sacramentally the divine pardon to the confessing person supposed to have right dispositions. We make no attempt to discuss this system in detail; to point out its terrible risks to both penitent and "confessor," risks indicated only too well in the minute and often deplorable rules for the confessor current in the Roman Catholic Church; nor to speak of the too often futile and perfunctory character of "penances." We only note one special spiritual fallacy in the system; that the *absolvo* is held to be

THE DOCTRINE OF THE MINISTRY. 225

rightly received, even if the penitent is not *contrite* (lovingly sorry for sin as sin), provided only he is *attrite* (conscious of the disgracefulness of the sin, or alarmed at its coming retribution, in a way to stay the actual sinning: *Canons, etc., of Trent*, Sess. xiv., c. 4). Attrition and penance are, as it were, the equivalent of contrition. It is obvious how gravely such a theory deviates from the Scripture doctrine of repentance.

Yet the system, grievously in error as it is, is related to truth. The Christian pastor, as the commissioned minister of the Word, *has* an important absolving function. The proof of this lies not in Joh. xx. 23 (Matt. xvi. 19, xviii. 18, have a quite different reference), for there the whole Church appears to be addressed, not only the pastorate.[1] It lies in the pastoral commission generally. So far as pastoral absolution refers to the outward order of the Church, the presbyter must in a great degree be the responsible guardian of order and ordinances (1 Tim. iii. 5), with the entrusted function of admission and exclusion, to be constitutionally used. And so far as it refers to the inward sphere, to the divine pardon, the pastor, as the *commissioned* "messenger, watchman, and steward," will not only, as every Christian man and woman may and should, point the burthened soul to the revealed secret of peace in the Word of God, but will announce the certainty of pardon to the true penitent with just that *authority* which belongs to his divinely instituted office. His absolution, in this sense, is no more *prophetic* as regards insight into the individual than the private Christian's is. But he is the representative of that sacred monumental ordinance, the

[1] See Westcott on the passages in *The Speaker's Commentary*.

Ministry, founded by Christ Himself. And that fact, though it cannot make divine truth truer in itself, can, and should, and (in proportion to the man's spiritual correspondence to his office) will, make it specially certain to the penitent, specially tangible to faith.

SUPPLEMENTARY.

HISTORY OF THE CONFESSIONAL.[1]

In the primitive Church the three great sins, murder, adultery, apostasy, excommunicated the offender *ipso facto* on discovery; though never without hope of readmission.

Cent. ii. The re-admission was either denied wholly, or granted only once. Re-admission (to communion) was the one mode of absolution.

Cent. iii. Origen advises, in cases of burthen of conscience, the consultation of the clergy.

Cent. iv. An official, the Penitentiary, at Constantinople, receives private confessions of burthened consciences, and reports them to the Church, for public prayer for divine pardon. The office, however, on account of certain scandals, was by Chrysostom's time abolished. He constantly exhorts to confession to God, with or without human aid.

Cent. v. Leo the Great, of Rome, ordains that it is sufficient that the priests should know the offences, and ask prayer in general terms. Re-admission (for which no verbal form was used) is to be by the bishop, *except on the death-bed*.

Cent. vii. The classification of sins, and commutations of penalty due, began at this period to be elaborated. About

[1] We are much indebted to a Sermon before the University of Cambridge, by Dean Reichel, now (1889) Bishop of Meath; published, with full quotation of authorities, under the title, *History and Claims of the Confessional*.

THE DOCTRINE OF THE MINISTRY. 227

now was composed the original of the Prayer following the Absolution in our Visitation of the Sick (which see). It was to be said by the priest with the penitent in public at the altar.

Cent. xiii. Innocent III. ordains, 1215, that private confession and absolution shall be necessary in order to *retain* communion—a principle wholly different from the primitive. In 1268 the "indicative" formula, *absolvo te*, as against a solemn prayer for pardon, was pronounced alone effectual.

Cent. xiv. The words, "Whose sins thou dost remit, etc.," were introduced into the ordination of presbyters. They had been used before in the ordination of bishops; plainly with reference to the bishop's function (see above, cent. v.) of re-admission to communion.

It will be observed that the solemn exclusion from or admission to the Holy Communion is the thing mainly in view in much of this legislation. Even among Roman Catholic theologians many have held that the *absolvo te*, indicative and positive, refers not to the divine pardon, but to the Church's pardon, so to speak. Such is the true reference of it in the Anglican Visitation of the Sick. The presbyter has received, and thus exercises, the responsible function of solemnly reinstating the perhaps dying penitent, then and there, into Church communion, or of assuring him of his part and lot in it. It will be observed that even this is to be done only at the sick person's own desire.

GRACE OF ORDERS.

In the ideal of the Christian ministry, the minister is a man, on the one hand, inwardly called by the Spirit, and given by the Lord, for the sacred work; on the other, recognized as such by the Church, and sent forth with its solemn blessing, attestation, and, so to speak, counter-signature upon the heavenly commission. Such a sending is in itself a seal of the divine call, and, as such, a special occasion, to the believing recipient, of all the grace needed for his work. But no ordination can so "give the Holy Ghost" as that by virtue of it the man, not otherwise spiritual, shall become so, or, being already spiritual, shall for certain acquire new and supernatural discernment of character, or of doctrine, influential power, or the like. In 1 Tim. iv. 14 we do not know for certain what the "gift" was. And it was given "by *means of prophecy, with* the laying on of the hands of the presbytery." Joh. xx. 21-23, as we have said, is a commission rather to the Church than to the pastorate. Archbishop Whitgift says well: "The Bishop, by speaking these words ['Receive the Holy Ghost,' etc.] doth not take upon him to give the Holy Ghost, no more than he doth to remit sins when he pronounceth the remission of sins; but by speaking these words of Christ [Joh. xx. 22, 23] he doth show the principal duty of a minister, and assureth him of the assistance of God's Holy Spirit if he labour in the same accordingly" (*Works*, Parker Society, i. 489).

Episcopacy.

The *title* bishop (*episcopus*, "overseer") does not in the New Testament denote a minister ruling over other ministers; this is generally admitted. The New Testament *episcopus* is the overseer of not the shepherds but the flock. One local church (Phil. i. 1) might have several such "bishops." But this leaves the question quite open whether such a ruling ministry, however *named*, existed under immediate apostolic sanction. That it did so may, we think, be safely inferred, as follows.

By the close of cent. ii. a definite "episcopacy,"

THE DOCTRINE OF THE MINISTRY. 229

in the later sense of the word, appears practically everywhere in the Church.

And the word *episcopus* is used in this connexion (e.g., by Irenæus) without the knowledge, seemingly, of a previous other use. As early as 110 (probably) the ruling *episcopus* appears, in the Ignatian Letters, as a most important factor in Church life, at least in a large circle of churches. Early Church history presents us consistently thenceforward with the same general constitution.[1] Now between Ignatius and St John the interval is not great; say thirty years at most. It seems unlikely, to say the least, that so large an institution of order should have arisen, apparently unopposed, without some definite apostolic precedent. Such precedent we find in the New Testament (*a*) in the presidency of Apostles during their lifetime (e.g., of St Paul at Corinth, and at Ephesus); (*b*) in that of their immediate delegates (perhaps appointed *pro tempore*), as Timothy and Titus; (*c*) in that of James the Less in the mother-church (Jerusalem) of Christendom—a presidency more akin to later episcopacy than anything else in the New Testament. We further find that all early indications point to Asia Minor as the scene of the chief development of primeval episcopacy, and to St John at Ephesus as in a sense its fountain head. It is as least possible

[1] Some important details vary. At Alexandria, till at least 260, the bishop was chosen by the presbyters from their number, and ordained by them. In at least some other churches presbyters could ordain presbyters, with the bishop's formal sanction. In the church of St Patrick (cent. v.) in Ireland, and of St Columba (cent. vi.) in Scotland, the bishops were necessary to ordination, but not necessarily rulers at all. The chief of the Scottish Church was the Abbot of Iona. See Boultbee, *History of Church of England*, p. 25.

that he, when he took up his abode in Asia, began or developed there the *régime* he had known at Jerusalem, and that his example (if not precept) was rapidly and widely followed.

Meanwhile there is reason to think that the episcopate rather grew out of the presbyterate, in the order of Providence, than otherwise. The primeval bishop was not so much of another order as first of his order, for special functions of government and ministration. Such is St Jerome's view, (*on Titus*, i. 5), cent. v.; and he regards the bishop as being what he is, not by direct divine law, but by "the custom of the Church."

On the whole, the *data* of the New Testament and of the next earliest records confirm the statement of the Preface to the English Ordinal, that "from the Apostles' time there have been these orders of ministers in Christ's Church, Bishops, Priests, and Deacons." On the other hand, in view of the sublimely spiritual character of the Church in its true idea, and of the revealed immediate union of each member with the Head, by faith, and of the reserve of the New Testament, we are not authorized to regard even apostolic organization as a matter of the first order in such a sense as that we should presume to unchurch Christian communities, holding the apostolic faith of God in Christ, but not fully organized on what we believe to be the apostolic model. And we should take good care not to develop that model for ourselves into unlawful proportions; as in the theory that the bishop is the normal *channel of grace* to the lower clergy and the people. On the other hand, no thoughtful Christian will wish to forget the sacred obligations and benefits of external harmony, and of continuity and unity of organization, things meant to yield only to yet greater claims from the side of the highest spiritual truth.

We append a few statements of opinion on Episcopacy, in the direction of liberal moderation, by Anglicans of cent. xvi.-xvii. (See Goode, *Divine Rule*, etc., vol. ii., pp. 236-348 ; ed. 1853.)

Jewel (Bishop of Salisbury, 1560-71), *Defence of Apology*, II., ix., § 1 ; v., § 1, dwells on the essential oneness of presbyter and bishop, and maintains that even were the continuity of English episcopal succession broken (as the Romanists held) it could be restored *from within.*

Whitgift (Archbishop of Canterbury, 1583-1604) meets the Presbyterian's claim that their system was *jure divino*, not by a counter-claim for episcopacy, but by the assertions (*Defence of Answer*, etc.) that (*a*) no one certain and perfect form of government is prescribed in Scripture to the Church of Christ ; (*b*) the essential notes of the Church are only the true preaching of the Word of God and the right administration of the Sacraments.

Bancroft (Bishop of London and then Archbishop of Canterbury, 1597-1610), at a conference of bishops (1609) before the consecration to Scottish sees of certain clergymen in presbyterian orders, maintained, in answer to a doubt raised by Andrewes (then Bishop of Ely), that there was no necessity for their re-ordination (as presbyters), " seeing where bishops could not be had, ordination by presbyters must be esteemed lawful " (Abp Spotswood's *History*, iii. 209, ed. 1851). Andrewes concurred. Bancroft held very high views meanwhile of the vital necessity of episcopacy to the Church ideally.

Hall (Bishop of Exeter and then Norwich, 1627-56) Laud's chosen literary defender of Episcopacy, writes (*Defence of Remonstrance*, § 14 ; and cp. his *Peacemaker*, § 6), " I, onewhere, reckon Episcopacy amongst matters essential to a Church; anotherwhere, deny it to be of the essence thereof. [But see] the distinction that I make expressly between the Being and the Well-being of a church: affirming that those churches to whom this power and faculty is denied lose nothing of the true essence of a church, though they lose something of their glory and perfection."

Andrewes (Bishop of Ely and then Winchester, 1609-28) writes to Du Moulin, 1618 (Letter ii.): "Though our government be by divine right, it follows not either that there is no salvation, or that a church cannot stand, without it. He must needs be stone blind that sees not churches standing without it; he must needs be made of iron . . . that denies them salvation."

Ussher (Archbishop of Armagh, 1624-56): "An ordination made by such presbyters as have severed themselves from those bishops unto whom they have sworn canonical obedience cannot possibly by me be excused from being schismatical. . . . Yet for the testifying my communion with those churches (of France and the Netherlands), which I do love and honour as true members of the Church Universal, I do profess that with like affection I should receive the blessed Sacrament at the hands of the Dutch ministers if I were in Holland, as I should do at the hands of the French ministers if I were at Charenton" (*Works*, i., 259, ed. 1847).

Cosin (Bishop of Durham, 1660-74), when actually in exile at Charenton, attended the Huguenot sacrament, and wrote to a friend (Mr Cordel, Feb. 7th 1650), who had scruples on the point: "Considering there is no prohibition of our Church against it (as there is against our communicating with the Papists, and that well grounded upon the Scripture and will of God) I do not see but that you . . . may (either in case of necessity . . . or in regard of declaring your unity in professing the same religion . . .) go otherwhiles to communicate reverently with them of the French Church" (*Works*, Anglo-Cath.

THE DOCTRINE OF THE MINISTRY. 233

Library, iv., 407. See also the extract from his Last Will, *ibidem*, i., xxxii).

See at large Goode, as above; Dean Perowne, *Church, Sacraments, and Ministry;* and *The Huguenots and the Church of England,* a Sermon before the University of Cambridge (1885), by the Rev. J. de Soyres.

Our purpose in this brief collection will not be mistaken. At the present day we meet everywhere the two opposite forces of ecclesiastical anarchy and of a theory which unchurches all Christian societies not of the episcopal regimen. We have sought to deal with the first above (p. 208). No better means of dealing with the other appeared than the quotation of the weighty and well-balanced utterances of men who were no hesitating Anglicans, and not modern controversialists.

As we leave the subject of the Doctrine of the Ministry, let it be remembered that the very last purpose of the divinely founded Ministry is to absorb, or to repress, the energies of the Church at large for witness and service. The words of Eph. iv. 12 are memorable: "He gave some . . . as pastors and teachers, *with a view to the equipment of the saints for* (*their*) *work of active service, for* (*their*) *upbuilding of the body of Christ.*"

CHAPTER XI.

THE DOCTRINE OF THE SACRAMENTS.

"SACRAMENTS ordained of Christ be not only badges or tokens of Christian men's profession, but rather they be certain sure witnesses and effectual signs of grace and God's good-will towards us, by the which He doth work invisibly in us, and doth not only quicken (*excitat*), but also strengthen and confirm our faith in Him. . . . The Sacraments were not ordained of Christ to be gazed upon, or to be carried about, but that we should duly use them. And in such only as worthily receive the same, they have a wholesome effect or operation. But they that receive them unworthily purchase to themselves damnation, as St Paul saith" (Art. XXV.).

The Latin word *Sacramentum* was long used loosely by Latin Christian writers, so as to include nearly anything sacred, e.g., a revealed truth (*mysterium*). By a large consent of the Christian Church, however, the word is restricted to denote such Christian rites as have an immediate divine institution and a revealed connexion with the conveyance of spiritual blessings. Baptism and the Supper of the Lord alone answer this description. They thus stand in a sacred position of their own.

The Roman Church reckons Confirmation, Penance, Extreme Unction, Ordination, and Marriage, as con-

DOCTRINE OF THE SACRAMENTS. 235

stituting with Baptism and the Supper the Seven Sacraments, each instituted by Christ, and each " a visible sign of an invisible grace, instituted for our justification," i.e., in the medieval sense of justification, " for our acceptance and purification." With great ingenuity, but in vain, proof is alleged that each of the five rites has the authority of Christ as to its " matter," or element, and its " form," or efficacious verbal formula. (See Boultbee, *On the Articles*, pp. 212-16 ; and Jenkins, *Romanism*, pp. 87-101.)

As regards the efficacy of Sacraments in general, the medieval theology holds[1] that the Sacraments so contain grace that the reception of the Sacrament is the reception of the grace, *ex opere operato*, and that grace cannot be obtained by other than sacramental channels, certainly not by faith in the divine promise alone (see *Canons, etc., of Council of Trent*, Sess. vii., c. 6, 8). The medieval idea of " grace," in the sense here in view, is of a mysterious somewhat, an almost physical agent, capable of being contained and carried by a material vehicle, and which, received into the soul, gives it a new " habit " (*habitus*), a new *cast*, such as will come out (not of itself, but under proper impulses) in holiness and righteousness. Grace, " habitual grace," which, on this theory, only sacraments can infuse (so that *they alone* are, in this sense, "*means of grace*"), is thus nearly akin to " new birth," " new nature." Thus baptism infuses grace in the form of new birth; while it needs other impulses, divine or human, or both together, to call out the new born " habit " into holy action. (Mozley, *Baptismal Controversy*, Pt I., ch. vii.)

Do we gather from Scripture that this theory

[1] Not without exceptions. It was held by many that Matrimony conferred no grace.

rightly represents the function of Baptism and the Eucharist? We think not. Let us make a brief enquiry, and with special recollection of the need here of watchfulness over fairness, truth, and peace of spirit as before God, in view of the controversies which have so long agitated this sacred region.

The New Testament passages which beyond doubt deal with Sacraments are not very many. We put aside, by the words "beyond doubt," the discourse of our Lord, Joh. vi.; a passage about which wide differences of interpretation (in this respect) have existed in all periods (Waterland, *The Eucharist*, ch. vi.), and which cannot be proved exegetically to refer directly to the Eucharist. We cannot similarly exclude (as has been done) Joh. iii. as not referring to literal Baptism in the word "water." The collocation there of that word with "Spirit" seems clearly to point to something so far not of the spiritual order; while yet the question remains, of course, *what* is the connexion of the water with the new birth. Besides this passage, we have our Lord's parting command to His Church to baptize in the Triune Name (Matt. xxviii. 19; cp. Mar. xvi. 16), and many places in the Acts, recording the practice, and here and there indicating the doctrine ("for the remission of sins," ii. 38; "wash away thy sins," xxii. 16). In the Epistles eight or nine places deal with Baptism, teaching that in it we are baptized into our Lord (Gal. iii. 27), into His death, into His grave (Rom. vi. 3, 4; Col. ii. 12); raised with Him (Col. ii. 13); clothed with Christ (Gal. iii. 27); saved, that is, saved by the answer of a good conscience in it (1 Pet. iii. 21); all knit into one body (1 Cor. xii. 13). The Church is (Eph. v. 26) "sanctified and cleansed by the laver

DOCTRINE OF THE SACRAMENTS. 237

of the water, attended, or conditioned, by an utterance" (of the divine name and promise). Baptism is the "laver of new birth" (Tit. iii. 5). On the other hand, baptizing appears as a work secondary to preaching the gospel (1 Cor. i. 17). The Second Sacrament appears rather more rarely in didactic passages. We have in the Acts five mentions, without comment, of the Breaking of Bread (ii. 42, 46, xx. 7, 11, xxvii. 35). We have in the Epistles two great didactic passages, only two, but fuller than any baptismal passage (1 Cor. x. 16-21, xi. 17-34). There we gather that the "cup of blessing" is the common partaking of Christ's Blood, and the Bread, broken, of His body; that the partakers of the one bread, or loaf, are as such one body; that the Cup and the Table (so called, not altar) are the Lord's; that the Ordinance is the Lord's Supper [1]; that it is done "in remembrance of Him" (below, p. 264); that the partakers "show," announce, proclaim, "the Lord's death, till He come;" that to partake unworthily is to be "guilty of His body and His blood," committing a sin which calls down "judgment," because of "non-discernment of the Lord's Body." There is a possible further reference to the rite in 1 Cor. xii. 13; "We were all made to drink into one spirit." Then, above all, we have the holy fourfold Record of the Institution (Matt. xxvi.; Mark xiv.; Luke xxii.; 1 Cor. xi.), from which we gather the ruling fact that the Lord's Supper stands in immediate, indissoluble connexion with His *Death;* that the Bread is the Body not under *any* aspect, but as "given," being given, yielded up in sacrifice "for us;" that the Wine is the

[1] The passage *as a whole* clearly includes under this name the Eucharistic Rite proper, not only the Agapé.

Blood not under *any* aspect, but as "shed," being shed, "for us," as the Blood of Covenant.

Such is the special New Testament material for sacramental doctrine. It will be seen that its bulk is not great. It is amply enough to secure the believing reader's deep and reverent attention. But it is not enough to justify the inference that the holy rites stand in the front, so to speak, of Christianity. If they do stand there, it is a strange paradox that large tracts of the New Testament are as a fact silent about them, just where emphatic mentions might be looked for; e.g., the Epistles to the Ephesians and to the Hebrews.[1] And meanwhile the New Testament directly cautions us against the risk of allowing even divine rites, whatever their function, to obscure the function of the moral, spiritual action of the soul (1 Cor. i. 17, x. 1-13; 1 Pet. iii. 21; cp. Mar. xii. 33, 34; Joh. iv. 23, 24; Rom. ii. 25-9). The Scripture, certainly, is far more ample and emphatic on Grace than on the Sacraments of grace; on the efficacy of penitent faith directed with profound simplicity to God and Christ, rather than on that of the administration of divine ordinances. And we believe this fact to be a pregnant and directive fact for this whole enquiry, in which sometimes investigation seems to approach first Sacraments, then Grace, instead of taking the true order.

The Sacramentalism of the New Testament will not be viewed aright if viewed in isolation from that

---

[1] That Heb. xiii. 10 refers to the Holy Table is by the context extremely improbable. See Kay, in the *Speaker's Commentary*; and Lightfoot, *Philippians*, p. 265, note. Did the Writer mean to designate the Table "our altar," it is, to say the least, difficult to explain why, in view of the special perplexities of his readers, he did not make *very much more* of the fact.

DOCTRINE OF THE SACRAMENTS. 239

of the Old. The Gospel Sacraments are most sacred parts of a sacred whole, the sacramental Idea pervading Scripture. From the beginning onward the covenantal Idea appears, and everywhere, at its side, the sacramental Institution; "certain sure witnesses and effectual signs of grace and God's good will," "whereby He doth work invisibly in us," in the world of thought and will, "and doth not only arouse," as by a vividly presented object of sense, "but also confirm," as by its revealed designed significance, "our faith in Him;" working on the soul by way of divine (nothing less than divine) attestation and ratification. Perhaps the Tree of Life to Adam, certainly the Rainbow to Noah, Federal Sacrifice (Gen. xv.) and Circumcision (Gen. xvii.; Rom. iv. 10, 11) to Abraham, the Passover Sacrifice and Feast to Israel; are all instances of one idea—the giving of an external, and usually lasting or recurring, divine sign along with a divine promise.[1] It is the same thing, in its last and noblest development, when at length the eternal Covenant appears fully revealed, and brings with it its Laver, its Bread, its Cup.

Taken thus in harmony with the long past of the ways of God, the Christian Sacraments are, as to their place in Christianity, as intelligible (we use the word most reverently) as divine. They are in plain harmony with the first truths and inmost genius of that Gospel of sovereign and mysterious grace, of direct spiritual contact between God and believing man, of which they are the Sacraments. It would be an anomaly, requiring quite peculiar evidence, if the crowning Dispensation of salvation should depend for its spiritual efficacy not less but more than earlier Dispensations (as that represented

[1] See Bp Hopkins (cent. xvii.), *Doctrine of the Covenants.*

in the Psalms and Prophets) on bodily actions and receptions. It is in proportion at once with the Old Testament and the Gospel that the two physical Institutions of the Gospel (the phrase will be understood) should have a work to do precious, venerable, holy, divine, but a work of not infusion but attestation; as divine Seals upon the eternal Covenant, working in the line of humble but luminous faith, and in entire accord with the observed phenomena of that manifested Life of Grace which is the "intrinsic final cause" of the Gospel.

Thus let special sacramental study be approached in the line of pre-evangelical sacraments. It is a line not much followed at present; but in earlier times it was not so. Bernard (cent. xii.) speaks (*Sermo in Cœnâ, Opera*, ed. Paris, 1839, vol. i., p. 1948) of Circumcision as the "former sacrament" of the grace of Baptism. And Mozley (*Bapt. Controversy*, Pt i., ch. vii. and Note 19) very fully illustrates the antiquity of such views as against a later tendency to depreciate the grace and the sacraments of the Old Testament.

That the Christian Sacraments *are* covenanting rites appears clearly from the words of the Institution of the Eucharist. In every account the Cup, the sacramental Blood, is "of the Covenant, the New Covenant;" while the whole rite is linked indissolubly to the covenant sacrifice and feast of the Passover. And the connexion of Baptism with "the Name" of the Christian's God speaks to the same fact. In each rite God in Christ attests and ratifies His relations and gifts of life and peace with His true Israel, individually and also as to the community. The *community* is especially prominent in the eucharistic rite, whose significance is quite expressly connected (1 Cor. x.) with *common* partici-

DOCTRINE OF THE SACRAMENTS. 241

pation; a fact recognized by our Church in the strict prohibition (see Rubrics after the Communion Office, and after the Communion of the Sick) of a solitary Eucharist, even in the hour of death.

The covenant-sealing work of Sacraments was the ruling view of the framers of our Articles and Offices, in their maturest convictions. It is instructive to read, in illustration of this, the three Sacramental Sermons of Bullinger (vol. v., Parker Society,) in which that view is largely expounded. Bullinger, though a foreigner, was a chosen friend of the Anglican reformers, and specially esteemed by them as a sacramental teacher. And in the reign of Elizabeth his doctrinal sermons (*Decades*, sets of ten) were systematically imposed by Convocation on the less educated clergy as their authorized body of divinity. Bullinger is equally earnest to preclude a false mysteriousness of theory, and to enjoin a deep while intelligent reverence in use.

In our conviction, this view of the function of the holy Sacraments secures as no other view does just those two objects. In this view, alike at the Font and at the Table, the conception and expectation of blessing will be as clear and as purely spiritual as when the "means" used is, for instance, the Scripture, or secret prayer. Yet will the Sacrament have a peculiar and inestimably precious function. In it, as in nothing else, God in Christ, through ordered human ministration, but most really, is present to meet spiritual faith with material token, stepping out of His invisible and spiritual region of action just so far as to touch, as it were with a sensible contact, the believer in his faith. The Water is not transubstantiated, nor transformed, into the Spirit, nor the Bread and Wine into Christ (see further below, p. 260). But the Water, the Bread, the Wine, are not bare signs, mere occasions of reminiscence, however tender. They are the personally given Warrants and Witnesses of eternal realities; such that as surely as they are used in faith, so surely are the blessings faith seeks certified, not by man but God, definitely, specially, infallibly, to the user. The hour of communion is thus indeed an hour with God, with the Son of God, "who loved us and gave Himself for us." It is a blessed hour of remembrance, of meditation; but far more. It is an hour in which He speaks to us, and as it were sensibly touches us, in the ordinance of, not our invention, but His command. The holy Bread, the holy Cup, are received as from His hand, as truly (to faith) as they were received at the first Administration. The disciple literally in them "touches his salvation," in its attesting and lawfully conveying Seal. He goes forth fed and refreshed with Jesus Christ, who has thus solemnly made over to him anew His sacrificed Body and His outpoured Blood; that is, His finished Sacrifice, bearing its "innumerable benefits" (below, p. 260).

This view is no modernism. In one well known passage St Bernard thus describes the special function of Sacraments (*Sermo in Cœnâ*, c. 2, as referred to above, p. 240): "A sacrament is a sacred sign, or sacred mystery (*secretum*). Many things are done for themselves alone; but other things in order to designate something else, and are themselves called signs, as they are. To take an instance from common life: a ring is given for the ring's sake, and there is no significance; it is given to invest an heir in some inheritance, and it is a sign. The recipient can in that case say, The ring avails nothing, but

DOCTRINE OF THE SACRAMENTS. 243

yet is it the inheritance which I sought. In this manner the Lord, drawing near His passion, took means so to invest His people in His grace, that the invisible grace might be granted (*præstaretur*) by some visible sign. To this end were all sacraments instituted. . . . Investitures vary with the things in question; for instance, a canon is invested by (*per*) a book, an abbot by a staff, a bishop by a staff and ring." The function of the sacrament here is that of lawful attestation, obsignation, conveyance, after the manner of title-deed. It is remarkable that a century later this passage of "the last of the Fathers" was criticized by Aquinas (*Summa*, iii., lxii., i., § 3), as inadequate, as making the sacrament a (legal) sign only, whereas "by many testimonies of the saints" it was a "cause of grace."

The statements of Bernard afford, as we venture to believe, a clue to an inner or underlying meaning in much (we certainly do not say all) of the exalted language of the ancient Church about the Sacraments. From the very first, even in the New Testament itself (cp. Gal. iii. 26 with 27), language tended, because this is a deeply natural tendency, to speak of the sign and seal in terms of the thing signed and sealed, of the Sacrament in terms of the Thing (*Res*); so that Baptism came to be called "regeneration," "illumination," and the like, while all the time it was possible to receive the Sign without the Thing, and the Thing without the Sign (as Cornelius did, Acts x.). As time went on, it proved only too possible for the visible and tangible in religion to overlay the related spiritual and eternal; and so it was with the Sacraments. But witnesses to the original idea were still not wanting. In the patristic treatment, e.g., of Baptism (Mozley, as quoted above) it is remarkable that regeneration and kindred terms, however close their identification with Baptism, are usually treated as meaning not merely changes of status, or gifts of latent faculty but *actual and positive changes of character* from evil to good, from love of sin to love of holiness. Such language is difficult, we think impossible, to reconcile, in a sacramental theory, with facts, unless the theory be that indicated in St Bernard's words. And so far the presence of such language in the Fathers is a witness to what at least *had been believed* of the work of Sacraments. So we think is the primitive custom of administering Baptism by preference at Easter and Whitsuntide. If the holy rite is the infusion of new birth and nature, its delay by a day, by an hour, much more by months, is terrible. Not so if it is the solemn sealing of a covenant, whose internal realities rise above limits of date and season. And this view comes out, as it seems to us, in the discussions of the Schoolmen themselves. Lombard (cent. xii.) examines the work of Baptism in his *Sententiæ*, in a passage full not only of subtle thought but of strong common sense. One statement is remarkable (*Lib.* iv., *Dist.* iv., § 7): "Do not wonder that the Thing sometimes precedes the Sacrament, since sometimes it follows long after."

Much that we have said as to this aspect of language has reference to baptismal doctrine. But it bears equally on eucharistic; for the Sacraments are things of one kind. The late Dr T. S. L. Vogan (*True Doctrine of the Eucharist*) has shown, with much wealth of proof and strength of reasoning, that views now widely current on the Holy Communion (e.g., that in or with the Elements in the Eucharist, there, where they are, is the "Real Objective Presence

DOCTRINE OF THE SACRAMENTS. 245

of the glorified Body of Christ, and that the blessed rite is a sacrifice of peace and propitiation), are not only not the meaning of Holy Scripture, but not the teaching of primitive antiquity when words come to be weighed. See by all means his work, especially chapters v.-xiv. The older and classical work of Waterland, *On the Eucharist* (early cent. xviii.), bears in the same direction. Much of his enquiry and discussion, highly technical in parts, comes to the Bernardine view, if we may call it so, to which full reference is made by Waterland, ch. vii. One remark which he makes (at the close of chap. vii.) on the theory of Transubstantiation is a key to much of his teaching. He says that it is a needless theory, for "will nothing satisfy, except the wax and parchments [of a deed or conveyance] be transubstantiated into *terra firma?*"

We have said above, what our older divines fully owned, that the Sacrament is often spoken of in terms of the Thing. This, carefully remembered, explains an observable fact in much of the Anglican theology of cent. xvi., xvii. The teachers of that time habitually use the highest and noblest language about Baptism. " Our second birth is by the water of baptism," says Cranmer, for instance; and the quotation might be paralleled indefinitely. Yet these same writers, when speaking to individual consciences, speak of justification, and of regeneration, very much as the modern " Evangelical " might do. It was Cranmer who composed the Third Homily. Bishop Hall (*Works*, vi., 249, ed. 1837; see the passage) says, "Christ dwells in our hearts by faith; a man may have a saving faith before baptism." And Ussher (*Body of Divinity*, ch. xlii., ed. 1841) has this remarkable passage: " We may rather deem and judge [as against the theory that in the baptism of infants a 'habit of grace is infused'[1]] that baptism is not actually effectual to justify and sanctify until the party do believe and embrace the promises. . . . Baptism . . . is a seal of the righteousness of Christ, to be extraordinarily applied by the Holy Ghost, if [the infant] die in its infancy; to be apprehended by faith if it live to years of discretion. So that as Baptism administered to those of years is not effectual, unless they believe; so we can make no comfortable use of our baptism administered in our infancy, until we believe. . . . All the promises of grace were in my Baptism estated upon me, and sealed up unto me, on God's part; but then I come to have the profit and benefit of them, when I come to understand what grant God, in Baptism, hath sealed unto me, and actually to lay hold on it by faith."

In the same spirit speaks the learned and saintly Beveridge. His language about the dignity of Sacraments is most exalted, but when he comes to enforce the need of Regeneration (Sermon lxxiii.) in practical preaching, he scarcely alludes to the font, but makes his whole appeal take the line of the enquiry, "Are you bringing forth the fruit of the Spirit? For there, and only there, is the sure proof that you have ever been born of Him." (See *Addenda*, p. 268.) So Jeremy Taylor (*On the Spirit of Grace*, Sermon i.), addressing unspiritual church-goers: "They were washed with water, but never baptized with the Spirit. . . . They would think the preacher rude if he should say they are not Christians, they are not

[1] "For if there were such a habit of grace infused, it could not be so utterly lost, or secreted, as never to show itself but by being attained by new instruction."—*Ibid.*

DOCTRINE OF THE SACRAMENTS. 247

within the covenant of the Gospel. But it is certain the Spirit of manifestation is not yet upon them; and that is the first effect of the Spirit whereby we can be called sons of God. . . . If the Spirit be in you, you are in It. . . . If the Holy Ghost be not come on you to great purposes of holiness, . . . ye are yet in the flesh." The great Hooker uses language (*Eccl. Pol.*, bk v., cc. 58-65) of the highest technicality about holy Baptism, and *seems* to assign to it (we do not think, by the context, that he really does so) the function of positively beginning the sanctified life where that life begins at all. Yet when he, like Beveridge and Taylor, speaks to living men, he speaks otherwise, because from another point of view. In his two *Sermons on St Jude* 17-21 (Ser. i., § 4), he depicts (surely from his own consciousness) the experience of a true conversion, in words which might be used by a Whitefield, or a Wesley; and concludes: "If the Spirit have been thus effectual in the secret work of our Regeneration unto newness of life . . . we say boldly with the blessed Apostle, 'We are not of them which withdraw ourselves unto perdition, but of them which follow faith to the salvation of the soul.'" Long before Hooker, Augustine had written (on 1 Joh. v., § 7): "Let all be baptized, let all enter the Church walls; the children of God are only distinguished from the children of the devil by love. They who have not love are not born of God."

Certain points of detail connected with both the holy Sacraments, and with each, are briefly noticed below. We conclude our general treatment with the confession of belief that in the whole study two drifts of opinion are to be watchfully, while in a spirit of holy charity, avoided. One goes towards making them *the* means of grace, channels *sui generis* for the infusion of divine nature and life. The other goes towards making them *mere* symbols, illustrations, occasions of recollection. It is not so. They are not creative, but obsignatory. They are not human, but divine.

SUPPLEMENTARY.

CERTAIN POINTS OF SACRAMENTAL DOCTRINE.

SACRAMENTS IN GENERAL.

The Church Catechism (in its sacramental section, added 1604; drawn up by Dean Overall, on the basis of the Smaller Catechism of Dean Nowell) is verbally ambiguous on the word Sacrament; see the second and third answers. But it is plain that the first of these two is the stricter and defining statement. The other will naturally describe the word in a larger and derived sense; the sacramental institution, or occasion. Art. XXIX. is sufficient witness that the sign *may* be wholly disconnected from the grace.

"*A means whereby we receive the same.*" These words of our Catechism are never to be forgotten. The question remains, however, what class or kind of means? The word "means" may equally denote *either* lawful "conveyance," as of title (see above, p. 242) to inheritance or possession, *or* infusion, as of substance or nature. We think that the former alternative is indicated as the intention of the passage, by the cast of the theology (above, p. 241) on which, as a whole, this part of the Catechism was based. Nowell's Longer Catechism, sanctioned by Convocation, 1570, fully explains the work of sacraments, and makes no reference to infusion of life or nature. Their function is: (*a*) "that God's promises may be presented to our senses, that they may be confirmed to our minds without

DOCTRINE OF THE SACRAMENTS. 249

doubting ; " (*b*) " that they should be certain marks and tokens of our profession." Meanwhile he says of them just below, "by the one we are born again, and by the other we are nourished unto everlasting life " (ed. Parker Society, pp. 205-207).

We may say that the Sacrament is " a means whereby we receive," inasmuch as it is the divinely given ordinance of institution (p. 242), in which the worthy receiver sees and touches, as it were, the Hand that consigns to faith the gifts of life and peace ; in which he receives from it, as in a holy " deed," his possessions. It is " a pledge to assure us thereof," in closest connexion with that fact. As it is God's ordinance of institution, so faith, taking and pondering it, finds it its powerful present "excitation and confirmation," and also its "pledge" of a glorious *future*. (See further *Addenda*, p. 268.)

" *Generally necessary to salvation*." The word "generally" cannot here mean strictly "universally" ; for no one, certainly in Western Christendom, holds this of the Eucharist in the case of infants. See further the important third Rubric (based on St Augustine) after the Office of Communion of the Sick ; and, with regard to the "necessity " of Baptism " *where it may be had*," see the Comment on the Gospel in the Adult Baptismal Service. The word "necessary" is to be interpreted in relation to the divine blessings " conveyed " in the two Sacraments, compared with those conveyed in the alleged other five Sacraments. Without death to sin and life to righteousness, and without the Body and Blood of Christ, there is no salvation ; not so without " grace of orders," for instance. And as in the order of the Church Visible the two Sacraments are the divine counterparts of those absolutely necessary graces, they are, in relation to that order, generally necessary.

Language of Ceremony. Ceremony, by a general law of language, freely borrows the terminology of the facts related to it, but only in a certain sense. A man may be ceremonially "made" king before he *actually* "becomes" king (so David, 1 Sam. xvi.); or again, after he *actually* "has become" king, as at almost every coronation. This is not accidental or arbitrary, but has to do with the permanent relations between facts and their symbols and seals. Meanwhile symbol and seal have a great work to do, only not the work of *origination*.

As regards the origination of grace, so to speak, by sacraments, our Articles nowhere speak of it, nor does the sacramental part of the Catechism. On the words "in my baptism," at the beginning of the Catechism, see just below.

On the word "in":—"*in* my Baptism"; "our spiritual food and sustenance *in* [the Lord's Supper]." The phrases are ideal, mystical. "*In*," in sacramental language, is not a synonym for "*at*" so as decisively to tie the reception of the Grace to the moments of the Sacrament. Those moments have indeed a most special sacredness and blessing for the faithful recipient of the holy Elements. But the analogy of the words "in circumcision" (Rom. iv. 10) indicates, as the essential meaning of these phrases, *connexion with the covenant* thus sacramentally signified and ratified. And the inmost principles of the Gospel of grace warn us against the least needless pressure of conditions of time and place in the matter of reception of the life eternal.

The Scholastics, in discussing the blessings of adult baptism, argued with much subtlety that the moment of the rite cannot be the moment of "justification" (which with them means, practically, regeneration). For the sincere catechumen is already *justus* before God, as already repenting and believing; and the insincere can only become *justus* later, on repenting and believing, when, and not before, the covenanted blessing of justification becomes his.

See on this whole question the important discussion of Mozley, *Bapt. Contr.*, Pt ii., ch. ix.; and cp. Pt i., ch. ix.

DOCTRINE OF THE SACRAMENTS. 251

Extension of the Incarnation. One important and influential view of the Sacraments may be stated somewhat as follows. Our Lord, by His holy Incarnation, provided for the re-creation in us of the whole Nature of which He became the Second Head, and of course therefore for the re-creation of flesh as well as spirit. Now as His Incarnation was no mere abstract, or spiritual, " becoming flesh," so the impartation of its blessings must be by means not only spiritual but physical. In the Sacraments the physical and spiritual so concur that by them man in his double nature is put into not partial but complete vivifying contact with the Incarnate Glorified Lord in His whole Being (see *Addenda*, p. 268). This refined and in some respects beautiful theory, seems, however, to lack solid support from Scripture, though related to some of its deepest truths. The share (yet future, Rom. viii. 23) of the body in redemption, and the connexion of our union with Christ with the present sanctification and future glorification of the body, are truths most surely revealed. But Rom. viii. 11, a pregnant verse in a context full of primary truths bearing on this problem, indicates to us that in the order of grace the body is, as it were, approached *through the spirit;* that its glorification will be "by," or "because of," the present inhabitation of the Holy Spirit in the saint, such an inhabitation as has to do with his " minding the things of the Spirit " (ver. 5). His body meanwhile, as to actual conditions, is " dead, because of sin " (cp. 2 Cor. iv. 16), in a sense antithetical to that in which "the Spirit is life" (ver. 10). And when that body is " sown " it is " not that body that shall be " (1 Cor. xv. 37). With the Incarnate and Glorified we are indeed one, in our whole being, so that our whole being shall share the transfiguration due to that union. But that union is by the Holy Spirit alone, not by the subsidiary way of physical or quasi-physical contact with the Glorified Body of the Redeemer, however the idea of such contact may be subtilized. (See above, p. 135.)

Holy Baptism.

"Baptism is not only a sign of profession, and mark of difference, whereby Christian men are discerned from others that be not christened (*a non Christianis*), but it is also a sign of Regeneration or New Birth, whereby, as by an instrument, they that receive Baptism rightly (*rectè*) are grafted into the Church" [defined Art. XIX.]; "the promises of the forgiveness of sin, and of our adoption to be the sons of God by the Holy Ghost, are visibly signed and sealed; faith is confirmed, and grace increased by virtue of prayer unto God.

"The Baptism of young children is in any wise to be retained in the Church, as most agreeable with the institution of Christ." (Art. XXVII.)

Certain Theories of the Work of Baptism. We have indicated already in outline one widely prevalent theory; that at and by Baptism, by the will of God, the recipient gets a germ of life eternal, not otherwise ordinarily given. This germ is held to be rather a faculty than a tendency; it not only may but will come to nothing but for after mercies of God. But when, in His after dealings, spiritual fruit appears, it is to the baptismal germ, to the then implanted framework of the new nature, that we are to go back for one great part of the cause. Not many years ago a man, awakened to divine faith and love, called to see his devout and holy pastor, and told his tale of peace and joy. "These are fruits of your Baptism," was the response. But it appeared that the new convert, "born again to a living hope," had not been baptized, and came to seek the blessing of Baptism.

We have sought already to point out what seem to us to be grave objections to the theory thus indicated, objections from the nature of the Gospel, and from the facts of life—a branch of evidence never to be forgotten.

Another theory, also widely influential, is that to the worthy recipient of Baptism are given, at and through

DOCTRINE OF THE SACRAMENTS. 253

the rite, as God's appointed vehicle, pardon of original sin and of all past sins; the certainty of the special presence of the Holy Spirit with the soul, specially to plead with it, and generally to renew it; and also eternal life, in the sense of glory to come, contingently upon persevering faith and obedience. Such is Baptism to the sincere adult, and this is the regeneration of Baptism. The insincere gets none of these gifts in present fruition; though he gets the real benefit of recognized connexion with the Church of Christ. As regards the infant, brought to Baptism, the gifts are always certain, because the infant can oppose no *obstacle to grace*. As life developes the will may, or may not, yield to the Spirit: the spiritual gift may, or may not, be followed by moral transformation. (Bishop Browne on Art. XXVII.)

A serious difficulty in this view appears to us to be that it takes a lower idea of regeneration, new birth, divine spiritual filiation, than the Scriptures. A regenerate person in this view might be, and alas too often is, one who has never shown the least special yielding to the Holy Spirit's power; who has always ignored or resisted it. But both Scripture and on the whole the Fathers (see above, p. 244) connect with regeneration, and the large mass of kindred phraseology ("child of God," etc.), the idea of actual moral goodness,—not the mere *faculty*, but the seen *character*; the state of a really changed heart. And it is to be observed further, that the view of infant regeneration as secured by the *absence of obstacle* is nowhere stated in our Articles, or Services, or Catechism. It was noted as an innovation in England early cent. xvii.

Another view is, that the function of Baptism is to convey an outward *status*, to induct into Church privileges, to give to the recipient a position in which Gospel promises are, by an act of divine appointment, brought specially near for use, so that whatever belongs to the Church Visible is lawfully and already possessed for use. This very nearly approaches the last view, only with the important difference that it does not teach the definite and special dwelling of the Holy Spirit with or in the baptized. The same difficulty occurs here as in the other case; that of the use of the word Regeneration. See further below, p. 255.

To us, no view of the work of holy Baptism more commends itself than that of Archbishop Ussher, given above (p. 246). We may call it the federal view. The immemorial ritual of Baptism reminds us that from the earliest days, not to speak of Scripture itself (above, p. 240), Baptism has been viewed as a federal covenanting transaction. And in Scripture, *in cases of covenanting*, there is a tendency (not arbitrary, but natural) to use positive terms, and *in the present tense*, about things which from another point are contingent and future; the visible token being taken for the coming reality (e.g., Gen. xv. 18; Exod. xxxiv. 10, 11).

The federal view may be briefly stated as asserting that the promises of grace and salvation are assured to the recipient (child or adult), under the new and better Covenant, by its divine Christian Seal, which is to be used in humble boldness by faith, either then and there by the conscious adult Christian, or in due time by the then unconscious child.

Remission of Original Sin in Baptism (Homily iii.). This mysterious gift (Mozley, *Bapt. Contr.*, Pt i., ch. iv., calls it "incomprehensible forgiveness," because it is of "incomprehensible sin") has been widely and anciently held to be given specially "in" Baptism, even where other gifts, as of true regeneration, were not given. Our Church refers to it in Hom. iii., but does not anywhere define it dogmatically. It cannot be said to be a direct revelation, as regards any distinction it implies between remission of sin and remission of sins. We may venture to say that its practical significance, as presented for our assent, is that Baptism is the divine sacramental attestation that, in and through Christ, man, as man, despite the Fall

DOCTRINE OF THE SACRAMENTS. 255

and its mysterious results of inherited guilt, is wholly welcome to come personally to God in Christ.

Joh. iii. 1-8. This great passage includes a distinct allusion (above, p. 236) to the baptismal rite. But it does not say that the concurrence of the Water and the Spirit is necessary, or even normal, certainly not in point of time. And it lays down with divine emphasis the principle that in *every case* (ver. 8) of spiritual regeneration two facts concur, whatever are the other conditions; (*a*) *sovereignty and mystery*, "the wind bloweth where it listeth; thou knowest not whence or whither"; and (*b*) *verifiable result*, "thou *hearest the sound thereof.*"

Ecclesiastical Regeneration. We have indicated above (p. 253) the view which may be thus designated. We refer to it here to remark that it is a true view just so far as it is held in relation to the doctrine of the Church as invisible and the Church as visible (above, p. 202). As there is Church and Church, Body and Body, so, and only so, there is Regeneration and Regeneration. The outward and visible may, and ideally should, coincide with the spiritual and real. But, alas, it does not do so actually, in too many instances. In *all instances*, however, the outward rite has a real and true relation to the outward and visible aspect of the Church, and has from this point "much profit every way." But this leaves untouched the question what, really and ultimately, does New Birth mean, and what makes it, and what shows it. And this question is supremely important.

Confirmation of the Baptized. This rite appears so early in Church History as to warrant its derivation from the apostolic laying on of hands in the reception of (not the graces of faith, hope, and love, but) the miraculous *charismata;* which do not appear in Scripture to have been ever received through any but the Apostles (p. 142). As our Service stands, it is practically the completion, or realization, of Baptism; the baptized openly and ceremonially acknowledging his baptismal covenant engagement. And the chief Pastor both beseeches from the Lord the developed power of the Holy Spirit in the soul—thus claiming in faith its baptismal covenant heritage—and assures it, in the name of the Church, by the apostolic manual act of imposition, of the certainty of the divine promise. Confirmation is *just not* a sacrament, because lacking the Saviour's institution. But it carries all the weight of attestation and "conveyance" (p. 243) that can be given by apostolic suggestion and primeval practice. It may be viewed, *inter alia*, as the quasi-sacrament of what some Christians call the " second blessing ; " the realization of the highest life of the new-born soul in the more fully received power of the Spirit.

Infant Baptism. It is well known that a large body of Christians, since cent. xvi. especially, maintain that Baptism is only for those already believing. In our view the question is very nearly reduced to this : is Holy Baptism a covenanting ordinance ? If it is, as we think most assuredly it is, then both the analogy of the Abrahamic covenant (*of grace*, Gen. xvi.), and the express words of the New Testament (Acts ii. 38, 39 ; cp. 1 Cor. vii. 14), indicate that in some sense, and certainly up to the length of a right to outward Church privileges, the children of the already members of the covenant are within it. And if so they have a right to its visible seal.

In the New Testament we have not indeed any mention of Infant Baptism. But we find not the least explicit caution against it, and no injunction to Christian parents to prepare their children for Baptism. There is, on the other hand, at least high probability that existing Jewish usage made it regular for a proselyte to be baptized *with his children* (Wall, *Infant Baptism*, Introduction). The whole analogy of circumcision (which is surely present to St Paul's mind, Col. ii. 11, 12) goes in the direction of Infant Baptism ; and makes it fair to say that the silence of our Lord is much more for than against Infant Baptism. It may fairly be said that the commission, Matt. xxviii. 19,

if we may for the moment imagine it given by Moses, not
Christ, might have run ; "Make disciples of all nations,
and circumcise them into the name of the God of Abraham,
Isaac, and Jacob"; and that this would not have excluded,
but implied, infant-circumcision as the extension (which
it was) of adult.

It is true that few certain notices of Infant Baptism are
to be found before cent. iii., and that Tertullian even seems
to deprecate it (*de Bapt.*, c. 19). Much later still, devout
Christians, like Monnica, Augustine's mother (cent. iv.),
often postponed the Baptism of their children (though
getting them initiated as catechumens) till evidences of
conversion appeared. But we think the evidence against
the *primeval use* of it quite insufficient, and that such
practices as Monnica's arose not a little from an oblivion
of its covenantal function and an exaggerated view of its
purifying power *opere operato*.

Meanwhile, observe the very temperate language of Art.
XXVII. on the subject. And Infant Baptism is not in
such a sense "of faith" that the Christian who reverently
declines its use for his children is therefore heretical.
Dr Wall, whose *History of Infant Baptism* (1705) received
the thanks of Convocation, entirely declines to make it
thus *de fide*. He pleads, on that very ground, with the
Baptists of his day not to break with the National Church
on this point. Were he in a country where the national
Church was not pædo-baptist he would seek Infant Baptism, in conscience, for his children, but he would attend the
Communion Table of the national Church (vol. ii., ch. xi.).

Sponsors in Baptism. This institution is traceable to
Jewish usage (Wall, vol. i., p. 35). Tertullian (late cent. ii.)
refers to it as an established Christian institution. The
purpose is partly theoretical and doctrinal, to signify that
the candidate is brought to Baptism, not in virtue of
merely physical descent, but because of Church connexion,
which gives a reason why parents should not be sponsors ;
partly practical, to secure in a special way fuller Christian

influence for the baptized. In Infant Baptism the child is treated, symbolically and federally, as a cetechumen; and this aspect of the rite (an aspect the exact opposite to superstition) is kept prominent by the answers given *pro tempore* in its name by the Sponsors. Those answers are formally and ceremonially "taken over" by the baptized at Confirmation. It is almost needless to say that morally and spiritually they are to be "taken over" so soon as reason and conscience can at all understand their import. The thought that the Sponsors till then, or till Confirmation, bear the moral responsibility for the child is not an uncommon one among the people; but it is of course an illusion. The sponsorial responsibility is most real and solemn, but (see the language of our Services) widely different from this.

Order of study. Observe that our Articles and Catechism *study Baptism first in the adult*, then in the infant, not *vice versâ*. Ideally, the baptized person "seeks the faith," is instructed, admitted as a believer, and so baptized. So, ideally, the Israelite (if Abraham was his prototype) was circumcised. But the ideal, as in many another case, while remaining a testimony and exposition of principles, ceased at once in Circumcision, and (as we believe) in Baptism, to be the rule of usage. We baptize infants because of the Covenant; we study the Covenant, and its terms, and seals, in the adult.

Sprinkling or Immersion. Baptist Christians hold that entire bodily immersion is *absolutely essential* to Christian Baptism. We believe this to be untenable by Scripture. True, Scripture indicates a *usage* of immersion in the apostolic missions, very plainly. And it connects Baptism with our Lord's Death, Burial, and Resurrection, doctrinally. But characteristically it gives no directions in detail how to baptize; and it seems more scriptural to believe that any "washing" with the prescribed Element, in the Blessed Name, is (though a *minimum*) valid, than to hold that the covenanting ordinance depends for validity

DOCTRINE OF THE SACRAMENTS. 259

on the literal immersion of the person. It is remarkable that the earliest sub-apostolic account of Baptism (*Teaching of the Twelve Apostles*, ch. vii.) expressly provides for "pouring water on the head" where immersion cannot be had. The Church of England makes immersion her first alternative, meanwhile, in the baptismal rubrics.

THE HOLY COMMUNION.

"The Supper of the Lord is not only a sign of the love that Christians ought to have among themselves one to another; but rather it is a Sacrament of our Redemption by Christ's death: insomuch that to such as rightly (*ritè*), worthily, and with faith, receive the same, the bread which we break is a partaking of the Body of Christ; and likewise the cup of blessing is a partaking of the Blood of Christ.

"Transubstantiation (or the change of the substance of bread and wine) in the Supper of the Lord, cannot be proved by Holy Writ; but it is repugnant to the plain words of Scripture, overthroweth the nature of a Sacrament, and hath given occasion to many superstitions.

"The Body of Christ is given, taken, and eaten, in the Supper, only after an heavenly and spiritual manner. And the means whereby the Body of Christ is received and eaten in the Supper is Faith.

"The Sacrament" (observe the exact use of the word) "of the Lord's Supper was not by Christ's ordinance reserved, carried about, lifted up, or worshipped." (Art. XXVIII.)

"The wicked, and such as be void of a lively faith, although they do carnally and visibly press with their teeth (as St Augustine saith) the Sacrament" (again note the word) "of the Body and Blood of Christ, yet in no wise are they partakers of Christ; but rather, to their condemnation, do eat and drink the sign or Sacrament of so great a Thing." (Art. XXIX.)

"The offering of Christ once made is that perfect

redemption, propitiation, and satisfaction, for all the sins of the whole world, both original and actual ; and there is none other satisfaction for sin, but that alone. Wherefore the sacrifices of Masses, in the which it was commonly said, that the Priest did offer Christ for the quick and the dead, to have remission of pain or guilt, were blasphemous fables, and dangerous deceits." (Art. XXXI.)

The Body and Blood of Christ. The devout and accurate study of these sacred words in their sacramental use is a pre-requisite to all true eucharistic teaching. To ascertain their divinely-intended meaning we go of course to the four Records of the Institution ; by SS. Matthew, Mark, Luke, and Paul. We find that SS. Matthew and Mark give only, "Take, eat; this is My Body ; " St Luke, "This is My Body, which is being given for you ; this do in remembrance of Me ; " St Paul, "This is My Body which is being broken for you," or simply, "which is for you" (the reading is questioned ; but even in the latter reading the omitted word is implied by the previous context). Again, SS. Matthew and Mark give, "This [Cup] is My Blood of the New Covenant which is being shed for many " ("for the remission of sins," adds St Mark) ; St Luke, "This Cup is the New Covenant in My Blood which is being shed for you ; " St Paul, "This Cup is the New Covenant in My Blood ; do this, as oft as ye drink it, in remembrance of Me."

In interpretation, we must take *the longer forms.* And these show us that the Body in the Eucharist is not the Body absolutely, but the Body regarded as being "given for us." And the Wine (which indeed is not verbally mentioned) is not the Blood absolutely, but the Blood regarded as being "poured out for many, for the remission of sins." It is "the Cup of the New Covenant in Christ's Blood as being shed for us ; " " the New Covenant in His Blood."

Further, we find the two Elements, two utterances, and two deliveries, side by side, but *separate;* the Blood separate

DOCTRINE OF THE SACRAMENTS. 261

from the Body. At the blessed moment of the first Lord's Supper our Lord and Saviour was living Man, His blood flowing in His veins. The qualifying words, used at such a moment, were all significant. He was putting Himself before His disciples as already in the then fast approaching state in which the Blood should be parted from the Body; that is, in the state of death. In that state the holy sacrificed Body, given for us, would be apart, and the holy Blood, poured out for us, apart. The separation of the Elements, along with the full words of delivery, is eloquent of the state of Death.

Thus indeed, "as often as we eat that bread and drink that cup, we proclaim, tell forth" (καταγγέλλειν, see below, p. 264), as our creed and our peace, "*the Lord's Death, till He come.*"

The words, thus studied, give no real support to certain famous theories of the Eucharist, which yet claim to be above all things jealous of the words. The Roman doctrine[1] is that at consecration the "Substance" (i.e. essence, supposed to underlie all "accidents" or physical manifestations) of the whole glorified Christ, Body, Blood, Soul, Spirit, Deity, *takes the place of* the "substance" of the bread and wine, so that every particle of each Element is He, as truly as His glorified Person on the throne is He; and is likewise to be worshipped. The doctrine of Luther was that, at consecration, "in, with, or under the bread is the Glorified Body;" but Luther did not teach "eucharistic adoration." A widely prevalent teaching in the English Church now is that the consecrated bread "has under its form the presence of the Glorified Body;" and that Christ is to be adored accordingly as in the Elements —a very different thing from adoring Him as present in His ordinance, as He is present in every other ordinance, e.g. in prayer, private or public, and in His Word. The words

[1] *Transubstantiation* (the word dates from late cent. xi.) was first definitely *approached* cent. ix., by Radbert, more distinctly *taught* in the Church cent. xi., *imposed* as *de fide* 1215.

of Institution give no real support to any of these views. Let those words be fully preserved in our interpretation, and let the sacred Blood have its place of *distinct* and *equal* honour, and it will be seen that a very large range of inferences, sometimes taught as if directly revealed truths, prove to have no basis in the words of the Lord Himself. His words point directly, not to Glory, but to Death; not to the Throne, but to the Cross; to Propitiation, Atonement, Sacrifice, Offering, there completed for ever.

It is observable that under the often glowing language of the Fathers this aspect of the Eucharist is on the whole in view. They see in the Elements not Christ as He is, but the Body and Blood of Christ as He was, and is (actually) no more, for us (see Vogan, *True Doctrine of the Eucharist*, Pt i., ch. xiv.). So do our Reformed Anglican divines till well within this century (*ibid.*, ch. xv.). So certainly does our Church in Liturgy, Articles, and Catechism.

It is clear that in this view a Presence of Christ *in the Elements* is not to be sought. For "the Body and the Blood" are not the equivalent for Christ. They are not the whole Christ, but those parts of His blessed Constitution whose separation testified His Death. And again, that state of them and of His constitution is for ever past. As to actual being, as a state, it is no more. It therefore cannot be "there," except "in a certain manner." That manner is sacramental, mystical. The Elements which He ordained to represent validly to His true disciples His Body as slain for them, and His Blood as shed for them, now eighteen centuries ago, are most truly "there," as His warrant and conveyance to their faith of all the benefits of the Passion. *In that sense*, the Body and the Blood are there, and in no other sense at all revealed.

The words of Waterland (*On the Eucharist*, ch. vi.) are remarkable. "Spiritual feeding in this case, directly and

DOCTRINE OF THE SACRAMENTS. 263

primarily, means . . . the eating and drinking our Lord's Body broken and Blood shed; that is, partaking of the Atonement made by His death and sufferings; this is the ground and basis of all the rest. . . . The foundation of all our privileges is our having a part in that Reconciliation."

Waterland insists, as of course he must, on our blissful union and communion with the Glorified Lord, and how this has a holy and delightful connexion with the Eucharist. But he points out that the connexion is not direct, but indirect. Directly, we "feed on" Christ *as He was*, or more strictly on His Body and Blood *as they were*; upon the finished Work of Calvary, as our avenue to all other blessings, "the innumerable benefits of His Passion." "To be refreshed with His Body and Blood" is thus a phrase which points, directly, not to the infusion of His life-power, but to the reconciliation, peace, and joy of our acceptance in Him slain for us. Meanwhile, let the disciple never forget that the eucharistic hour is meant to be a sacredly special occasion of that exercise of faith by which indeed we "*feed on* HIM" in the *whole range* of what He-is-to us.

The word "is." It is quite certain from the context, in the Three Gospels, and 1 Cor. xi. 1, that this word must be interpreted not literally but "in a certain manner." For the words are not only, "This *is* my Body," but also, "This Cup *is* the new Covenant." The Roman and kindred interpretations, (as Vogan shows,) in jealousy for the letter really wander remotely from it, to support a theory which it only negatives. But the important point to notice is that the use of the word "*is*" here by our most Blessed Lord must be understood "in a certain manner," not arbitrarily, but by a law of that human speech which He, the Man of men, used most truly of all men. For wherever in human speech the word "*is*" connects two nouns or thoughts not obviously homogeneous or identical, it is invariably understood "in a certain manner," that is, it needs explanation. "This Cup is the Covenant" is a linguistic phrase of the same order as, "This note is a thousand pounds." Here we think Dr Vogan stops somewhat short of his own just conclusions. He simply declines, in deep reverence, to interpret the "*is*" at all. But may we not say that to seek an interpretation of "*is*," is as much, or little, irreverent, as to interpret "My Body and My Blood"?

But let his book by all means be read with earnest care; it will repay the labour. An able *resumé* of its main argument will be found in a pamphlet by the late Dr Boultbee, *The Presence of Christ in the Lord's Supper*. See too a book little noticed, but well worthy of attention, *An Exposition of the Lord's Supper*, "by a Presbyter of the Church of England;" and *The Finished Offering of Christ*, by the Rev. C. H. Waller.

"*Do this in remembrance of Me;*" lit., "*unto My remembrance, or memorial.*" The word ποιεῖν (*do*) is frequently used in the LXX. for the "doing" which in the case of a sacrifice means "offering;" and the LXX. use ἀνάμνησις (*reminiscence*) *once only* (Lev. xxiv. 7; elsewhere, μνημόσυνον) for a sacrificial "memorial." It has been held accordingly that the words of our Lord should be rendered, "Offer this to be My" (as distinguished from a Mosaic) "sacrificial memorial" (before the Father). But the word ποιεῖν is *never* used elsewhere *in the New Testament* in sacrificial connexions. And if the Lord's words had borne a sacrificial meaning it is surely inexplicable that the New Testament should be so entirely reticent as it is (above, p. 223) about a sacerdotal function of the Christian ministry. Observe further the connexion of thought in 1 Cor. xi. 25, 26; the "*for*" in ver. 26. St Paul plainly means that to "show" (literally, and far better, "proclaim," as messengers or preachers, to each other and the world) "the Lord's death, till He come," was the way to carry out His precept about His ἀνάμνησις. It has been said that to "proclaim" there means our pleading, asserting the fact of, His Sacrifice, *before the Father*. But the verb καταγγέλλειν is frequent in the New Testament, and invariably elsewhere in it bears the common meaning of telling news to human hearers.

Bp Chr. Wordsworth renders Luke xxii. 19, "*for the recordation of Me;*" and says: " ἀνάμνησις is not simply remembrance, which may be involuntary, but a deliberate inward act of the will, showing itself by outward signs." See his whole note, and that on "*Do this*," just before it.

The Hour of Communion. St Augustine, *Epistt., lib.* ii., *ep.* liv., speaks of the practice of *fasting* communion as apostolic, and due to the teaching of the Holy Spirit. And the obvious inference would be against communicating *after the morning.* But Augustine is not borne out by facts. In Egypt there were evening Communions after meals (Socrates, *Hist. Eccl.*, v. 22). This was noted as singular, but it was the singularity of a very eminent Church. Chrysostom speaks of Communion after eating with deprecation, but quite without horror, and blames those who turned away because they had eaten. Cyprian notices without blame the use of wine in the evening, at Communion, by a sect (the Aquarians) who used water in the morning. The *Teaching of the Twelve Apostles* speaks of the receiving the Eucharist "after being filled "; words whose natural meaning is, "after a meal," i.e., after the Agapé. Bp Lightfoot, on Ignatius, *ad Smyrn.*, c. 8, says : " In the apostolic age the Eucharist formed part of the *Agapé.* . . . This appears from 1 Cor. xi. 17 *seq.* . . . from which passage we infer that the Eucharist came, as it naturally would, at a late stage in the entertainment." See too Acts xx. 7, with Wordsworth's note. It appears highly probable that the change to morning Eucharists took place in deference to an edict of Trajan's (early cent. ii.) against *hetæriæ* —guilds, or clubs; an edict which would have included in its scope the Christian *Agapæ*. These, as not of divine ordinance, were probably laid aside for a time ; to

be resumed later (as they were) apart from the Eucharist
And so the Eucharist was attached to the morning Sunday
service.

We are much indebted to a learned paper by the Rev.
N. Dimock, in *The Churchman*, March, 1886.

Attitude at the Holy Communion. The Ordinance supposes the LORD to be Master of the Feast; it is His Table (1 Cor. x. 21, xi. 20). Mediately, by the ministry of His Church, but most truly, HE, as at the first Eucharist, says, "Take, eat ; drink ye all." In this sense He is indeed "really present."[1] And as really present He is to be reverenced and adored. Our Church enjoins us accordingly to *kneel*; guarding and explaining her practice in the last Rubric (as authoritative as any other) after the Communion Office. It is the custom of some Christians to *sit*, on the supposition that the Apostles *reclined* (Luke xxii. 14, etc.). In the earliest *picture* of the Last Supper, A.D. 586 (Marriott, *Vestiarium Christianum*, p. xxvi.) the Apostles appear reverently *standing*.

Non-communicating attendance was unknown in the primitive Church (Bingham, *Antiquities*, Bk xv., ch. iv., § 1, 2).

It is not willingly that we close these notes, and leave this sacred subject, and conclude this little book, with discussions which pointedly refer to differences and controversy. Let us at least, by way of actual conclusion, in some of the most ancient liturgical words still used in the Christian Eucharist, "Lift up our hearts unto the Lord." To HIM,

[1] Though not in the sense of the technical phrase *Realis Præsentia;* i.e. the actual and unfigurative "presence," with and in the Elements, "of the Thing" (*Res*)—in this case the actual Body and Blood. That phrase, in connexion with the Eucharist, appears to be no older than early cent. xvi. See Vogan, *True Doctrine,* etc., p. 91. On the subject at large see a learned book, *Doctrine of the English Church on the Eucharistic Presence*, by the Rev. N. Dimock.

DOCTRINE OF THE SACRAMENTS. 267

directly to HIM, Son of the Father, Lamb of God, Lord of Resurrection, Head of the Church, Life of the soul, across and above all controversies between disciple and disciple, we will, and do, lift up our hearts, as He descends to dwell in them by His Spirit, and rule them for Himself. For Him we long, looking for Him to come again, "this same Jesus, in like manner as He went up into heaven." May not one word we have written, if His mercy will grant it, becloud that look, or chill that longing, for any follower of His. If He be pleased in sovereign kindness to grant it, may some words we have written direct and clear that look, and make that longing only tenderer and deeper, till He come.

ADDENDA.

P. 196.—"*The flesh*" and "*the old man*" (Rom. vi. 6; Eph. iv. 23; Col. iii. 9) are not identical. The writer ventures to quote his own comment on Eph. iv. 23 ("*Cambridge Bible for Schools*"): "On the whole, we may explain the phrase ['the old man'] by '*the old state*.' And under this lie combined the ideas of past personal legal position and moral position; all that I was as an unregenerate son of Adam, liable to eternal doom, and the slave of sin. To put off the old man is thus to quit these positions . . . to step into the position of personal acceptance and of personal spiritual victory; and that position is 'in Christ.'"

P. 223.—In Rom. xv. 16, St Paul uses sacerdotal terms, speaking of himself as a λειτουργός, ἱερουργῶν τὸ εὐαγγέλιον. But the passage is self-evidently figurative, poetic, in its wording. "The gospel," not an altar, is in view. This passage of St Paul's, with its non-literal meaning, may caution us in the interpretation of many patristic passages.

P. 246.—Beveridge thus writes, at the close of the Sermon: "The children of God . . . 'all things are theirs.' . . . Their minds must needs be at rest, and their souls as full as they can hold of all true joy and comfort. Who then . . . would not be regenerate, and made a child of God, if he might? And who may not, if he will? Blessed be God, we are all as yet capable of it; for now that Christ is . . . exalted . . . to give repentance and forgiveness of sins, if we do but apply ourselves to Him, and believe and trust on Him for it, His Father will be ours too; He will beget us again in His own likeness, and admit us into the glorious liberty of His own children."

P. 249.—"An outward . . . sign of an inward . . . grace, given," etc. (Church Catechism). A comma should stand after "grace." Durel (see our p. 223) renders here, *signum . . . spiritualis gratiæ*, quod *nobis datur*.

P. 261.—Many theologians teach definitely that the work of Baptism and the Eucharist is to communicate to the recipient, then and there, the "substance" (p. 261) of the Lord's glorified Body, which "substance" is nearly or quite identified with "grace." The matter of the "Sacrament" is thus as it were animated with the essence of the

"Thing." If the remarks made pp. 261-2 hold good, this view is quite precluded by the words of Institution.

The phrase Extension of the Incarnation is employed by Bp Jeremy Taylor (*Worthy Communicant*, i. § 2) ; but with him it denotes not such an infusion of "substance," but the application by the Holy Spirit to the worthy recipient of the blessings won for us by the Incarnation.

Taylor elsewhere (*Real Presence*, vii. § 8) writes as follows : " The benefit reaching to the body by the holy Eucharist comes to it by the soul ; therefore by the action of the soul, not the action of the body ; therefore by faith, not by the mouth. . . . All that eat are not made " Christ's body," and all that eat not are not disentitled to the resurrection ; the Spirit does the work without the Sacrament ; and in the Sacrament, when it is done, ' the flesh profiteth nothing.' . . . If the nourishment be wholly spiritual, then so is the eating."

INDEX TO SUBJECTS AND WRITERS.

ADAM, his headship, 64, 168, 175; a real personage, 153, 168.
——, the Second, 100.
Advent, pre-millennial, 113.
Agnosticism, 16.
Altar, is there a heavenly? 104.
Ἀνάμνησις, 264.
Anderson's *Human Destiny*, 94n.
Andrewes, Bp, 188, 231.
Angel of Jehovah, 24.
Angels judged, 117.
Anselm, 53, 63n, 90.
Antinomies of thought, 44, 158, 177, 180.
Apollinarius, 66.
Apostolate, 219.
Aquinas, Thomas, 53, 91, 243.
Arianism, 28, 60, 66.
Arminius and his theology, 45, 54.
Arnauld, 53.
Articles, Anglican, i., 10, 19; ii., 32, 57; vi., 216; xi., 187; xvii., 48; xix., 210, 252; xx., 214; xxi., 216; xxiii., 217; xxv., 234; xxvii., 252, 257; xxviii., 259; xxix., 248, 259; xxxi., 260; xxxiv., 214.
Assumptions (*data*) of Christian Theology, 2.
Assurance, 47.

Athanasius, 89, 148.
Atheism, 15.
Atonement, the word, 78.
—— of Christ, scope, 45; central importance, 75; elements necessary to true theory, 77; Scriptural phraseology, 78, 84; aspect Godward, 81; and manward, 81; application, 189; history of the doctrine, 87-92.
Augustine, 51, 52, 89, 96, 110, 123n, 149, 150, 207, 247, 265.
Augustinianism, 180.
Augustinus of Janserius, 53.
αὐτεξούσιον, 51.
Authority, grades of, 7.

BANCROFT, Abp, 231.
Baptism, at Easter, etc., 244; theories of its work, 252; right order of study, 258.
Basil, 148.
Baxter, R., 55.
Bernard of Clairvaux, 90, 151, 240, 242, 243.
Beryllus, 27.
Beveridge, Bp, 188, 246, 268.
Bigg, Dr, 148.
Bingham's *Antiquities*, 266.
Bishops, primitive Scottish and Irish, 229n.

INDEX TO SUBJECTS AND WRITERS. 271

Blood of Christ, 85.
Body and blood of Christ, 260.
Boultbee, Dr, 214, 229n, 235, 264.
Brahmanism, 15.
Brown, Dr D., 114n.
Browne, Bp, 253.
Buddhism, 15.

CALL of grace, 36, 182.
Calvin, 45, 53.
Carus, Rev. W., 55n.
"Catholic," the word, 212.
Catechism, English, 35n, 248.
Cave, Rev. A., 5n.
Ceremony, language of, 249.
Chalcedon, Council of, 67.
Charismata, 142, 219.
Charlemagne, 149.
Chiliasm, 110.
CHRIST, and His Church, 39, 64, 101; and Creation, 40, 70; His Glory, 57; Godhead, 58; Sonship, 58, 64; *Logos*, 59; Consubstantial with the Father, 60; Incarnate, 60; reality of His human experience, 62; yet He was impeccable, 62, 63n; His knowledge, 63; Second Man, 64; history of doctrine of His Person, 65-9; "Definition of Chalcedon," 67; is He the Archetypal World? 70; is He Archetypal Man? 72-4; His Atonement, 74-86; Merit, 80; Expiation, 82; relation of His Life to His Death, 83; His Blood, 85; *Pœna Vicaria*, 86; Descent into Hell, 92-6; Resurrection, 99; Second Adam, 100; Ascension, 101; Mediation, 102; Suretyship, Intercession, Priesthood, 103; Kingship, 105; Return, 106-9; history of belief about it,

109-14; Judge of man, 115; Life of the regenerate, 137; and their Sanctification, 192.
Christendom, reunion of, 209.
"Christian consciousness," 150.
Christianity, a part of theistic evidence, 17.
Chrysostom, 265.
Church, the, 35, 49; "visible," 129, 202; "invisible," 130, 202; unity, 202; Scripture view of it, 205; benefits of outward uniformity, 208; cautions, 209; "Notes of the Church," 210; "Catholic Church," 212; authority, 214.
Clement of Alexandria, 65, 96, 140.
Clement of Rome, 51, 88, 139, 147, 219.
Coleridge, S. T., 174.
Comforter, the word, 119n.
Communion, hour of, 265; attitude at, 266; not to be received in solitude, 241.
Communities addressed as in their ideal, 49.
Confessional, history of, 226.
Confession and absolution, 224.
Confirmation, 255.
Conflict, spiritual, 196.
Conscience, 164.
Conversion, 182.
Cosin, Bp, 231.
Councils, general, 215.
Covenanting, language of, 254.
Covenant of grace, 40, 41, 102.
Cranmer, Abp, 245.
Creationism, 165n.
Cyprian, 140, 223, 265.

DAWSON, Sir J. W., on Science and Scripture, 153n, 157, 169n.
Deism, 16.

INDEX TO SUBJECTS AND WRITERS.

Design and order, 11.
"Depravity," universal, 173.
De Soyres, Rev. J., 233.
Dimock, Rev. N., 266.
Diognetus, Epistle to, 88.
Dionysius of Alexandria, 110.
Doddridge, 53.
"*Do this in remembrance of Me*," 264.
Dorner, 91.
Dort, Synod of, 55.
Durel's Latin Prayer Book, 223*n*.

EDWARDS, Jonathan, 55.
——, Dr L., 81*n*.
Election, 36-55; necessary mystery of the subject, 37, 44; not capricious, 37; the work of the Father, 38; in the Son, 39; cautions, 42-8; moral import, 43; various theories, 48-51; history of opinion, 51-5.
Elôhim, the word, 24.
Ephesus, Council of, 67.
Episcopacy, 228; Anglican opinion on, 231.
Eusebius, 110.
Eutyches, 67.
Evil, origin of, 171.
Evolution, 154.
Evolutionary philosophy, 155.
Expiatory view of Christ's Death, 79; harmonizes with other views, 82.
Exposition of the Lord's Supper, 264.
"Extension of the Incarnation," 251, 268.

FALL of man, 169.
"Fall upward," 170.
Faith, 132, 137, 185; its work in sanctification, 191.
Father, the Eternal, 31-6; essentially Love, 32; is He the Father of all men? 34.
Field, Dean, 211.
"Flesh, the," 195.
Flint, Prof., 13*n*.
Florence, Council of, 149.

"GENERALLY necessary," 249.
"Generation, Eternal," 59.
Genesis i., ii., interpretation of, 153.
Germ of grace, 232.
Gnosticism, 26, 147.
GOD, 10-30; Infinite and Personal, 2, 13; testimonies to His existence, 10; Providence and Sovereignty, 18, 19; Unity, 20, 22; Claim, 21; relation to Time, 146. See further under *Christ Eternal Father, Holy Spirit*, etc.
Goode, Dean, 7*n*, 53*n*, 140*n*, 231, 233.
Grace, 47, 130; defined, 143; not universal, 128; medieval theory of, 235.
Gratry, Père, 13*n*.
Gwatkin, Mr H. M., 66.
Guilt, original, 175.
Guinness, Rev. H. G., 114*n*.

"HABIT," the word, 167, 170, 235.
Hagenbach, 69*n*.
Hall, Bp, 231, 245.
Harris, Dr, 13.
Hatherley, Lord, 7.
Heard, Rev. J. B., 162*n*.
"Heart, the," 164.
"Hell," the word, 92.
"Hell, descent into," 92-6.
Heredity, 158.
Heurtley, Prof., 68*n*.
Hodge, Dr A. A., 179*n*.
"*Homily of Justification*," 187, 254.

INDEX TO SUBJECTS AND WRITERS. 273

Homöousios, 60, 66.
Hooker, 129n, 187, 204, 211, 222, 247; an Augustinian, 54.
Hopkins, Bp, 239n.

IDENTITY, bodily, 100.
Ignatius, 51, 65, 147, 212, 213, 219.
Image of God, 157.
Immersion, 258.
Immortality, 159.
"In Baptism," 250.
Incarnation, 60-9; elements necessary to a true theory, 61; "divine-human personality," 62; history of the doctrine, 66-9.
Indwelling of Christ, 192.
Infants, baptism of, 256.
——, salvation of, 181.
"Inner man," 164.
Innocent VII., 227.
Inspiration, 140.
Intermediate state, 93, 98, 128.
Irenæus, 88, 96, 140, 147, 229.
Israel, restoration of, 108.

JANSENIUS, 53.
Jenkins, Rev. R. C., 213n, 235.
Jerome, 230.
Jewel, Bp, 23.
Judgment, the Last, 115, 118.
Justification, 183.
Justin Martyr, 65, 88, 140, 147.

KAY, Dr, 238n.
Kaye, Bp, 148n.

LAIDLAW, Prof., 163n.
Language, origin of, 168n.
"Larger Hope, the," remarks bearing upon, 94, 116, 128, 160, 178, 181.
"Last Day, the," 118.
Leo the Great, 226.
Lettres Provinciales, 53.

Liddon, Dr, 63n.
Lightfoot, Bp, 147n, 222n, 223 238, 265.
Logos, the word, 59.
Lombard, 53, 90, 244.
Lucian, 30.
Luther, 54, 187, 261.

MAN, 153-201; origin, 154; antiquity, 156; unity, 157; personality, 158; immortality, 159; constitution, 160; original state, 165; greatness of his nature, 166; "Son of God," 167; fall, 169; restoration, 177-200.
Manicheism, 26.
Marriott's Vestiarium, 266.
Marshall's Gospel Mystery, 93n.
Materialism discredited by physical science, 3.
Means of grace, 235, 249.
Mede, Joseph, 111, 112n.
Mediation and medium, 222.
Melanchthon, 54.
Memra, 59.
Merit of Christ, 80.
Millennium, 108-14.
Ministry, Christian, 217-33; growth, 218; succession, 221. See further under Episcopacy, Sacerdotalism, etc.
Mivart, Mr St G., 5n, 154n.
Monarchianism, 27.
Monnica, 257.
Montanism, 150.
Mystics, the, 91, 151.

"NECESSARY," 22.
Necessitarianism, 43.
Nestorius, 66.
Newton, J., 55.
Nicodemus, Gospel of, 96.
Noetus, 27.
Nowell, Dean, 248.

INDEX TO SUBJECTS AND WRITERS.

"OLD man, the," 268.
Orders, grace of, 227.
Ordinal, preface to English 230.
Origen, 88, 110, 147, 148, 226.
Overall, Dean, 248.
Owen, J., 135.

PANTHEISM, 14.
Paradise, 98.
Pascal, 53, 167n.
Pearson, Bp, 79n, 94, 96, 211.
Pelagius, 51.
Perowne, Archdeacon, 105.
———, Dean, 233.
Perseverance of the Saints, 46.
Personality, human, 2, 15, 158.
Philo, 59.
Photinus, 27.
ποιεῖν, 264.
Polycarp, 65, 213.
Polytheism, 14.
Prayer for the dead, 97.
Priest, the word, 223.
Prophecy, study of, 107-9.
Purgatory, 97.

QUESNEL, 53.

REAL Presence, 266n.
Reconciliation, 79.
Redemption, 35.
Reformers, Augustinians, 53.
Regeneration, 34, 182, 253, 255.
Reichel, Bp, 226n.
Resurrection, General, 118.
Reusch, Prof., 5n.
Revelation, divine, 4, 13.
Ridley, Bp, 207.
Righteousness, imputed, 188.
———, original, 159, 165, 166.
Rogers on the Articles, 211.
Rome, Church of, 213.
Rousseau, J. J., 83.

SABELLIANISM, 27.
Sacerdotalism, 221-3, 268.
Sacraments, Christian, 234-51.
———, Old Testament, 239.

Sacramentum, the word, 234.
Salmon, Dr G., 213n.
Sanctification, 190-9.
Schism, 214.
Schoolmen, 53, 250.
Scott, T., 55.
Scotus, 53.
Scripture, its characteristics, 4, 9; testimony of Christ to it, 5; finally authoritative, 7; its position in the Jewish Church, 122; inspired by the Third Person, 139.
Shedd, Prof., 53n, 165n.
Sheôl, 93.
Shepherd of Hermas, 147.
Simeon, C., 55.
Sin, a sense of, necessary to a true theology, 76, 77, 131, 150, 171; as guilt, 171; no "little thing" in God's sight, 80; not "a fall upward," 170; an insoluble mystery, 179; *original sin*, 173; how remitted in baptism, 254.
Sinlessness, 194.
Smeaton, Prof., 140, 150n, 151.
Smith's *Dict. Christian Doctrine*, 150.
Socini, the, 29.
Socrates the historian, 265.
Southall, Dr, 157n.
SPIRIT, THE HOLY, 119-51; Personality, 120; assumed in New Testament, 122; procession, 124, 149; work in Creation, 126; in mankind, 126; in the Church, 129, 141; in the man, 130; bond of union with Christ, 133; relation to Christ's Manhood, 134; Life-giver, not Life, 136; free, sovereign, 137; *non alligatur sacramentis*, 138; Inspirer of Scripture, 139, 150; His

INDEX TO SUBJECTS AND WRITERS. 275

work in Old Testament times, 144; "Vicar of Christ," 150; present study of His Person and power, 151; Fulness, 199; history of doctrine of the Spirit, 146-51.
Spirits in prison, 95.
Sponsors, 258.
Succession, 220.

TAYLOR, Bp Jeremy, 246, 269.
Teaching of the Apostles, 239, 265.
Tennyson, Lord, 158*n*.
Tertullian, 96, 140, 147, 150, 222, 223, 257.
Theophilus of Antioch, 140.
θεοτόκος, 67.
Tichonius, 207.
Toplady, 55.
Traducianism, 165*n*.
Transubstantiation, 261*n*.
Trent, Council of, 53, 213, 235.
TRINITY, THE HOLY, 19-30; the truth rather developed than announced in New Testament, 24; "immanent" and "economical," 24, 125; history of the doctrine, 26-30.
Trinity, the word, 30, 148.

UNION with Christ, 132, 183.
"Unitarianism of orthodoxy," 20, 58, 121.
Unitarians, 29.
Unity, the Divine, 20.
Universalism, 178. See "*Larger Hope*."
Ussher, Abp, 97, 232, 245.

VENN, 55.
Victim-state of Christ, does it continue? 105.
Visitation of the sick, 227.
Vogan, Dr, 244, 262, 264, 266.
Voltaire, 83.

WALDEGRAVE, Bp, 114.
Wall, Dr, 257, 258.
Waller, Rev. C. H., 100*n*, 141*n*, 219*n*, 264.
Waterland, 236, 245, 262, 263.
Wesley, 55.
Westcott, Prof., 60*n*, 64*n*, 140*n*, 225*n*.
Westminster Confession, 43.
White, Dr, 162*n*.
Whitgift, Abp, 228, 231.
Will, the, not forced by grace, 43; how free, 43, 49, 51, 164, 172, 175; Eastern and Western views of freedom of the will, 52.

INDEX TO SCRIPTURE REFERENCES.

⁎ *I owe this Index to the kindness of a correspondent, whom by accident I am unable (Feb. 1890) to thank by name.*

GENESIS.

CHAP.	VER.	PAGE
i.		157
	2	122, 126
	26	157
	26, 27	73, 152
ii.		157
	7	122, 126
	7-25	152
	8-14	153
	8-15	165
iii.	15	61
	5, 22	170
	22	160
iv.	1-16	178
v.	3	167
vi.	2, 4	95
	3	126, 127
ix.	4, 5	86
	6	158
	19	157
xv.		239
	18	254
xvi.		256
	10	24
xvii.		239
xviii.	25	115, 116
xxii.	12	24
	18	61
xxxi.	11-13	24
xli.	38	126

EXODUS.

CHAP.	VER.	PAGE
xv.	11	21
xxiii.	7	183
xxiv.	8	86
xxxi.	3	122
xxxiv.	10, 11	254

LEVITICUS.

CHAP.	VER.	PAGE
xvi.		75, 103
	30	86
xvii.	11	85
xxiv.	15	78

NUMBERS.

CHAP.	VER.	PAGE
vi.	24-26	24
xvi.	22	163
xviii.	22	78
xxii.	32	24

DEUTERONOMY.

CHAP.	VER.	PAGE
iv.	39	20
vi.	4	20, 186
vii.	7, 8	38
viii.	5	189
ix.	4, 6	38
xiv.	1	34
xxi.	8	86
xxv.	1	183
xxx.	15	178
xxxii.	39	20

INDEX TO SCRIPTURE REFERENCES. 277

JOSHUA.

CHAP. VER.	PAGE
v. 13	24
vi. 2	24
vii. 19	224

JUDGES.

CHAP. VER.	PAGE
iii. 10	122

1 SAMUEL.

CHAP. VER.	PAGE
xv. 22	209
xvi.	250
xxix. 4	79

2 SAMUEL.

CHAP. VER.	PAGE
i. 16	86
xii. 13	224
xxii. 32	20
xxiii. 2	122

1 KINGS.

CHAP. VER.	PAGE
viii. 46	173

2 KINGS.

CHAP. VER.	PAGE
xix. 15	20

1 CHRONICLES.

CHAP. VER.	PAGE
xxviii. 12	122

2 CHRONICLES.

CHAP. VER.	PAGE
xv. 1	122

JOB.

CHAP. VER.	PAGE
xxvi. 13	122, 126
xxvii. 3	122, 126
xxxiii. 4	126

PSALMS.

CHAP. VER.	PAGE
ix. 17	93
xvi. 10	92
xvii. 3	195
xxii. 1	78
27	127
xxv. 15	192
xxvii. 1-6	192
xlvii. 7	21

PSALMS (continued)—

CHAP. VER.	PAGE
l. 6	115
23	21
li. 5	173
10-12	145
11	122
13	182
lxvii.	108
lxxii. 14	86
lxxiii. 24	94
27, 28	178
lxxxii. 1, 6	20
lxxxvi. 10	20
xci. 1, 9	145
xciv. 12	189
xcix. 3	21
ciii. 13	34
civ. 13	122
30	123
cxvi. 15	86
cxxxviii. 7, 8	192
cxliii. 2	173, 184, 187, 195
cxlv. 9	33
cxlvi.-cl.	21

PROVERBS.

CHAP. VER.	PAGE
i. 23	122
viii. 22-31	71
xv. 24	178
xvii. 15	183

ECCLESIASTES.

CHAP. VER.	PAGE
xii. 14	115

ISAIAH.

CHAP. VER.	PAGE
vi. 3	24
5	58, 61
vii. 14	61
xxv.	108
xxxiii.	108
xxxv.	108
xl. 12-23	21
xlii. 8	20
xliv. 8	20
xlviii. 16	24
liii.	76, 139

INDEX TO SCRIPTURE REFERENCES.

ISAIAH (*continued*)—

CHAP. VER.	PAGE
liii. 6	36, 44, 78
8	86
5, 6, 10, 11	86
10-12	162
lx.	108
lxiii. 9	24
11	122, 145
16	34, 35, 145
lxv.	108
lxvi. 8	145

JEREMIAH.

v. 22	21
x. 7	21
xvii. 9	173
xxvii. 13	164
xxxi. 33, 34	41
xxxiii.	108
18-21	109

EZEKIEL.

xviii. 32	33
xxxiii. 11	33, 176
xl.-xlviii.	109

DANIEL.

iv. 35	164
vii. 13	64
22	117
xii. 2	178

HOSEA.

xiv. 9	178

JOEL.

ii. 28	127

MICAH.

v. 2	61
vii. 2	86

ZECHARIAH.

vi. 13	104
ix. 11	86
xiii. 7	61

MALACHI.

CHAP. VER.	PAGE
iii. 1	24, 40
17, 18	178

WISDOM.

ii. 23	158
ix. 15	160

ST MATTHEW.

i. 1	61
iii. 6	224
16	134
17	39
iv. 1	134
v. 1, 45	34
5	113
9	34
22, 29, 30	93
24	79
vi. 9	34
30	185
vii. 11	173
13-27	178
viii. 10	61, 185
29	117
30, 31	169
x. 15	115, 116
28	93, 163
xi. 25-27	23
27	59, 119
28	59, 132
xii. 31, 32	120, 121
36, 41	115
xiii. 20, 21	131
41, 42, 49, 50	108
43	34
xvi. 18	205
19	225
xvii. 11	178
xviii. 3	182, 205
8, 9	160
9	93
15-17	224
18	225
xix. 4-6	152, 154

INDEX TO SCRIPTURE REFERENCES. 279

St Matthew (continued)—

CHAP.	VER.	PAGE
xix.	28	117
xx.	28	75, 78, 84
xxii.	14	36
	31, 32	159
xxiii.	15, 33	93
xxv.		178
	10, 19, 21, 23, 46	107
	11-13, 30, 46	108
	19	110
	19-23	117
	32	115
	34-36	115
	41	117
	46	159
xxvi.		237
	24	77
	28	41, 86
	38	61
	39	61
	53	78
xxvii.	4	86
xxviii.	18	106
	19	236, 256

St Mark.

ix.	38-40	209
	47	93
x.	14, 15	181
	45	84
xii.	7	39
	32	20
	33, 34	238
xiii.	32	63
xiv.		237
	24	41, 86
xvi.	16	236

St Luke.

i.	31-35	61
	35	64, 134
ii.	52	61, 63
iii.	38	34, 64, 165, 167
iv.	14, 18	134
ix.	31	94
xi.	13	36

St Luke (continued)—

CHAP.	VER.	PAGE
xii.	5	93
	47, 48	116
xiii.	27	108
xix.	41	178
xxi.	20	41
	24	108
xxii.		237
	14	266
	19	265
	20	86
	22	164
xxiii.	43	92
	46	61
xxiv.	26, 46	76
	26, 44-46	77
	37, 39	162, 163
	39	101, 160

St John.

i.	1-4	57
	3	70
	9	45, 74
	12	34, 182
	13	34, 36, 164
	14	59, 60, 72
	18	39, 58
	51	64
ii.	19	99
	21	160
iii.		236
	1-8	255
	3	73, 173
	3, 5, 7	34
	8	36, 130, 133, 137, 183
	13	63
	16	32
	16, 19-21, 36	178
	34	134
	36	132, 159
iv.	21-24	109
	23, 24	238
	24	123
v.	18	58
	19-23, 26, 27	23
	20	39

280 INDEX TO SCRIPTURE REFERENCES.

St John (*continued*)—

CHAP. VER.	PAGE
v. 21	38, 51, 137
22	115
22, 24, 27	115
24	117
25	132
28	115
28, 29	107, 108, 160, 178
29	108, 115
40	164
vi.	236
35, 37	182
37	38, 132
37, 39	51
38	23, 32
39	107
39, 40, 44, 54	110
40	132, 137
44, 45	36
45	109
51	61, 75
53	85
53-56	86
70	38
vii. 38, 39	200
39	100, 102, 146
viii. 38	23
40	58, 61
42	34
58	58
ix. 35, 38	132
39	178
x. 15	45
18	78
26, 29	45
28	46, 47
28, 29	40
29	23, 38
xi. 35	61
xii. 41	58, 61
xiii. 18	38
xiv.	219
xiv.-xvi.	120, 146, 150
xiv. 3	107
16, 17	120

St John (*continued*)—

CHAP. VER.	PAGE
xiv. 16, 26	36
17	146
19	132
28	23, 59
xv. 1-5	133
6	47
16, 19	38
26	120, 124, 125, 137
xvi. 7, 8	120
8	47
8, 9	130, 131
8-11	127
24	137
xvii.	23, 48, 49
1	40
3	144
2, 3, 6, 9, 11, 12, 24	38
2, 3, 24	47
5	39, 61
5, 24	58
11, 15	36
17	36
24	36, 39, 40
xx. 21-23	228
22, 23	228
23	225
28	58
31	132
xxi. 22	58

Acts.

i. 2	134
2, 24	38
6	108
11	107, 118
16	139
ii. 16-21	127
23	38, 42, 75, 78, 164
24, 35	99
26, 27	92
33	103
33, 36	102
38	236
38, 39	256
42, 46	237

INDEX TO SCRIPTURE REFERENCES. 281

ACTS (*continued*)—

CHAP.	VER.	PAGE
iii.	18	77
	21	107, 178
iv.	10	75
	27, 28	164
	28	77
v.	3, 9	121
	28	86
	31	99
vi.		219
	3-6	217
vii.	48, 49	109
	51	121
	55, 56, 59	98
viii.	1	205
	14, 15	143
	21	205, 206
	29, 39	121
	35	75
ix.	15	38
x.		243
	19	121
	42	115
	44-46	143
xi.	14	95, 116
	30	217, 218
xiii.		220
	1	205, 217
	2, 4	121
	28-39	75
	30-39	99
	38-41	178
xiv.	23	217
xv.	2, 4, 6, 23	217
	9	191
	28	121
	41	205
xvi.	4	217
	6	121
	14	137
xvii.	26	157
	28, 29	34
	31	99, 115
xviii.	24-28	219
xix.	18	224
	32, 39, 41	205

ACTS (*continued*)—

CHAP.	VER.	PAGE
xx.	7	265
	7, 11	237
	17-35	217
	21	183
	23, 28	121
	28	75, 86, 205
	31	178
xxi.	11	121
	18	217
xxii.	16	236
xxiv.	15	108
	25	47, 115
xxvi.	18	191
	23	77
xxvii.	35	237
xxviii.	25	121, 139

ROMANS.

CHAP.	VER.	PAGE
i.	3, 4	61
	4	99
ii.	2-11	178
	5-16	115
	12	116
	14, 15	129
	16	108, 115
	25-29	200, 238
iii.	8	184
	9-18	185
	19	129
	19, 20	173, 185
	21-26	32
	23-25	75
	24, 26, 30	36
	25	86
iv.	5	36
	6	188
	7	78
	10, 11	239
	23, 25	132
	24, 25	99
	25	84
v.		168
	1	49, 132
	1, 11	190
	5	36

ROMANS (*continued*)—

CHAP.	VER.	PAGE
v.	6-9	75
	9	86
	10	79
	12-19	153
	12-21	175
	14	181
	20, 21	177
vi.		184
	1	184
	2	195
	3, 4	236
	4	195
	6	268
	9	99
	12	195
	13-19	198
vii.	4	195
	7-25	196
	12	197
	13	172
	22	164
	23, 25	164
viii.		48, 49
	1-11	130
	3	61, 84
	5	251
	5-8	173
	7	175, 195
	9	125, 195, 205, 208
	9, 11	103
	9-11	136
	10	251
	11	134, 135, 251
	13	195, 197
	14	139
	14, 15, 17, 21	34
	14, 16, 26, 27	121
	15	36
	17	40
	18-23	107
	21	108
	22	180
	23	35, 98, 160, 195, 197, 251
	26, 27	133

ROMANS (*continued*)—

CHAP.	VER.	PAGE
viii.	28	40, 44
	28, 29	41
	28, 29, 30, 33	37
	29	35, 38, 39, 200
	30	36
	30-33	36
	31-39	46
	32	32, 33, 78, 84, 171
	33	49, 117
	34	99, 102, 103
ix.		43
	5	58, 61
	6-25	37
	7	34
	19	164
x.	12-15	181
	13-15	95
	14, 15	116
xi.		108, 109
	2	38
	5-7	38
	6	143
	26	109
	33	180
	33-36	21
	36	19
xii.	6-8	217
xiii.	11	107
	14	192
xiv.	7-9	59, 200
	9	99
	10	115, 116
	15	45
xv.	16	203
	30	121
xvi.	1, 4, 5, 16	205
	25-27	21

1 CORINTHIANS.

i.	2	205
	17	237, 238
	23, 24	36
	24	182
	27, 28	38
	30	41, 132, 136, 191

INDEX TO SCRIPTURE REFERENCES. 283

1 CORINTHIANS (*continued*)—

CHAP. VER.	PAGE
ii. 9, 10	. 139
10	. 119, 121
14, 15	. 133
iii. 15	. 16
16	. 121, 136
iv. 4, 5	. 115
7	. 38, 43
17	. 205
v. 12, 15	. 176
vi. 2	. 117
3	. 117
13-20	. 160
14	. 110
17	39, 103, 132, 136
18	. 160
19	119, 121, 142, 200
20	. 78
vii. 11	. 79
14	. 256
viii. 11	. 45, 46
ix. 1	. 101
27	. 46
x. .	. 240
1-13	. 238
16	. 86
16-21	. 237
21	. 266
32	. 205
xi. .	. 237
1	. 263
3	. 39, 136
7	. 166
17	. 265
17-34	. 237
20	. 266
25	. 41, 86
25, 26	. 264
27	. 86
29-32	. 188
32	. 115, 178
xii. .	. 142, 218
3	. 58, 137
4-13	. 142
11	. 121, 137
12	. 39

1 CORINTHIANS (*continued*)—

CHAP. VER.	PAGE
xii. 13	. 236, 237
28	. 205, 217
28-30	. 143
xiii. 8	. 143
12	. 180
xv. .	. 107, 168
3	. 76, 77
3-11	. 75
8	. 101
9	. 205
14-18	. 77
20-28	. 106
21, 22, 45-49	. 175
22, 47	. 74
23	. 74
23, 24	. 113
23, 35-37	. 107
23, 47, 52	. 107
23, 50, 53	. 108
32	. 99
37	. 201, 251
42-44	. 201
44	. 160
45	. 100
45-49	. 153
47	. 64, 74
50	. 101
51, 52	. 118
52	. 201

2 CORINTHIANS.

CHAP. VER.	PAGE
iii. 6-8	. 41
iv. 10, 11	. 132
13	. 133, 137, 144
14	. 110, 201
14, 18	. 108
16	. 164, 251
v. 6, 8	. 201
7	. 201
8	. 93, 163
10	95, 115, 116, 160
14	. 75
15	. 200
17	. 34, 37, 133
19	. 45

INDEX TO SCRIPTURE REFERENCES.

2 CORINTHIANS (*continued*)—

CHAP. VER.	PAGE
v. 20	44, 79
21	62, 75, 80
vii. 1	163
viii. 7	143
9	143
xii. 2-4	98
xiii. 5	205
14	142

GALATIANS.

i. 2, 22	205
4	75, 84
13	205
15	137
16	73, 137
ii. 20	40, 84, 136, 191
iii. 13	75, 78, 83
17	40
26	200
26, 27	243
27	133, 236
iv. 4	61, 62
5	36
5, 6	34
6	125
v. 16, 17	195
16-25	198
17	195
24	196
25	133, 136
vi. 7, 8	178
14	75
15	34

EPHESIANS.

i. 3	40
4	37, 39
4, 7, 13	73
5	34, 36, 39
6	21, 36, 39
7	75, 86
10	78
10, 11	39
11	39, 42, 45, 164
15-23	199

EPHESIANS (*continued*)—

CHAP. VER.	PAGE
i. 20, 21	99
20-23	136
22	39, 205
22, 23, 25	58
ii. 1-3	173, 182
1-12	73
7	40
8	38, 133
8, 9	143
8-10	41
12	40
13	75, 86
iii. 3-12	32
8	58
9	70
11	40
14-19	192, 198
16	164
16, 17	136
19	58
20, 21	21, 194
iv.	218
3, 4	142
4	39
9	92
11, 12	217
12	233
15	39
15, 16	133
22-24	168
23	164, 268
24	133
30	121
v. 1	34
2	75
5	106
6	178
14	132
18	199
23	39, 268
25-27	45
26	236
vi. 10	193
11	192
16	191

PHILIPPIANS.

CHAP. VER.	PAGE
i. 1	217, 219, 228
21	201
23	93, 98, 110, 201
29	133
ii. 1	142
5-8	61
8	75
9-11	39
11	31, 57, 59
13	144
16	219
iii. 3	200
6	205
7-10	58
9	187, 189
11	110
18	178
18, 19	178
20, 21	107, 160
21	107, 108, 161
iv. 7	194
13	193
15	205

COLOSSIANS.

CHAP. VER.	PAGE
i. 9-13	199
10	194
13-17	58
14	86
14, 20	75
15	71
16	70, 71
16-18	39
17	40, 70, 71, 126
18	39, 99
18, 24	205
20	86, 178
ii. 11, 12	256
12	236
13	236
15	95
19	39
iii. 1-3	98
2, 4	108

COLOSSIANS (continued)—

CHAP. VER.	PAGE
iii. 4	107, 132, 136, 201
9	268
9, 10	168
iv. 17	217

1 THESSALONIANS.

i. 10	107, 190
ii. 16	95
iii. 13	107
iv.	112
14	99
14-16	107
14-v. 2	118
16, 17	107
17	110, 201
v. 2, 3	108
9, 10	107
10	75
12, 13	217

2 THESSALONIANS.

i. 7, 8	107
7-9	108
7, 10	107
12	40
ii. 1	110
13	37, 49
14	40

1 TIMOTHY.

i. 11	124
ii. 4	33, 34
5	61, 102
5, 6	84
6	45, 102
13, 14	153
14	169
iii. 1-13	217
5	225
15	205
iv. 1	121
14	217, 228
v. 1, 22	217
24	115
vi. 15, 16	21

2 TIMOTHY.

CHAP. VER.	PAGE
i. 6	217
9	38, 39, 41
12	132, 187
ii. 10	44
11, 12	75
18	107, 118
19	208
20	207
21	193
iii. 16	139, 141
iv. 1	115
8	107, 110

TITUS.

i. 5	230
5-8	217
ii. 13	58
14	75, 84
iii. 4	33
5	237

PHILEMON.

2	205

HEBREWS.

i. 2	70
2-8	58
3	103, 104
8	58
ii. 9, 14	75
9-18	61
14-17	58
iii. 3, 4	70
7	121, 139
iv. 12	59, 163
14-16	103
15	61
16	104
vi. 2	115
4-6	46
4-8	178
9	104
vii.	109
22	40, 78, 102

HEBREWS (continued)—

CHAP. VER.	PAGE
vii. 25	184
27	75
viii. 1	103, 104
3	104
3-5	105
6	40, 102
ix.	75
8	121, 139
9-14	164
11-28	75
12	105
12-14	86
14	134
15	40, 102, 103
15-22	41
25, 26	104
27	115
28	78
x.	109
2, 22	164
6	84
10, 12, 13, 14	104
10, 12, 19	75
11, 12	104
11-13	103
15	121, 139
16, 17	41, 183
19-29	86
26, 27	46
27	115
xii. 5-11	189
23	115, 162, 163, 205
24	40, 75, 86
25-28	108
xiii.	109
7, 17	217
10	238
10-12, 20	75
13	104
17	208
20	40, 41, 86, 99
21	99

JAMES.

i. 18	137

INDEX TO SCRIPTURE REFERENCES. 287

JAMES (continued)—

CHAP. VER.	PAGE
ii. 14-26	183, 186
iii. 2	195
6	93
9	73, 158
iv. 5	121
v. 8	107
14	217
16	224

1 PETER.

CHAP. VER.	PAGE
i. 2	36, 37, 38, 49, 136, 182
2, 11, 19	75
2, 19	86
3, 21	32, 99
4	108
5	36, 48
7	107
8	107
8, 9	46
11	125, 139
12	180
23	34
ii. 9	223
24	75
iii. 18	84
18-20	92, 94, 95
19, 20	128
21	236, 238
iv. 6	92, 95, 128
13	107
17, 18	178
18	195
1	75
1-4	217
1-5	208
4	107

2 PETER.

CHAP. VER.	PAGE
i. 2	133
4	35, 144
5-7	144
11	195
21	121, 139
iii.	112, 113
7	108, 115

2 PETER (continued)—

CHAP. VER.	PAGE
iii. 9	33
10-13	103
12, 13	107

1 JOHN.

CHAP. VER.	PAGE
i. 1	59
1, 2	61
7	75, 85, 86
8	195
ii. 2	45, 74, 75, 82
2, 3	78
5	194
19	130
27	139
28	107
iii. 1	200
1, 2, 9, 10	34
2	107, 200
4	188
6, 9	194, 195
9	34
16	75
iv. 2, 3	61
7	34
8, 9, 16	32
9	32, 58
10	75
17	115
v.	247
1	34
4, 18	34
6, 8	86
11	40
11, 12	132
12	135, 144
16	178
20	132

3 JOHN.

	PAGE
10	217

JUDE.

	PAGE
6	115, 117
14, 15	108
17-21	247

288 INDEX TO SCRIPTURE REFERENCES.

JUDE (continued)—

CHAP. VER.	PAGE
24	107, 195
24, 25	21

REVELATION.

CHAP. VER.	PAGE
i.	205
4	121
5	86
5, 7	75
6	223
7	108
17, 18	57, 99
20	217
ii.	134, 205
1, 8, 12, 18	217
7	98
7, 11, 17, 29	121
11	178
iii.	134, 205
1, 7, 14	217
6, 13, 22	121
11	107
14	71
iv. 11	18, 17, 126
14	71
v.	105
9	82, 86
9, 10	223
9, 12	75
vi. 9	162
16	105
16, 17	108
vii. 4-8	108
9	46, 94, 179
9, 17	105
14	75, 86
15	201

REVELATION (continued)—

CHAP. VER.	PAGE
viii. 16	139
xii. 9	
11	
xiii. 8	
xiv. 1, 4, 10	105
11	159
13	121
xvii.	111
14	105
17	164
xviii.	111
xix. 1	94
5	21
13	59
xx. 2-7	108
3	111
4	117, 162
4, 6	113, 114
7	112
7-11	108
10, 15	159
11	108
11-15	115
12	115
15	108
xxi.	109
1	108
1-8, 27	178
12	108
22, 23	105
xxii. 2-5	98
3	105, 106
12	108
14, 15	178
16	205
17	121

www.ingramcontent.com/pod-product-compliance
Lightning Source LLC
Chambersburg PA
CBHW060555230426
43670CB00011B/1828